BRAVE MEN

IN DESPERATE TIMES

BRAVE MEN

IN DESPERATE TIMES

THE LIVES OF CIVIL WAR SOLDIERS

John McKay

TWODOT®

GUILFORD, CONNECTICUT
HELENA, MONTANA
AN IMPRINT OF THE GLOBE PEQUOT PRESS

A · TWODOT® · BOOK

Text design: Jane Amara
Cover photo credits, from top down and left to right: Pvt. George A. Stryker, New York Regiment, Library of Congress, LC-B8184-10575 DLC; Pvt. Robert Patterson, Company D, 12th Tennessee Infantry, C.S.A., Library of Congress, LC-B8184-10038 DLC; Pvt. Edwin Francis Jemison, 2nd Louisiana Regiment, C.S.A., Library of Congress, LC-B8184-10037 DLC; Confederate soldier, Library of Congress, LC-B8184-10692 DLC; U.S. Sgt. Maj. Christian A. Fleetwood, 4th United States Colored Troops, courtesy Library of Congress; and portrait of a musician, 2d Regulars, U.S. Cavalry, Library of Congress, LC-B8184-10685 DLC, © Marius B. Péladeau Collection. All Library of Congress photos on the cover are from the Prints & Photographs Division, Civil War Photographs collection.

Library of Congress Cataloging-in-Publication Data
McKay, John, 1959-
    Brave men in desperate times : the lives of Civil War soldiers / John McKay. — 1st ed.
      p. cm.
    Includes bibliographical references and index.
    ISBN-13: 978-0-7627-2372-0
    ISBN-10: 0-7627-2372-6
    1. United States—Armed Forces—History—Civil War, 1861-1865. 2. Confederate States of America—Armed Forces. 3. United States—Armed Forces—Military life—History—19th century. 4. Confederate States of America—Armed Forces—Military life. 5. Soldiers—United States—History—19th century. 6. Soldiers—Confederate States of America. I. Title.
E607.M34 2006
973.7'4—dc22

                                    2006012102

Manufactured in the United States of America
First Edition/First Printing

CONTENTS

ACKNOWLEDGMENTS

T HIS BOOK WENT THROUGH SEVERAL UNEXPECTED PHASES AND MANY years of research and revision before coming to fruition, and I have many people to thank for their selfless contributions, verbal support, and encouragement. First and most important is my dear friend and editor for this and other projects, Erin Turner of Helena, Montana, who is solely and completely responsible for the best parts of this book; it quite literally would never have seen the light of day without her going above and beyond the call of duty.

As always, I am deeply indebted to my friends at the Atlanta History Center, who always seem to find an amazingly large number of resources for any question I ask of them; while their numbers are legion, the three who contributed most to this specific project were Gordon Jones, Erica Danylchak, and Beth Woodward. I am also grateful to the wonderful folks at the Georgia Department of Archives and History and the Southeastern Branch of the National Archives and Records Administration, who never failed to take the time to lend a hand, even in the middle of a major disruption, as both organizations moved to new facilities. The staff of the Photo Archives Division of the Library of Congress, the U.S. Navy Historical Center, and the U.S. Army Center for Military History were all most gracious in their assistance and support.

A number of people very kindly lent a large amount of help online, over the phone, and through the mail to provide assistance with the details that made the men in this book come alive: Hugh W. Barrow and Betty Jean Landers of Bowdon, Georgia; Bob Dame of Charlottesville, Virginia; Chinnubbie McIntosh of Sapulpa, Oklahoma; Carl Fallen and the wonderful men of the Col. Daniel N. McIntosh Camp #1378, SCV; Carrie Davison of Marvell, Arkansas; Steven Curtis of Illinois; and Jodie Goebel of New York.

I am grateful to my friend and fellow Civil War military historian Stephen Davis of Marietta, Georgia, who probably doesn't know to this day that a little thing he said to me in the midst of a bustling, over-crowded historians' panel (and repeated a few years later at another, wretchedly under-attended historians' panel) helped to make sure this project stayed alive.

Steve Narrie of the Northeast Georgia Civil War Roundtable, Julie Nix of Coal Mountain Elementary School, Lyn Hopper and Rebecca Stuckey of the Chestatee Regional Library System and the Dawson County Library, the Atlanta Literary Festival, the Forsyth County Friends of the Library, and the Friends of the Alpharetta Library groups were all very kind to invite me to speak during the course of this project, some on multiple occasions. Their audiences provided a wonderful sounding board, allowing me to gauge interest in the material I was uncovering and providing me with feedback that was valuable beyond measure.

It is a great honor to serve as a teacher at North Cobb Christian School, in Kennesaw, Georgia, where my students not only have the opportunity to live and learn literally in the middle of a great campaign and battle area of the war, but have the somewhat dubious opportunity to study with a historian obsessed with that particular war. There is a group of fine, intelligent, and upstanding young ladies and gentlemen at that school who have made my ministry to them a most joyful experience (even if they weren't always aware of it!): Michael Clayton, Kim Dannehold, Kalin Dreyer, Scott Edwards, Kaylyn Gilley, Ellen Hill, Meghan Hodges, Cosbie Hollenbeck, Wrenn Hoover, Joshua Hunter, Austin Jenkins, Cory Jones, Christen Sasscer, Matthew White, Stacie Wolf, and our beloved friend from Germany, Per-Elof Bergmann. I am also grateful to my colleagues and friends who have gone overboard to help me settle in at NCCS, encompassing the finest group of teachers I have ever had the joy to meet: Gayle Brainard, Vanessa Brown, Lee Campbell, Mark Cearfoss, Yelena Daniel, Dina Espenshied, Clancy Garner, Rachel Hedges, Peter Hensley, Linda Kern, Zach Kohlbacher, Greg Lawler, Amanda Ledbetter, Matthew Newton, Greg Scheck, Michael Swann, Amy Thompson, Cathy Troublefield, and Tara Turner.

Lastly, I give my greatest possible thanks, praise, and love for my wife and closest friend, Bonnie, who has been a constant and consistent source of support and inspiration, for this book and for my life. It is harder to find the words to express what she has done for me during my years of writing this book than it was to write the book itself. Since the day I began the first incarnation of this book, she has taken me from being broken by life and circumstance, led me by her own example to Calvary and the joy of discovering Christ, and walked with me in harmony before God since then. She has been my prayer partner, pathfinder, and exhorter, and is now preparing to enter full-time ministry beside me.

She is uncovering day by blessed day what it means to be a pastor's wife, and always has the ability to show the delight and peace that is beyond all understanding, no matter what problems, fears, or situations may arise. She is the best example of Proverbs 31 I could ever hope to see on this earth and always represents the best to our family of the qualities I tried to point out in this book; she is a brave woman in a fallen world, and she stands in the gap for the rest of us.

INTRODUCTION

I WAS A SOLDIER IN MY YOUTH, AS WERE MOST OF MY SOUTHERN MALE contemporaries. Even after six years of service in the Army and Army National Guard, I never saw a day of conflict, never heard a shot fired in anger, and never suffered any of the other pains of war, but again like so many of my Southern brethren, this was the destiny I was bred for. My earliest memories are of playing with toy guns and plastic helmets, getting a new "Army uniform" every year on my birthday, and consuming 1940s- and '50s-era war movies like so many kernels of popcorn. The house where I grew up, in quiet suburban Atlanta, was built on an old training ground used during both world wars, part of what was once called Camp Gordon. The trenches, bunkers, and even some barbed-wire barriers still remained in the thick woods, which provided a perfect setting to act out our military fantasies nearly every afternoon after school, rain or shine, cold or hot, just like we all imagined "real" battle would be like.

The American Civil War was still a living, breathing daily presence even in this twentieth-century suburban environment, and my friends and I would casually talk about our grandfathers and great-grandfathers, the units and commanders they fought with, and—since this part of Atlanta was near some of the great battlefields around the city—we sometimes walked the very ground they fought and died upon. We all expected that every one of us, without need to mention it, would repeat the military service our grandfathers, and our fathers and uncles after them, had performed. The Vietnam War was a looming presence. Some of us had brothers or cousins who had been there, and we all expected to end up in those same jungles one day. The fact that some of us might not return from those jungles, as our forebears had not all returned, was never a topic of conversation, other than in the form of humorous boyish harassment.

Being bred for war does not prepare one for a life of quiet civilian productivity, and in many ways sets up a sort of unstated yearning for the most destructive of all human endeavors—as if we could not fully be men without the searing forge of war on our souls. This is not just an intellectual curiosity; it is something that is central to the way this society shapes and views its men. John Eldredge in his book, *Wild at Heart*, talks about this masculine desire for adventure as not only an integral part of a man's creation, but one that gives him purpose and direction in life: "A man wants to be the hero to the beauty. Young men going off to war carry a photo of their sweetheart in their wallet. . . . You see, it's not just that a man needs a battle to fight; he needs someone to fight *for*." Eldredge also quotes the poet Ed Sissman commenting on what happens to a man who has missed his chance for war:

> *Men past forty*
> *Get up nights, Look out at city lights*
> *And wonder*
> *Where they made the wrong turn*
> *And why life is so long.*

This is precisely why war movies are often mockingly referred to as "guy movies," as the vast majority of men today in America, like me, have no direct knowledge of the experience of war, yet are drawn to it and sometimes consumed with curiosity about it. My own curiosity was to answer the question of how I would respond in battle. Would I have become one of the despised deserters, would I have cowered in fear in the bottom of my foxhole, or would I have been one of those to stand fast beside the colors while the enemy stormed in to kill us all?

This curiosity has shaped my professional life in no small way. I am a military historian by profession, an academic and teacher, accustomed to the cramped discomforts of archives and research libraries, my health affected by too many hours of sitting and reading poorly microfilmed records, and by too little exposure to air and sunshine. Yet I am driven to learn more and more by this insatiable curiosity. My particular obsession is with the American Civil War, as I not only grew up in the midst of one of the great campaign areas, but at least twenty-four of my relations fought for the Confederacy, four of them dying for the cause. One, Pvt. H.T. McKay, my father's grandfather, lived long enough to pass his stories of drill, march, and battle down to my father firsthand. His cousin, Pvt. J.H. McKay, was a cavalryman who was helping escort Jefferson Davis when he was captured at the end of the war—a fact that has opened more than a few doors in small-town museum collections! The rest were present in one or more of nearly every significant battle of both the Eastern and Western Theaters of the war.

All of this leads to the questions I hope to answer in this book: What was it like to be a soldier in combat during the Civil War? What was it like to be a poorly trained, ill-equipped, and un-uniformed militiaman in a state "army" trying to, literally, defend your own home? What was it like to be stuffed into a dank, dark, sweltering, three-foot-diameter iron tube, turning a crank to escape an enemy howling after you, all while thirty feet below the surface of Charleston Harbor? What was it like to be a Creek infantryman, slowly riding in to a Union post in the wilds of frontier Oklahoma, carrying the threadbare rags of what had once been your proud battle flag, knowing you were among the very last of the Confederates to surrender? What was it like to be a Prussian-born corporal, barely able to speak English, caught in the midst of a vicious street battle in Fredericksburg?

Most important of all, what was it really like, on a personal level, to be a soldier during the Civil War? What did the uniforms feel like on hot summer days, what did the food taste like, what did you do to entertain yourself over those long months in camp, how did the rifle feel in your hands when slick with sweat and gun oil, what was it like to pull the ramrod and draw a bead on an incoming enemy line, and finally, like my own great-grandfather's experience, what was it like to be a sixteen-year-old veteran infantryman, having the remains of your shattered leg cut off while lying atop a tavern table on a lonely mountain in Maryland?

In this book, we can explore on one level what the real "face of battle" was like for these men, and do so by looking through the lenses of twenty-one actual soldiers from that war. These men, by and large, have never had their stories told in print before, and with very good reason; there is very little in the way of records, official or otherwise, to be found in any known archive about them. We do know from battle reports, muster rolls, remaining unit photographs, artifacts in museum collections, family stories, and a handful of letters and diaries that these men did exist. From other sources we can piece some of their war experiences together, but there is not nearly enough information on any of them to provide even the barest hint of a full biography.

So, why were these men chosen? Precisely because of this nearly anonymous status, primarily, and because the relative celebrity of better-known lives would interfere with the attempt to personalize the experience for the reader. To illustrate this idea, could you, dear reader, ever imagine yourself as Robert E. Lee, atop Traveler, with Longstreet sitting on his horse at your side, while attempting to decide whether or not to launch the assault on Cemetery Ridge at Gettysburg? Of course not, not only because Lee's life has already been studied and written about nearly to death, but also because Lee himself is still seen as nearly equal to the

Almighty in some circles, and nearly as unknowable in most others. These lesser-known fighting men are equally worthy of both study and distinction, yet their very anonymity makes it easier to relate to what they did and experienced on a more personal level.

War is the epitome of all human cruelty and suffering, and as Sherman remarked long after his own war, it cannot be refined. We, or at least I, do not study military history in order to find great glory in the taking of some hill or some patch of ground, or raising one colored banner over another colored banner's possessions. Instead I find the greatest of humanity, of man's love for his fellow man, in these, the most depraved of circumstances. It is almost a cliché, but still overwhelmingly true, that men in combat after the first few fights usually don't stick around to gain glory, or medals, or women, or other such possessions, but do so because they cannot abide the thought of abandoning their friends. "We fought for each other" is a common refrain throughout modern combat histories—from the small band of beaten-up, freezing, and almost-ready-to-be-discharged Continental regulars who followed George Washington in a high-risk assault against a garrison of some of the world's toughest soldiers, to the equally small bands who stood by their regimental colors at Appomattox Courthouse and Durham Station, to the paratroopers who stood together despite impossible odds at Normandy and Bastogne, to the shunned infantrymen and Marines who sweated and bled together in the jungles, rice paddies, and mountains of Vietnam, only to come home to an even harsher and longer war.

Why these thoughts in a book about Civil War combatants? It is all connected, for if there is one thing that has always bound together any army throughout history, it is tradition and the formalized memory of unhappy times they went through together long ago. At this writing, we are engaged in the first major war of this new century. Once again young men are being asked by their country to stand to the colors and do their duty. One of the very first large units sent into battle was the storied 101st Airborne Division, whose "Screaming Eagle" shoulder patch bears the image of Old Abe, the mascot of the 8th Wisconsin Infantry, a Union army regiment that fought its way through Missouri, Kentucky, Tennessee, Mississippi, Louisiana, Alabama, and Arkansas. The Army's Special Forces and 75th Ranger Regiment each draw part of their heritage from John Hunt Morgan's Confederate Partisan Rangers, who raised hell far behind Union lines throughout the war, as well as from other "special operations" forces, like Andrew's Raiders and the crews of the CSS *H. L. Hunley*—all of whom paved the way for the military's acceptance of commando-style operations.

I mention all this for these reasons, and for yet another reason, the most important consideration of all. Even though most of the men discussed or mentioned in this book are long-forgotten and unheralded by most, it is their sacrifices, honor, and service that allowed the "great men" to have books, poems, and movies written about them, to have their images cast in bronze and stone, and to have their names recited in a droning manner by legions of schoolchildren over the past 140 years. There is nothing particularly wrong with this, of course, but it is the men in these pages who are the most important of all, yet the least recalled, and it is the height of tragedy to leave them and their many accomplishments to be forgotten. I do this, then, in remembrance of them.

QUEEN OF BATTLE: THE INFANTRY

Pvt. James K. Newton, Co. F, 14th Wisconsin Volunteer Infantry
Pvt. James R. Barrow, Co. B, Cobb's Legion Infantry

O N THE SUNNY MORNING OF APRIL 6, 1862, PVT. JAMES K. NEWTON OF Company F, 14th Wisconsin Volunteer Infantry (the "De Pere Rifles"), idled around his tent near Savannah, Tennessee, looking forward to another long, boring day of guard duty and drill. It was not the most pleasant way to spend his time, but it was a welcome alternative to the combat he knew awaited him in the coming days. Word filtering through the ranks was that the Confederate armies of the West were gathering in strength around the critical railroad crossroads at Corinth, Mississippi, 35 miles to the south, and that Newton's company would have to go down and dig them out of their trenches and redoubts sometime in the next few weeks. Rumors had sprung up around the camp that Rebel patrols, and even cavalry and artillery, had been seen as close as 10 miles down the nearby Tennessee River. Some of the wilder speculation had it that the Confederates were at that moment heading north to destroy the mighty Union army in their own camps along the river. Most of his friends laughed at the sheer folly of such an idea, as the once-feared Confederates had been sent running from every battle so far, abandoning both Kentucky and Tennessee in the process.

Private Newton's lazy morning routine ended suddenly when loud crashes of cannon fire erupted from somewhere south along the Tennessee River. The startled Wisconsin boys gathered around, speculating on what could have happened, when word passed through the camp that the "Secesh" had attacked in force and really were heading their way. Other rumors soon followed that fellow Wisconsin regiments had been cut to pieces, and that the entire Union army corps under Gen. Ulysses S. Grant, encamped 10 miles south of Savannah at tiny Pittsburg Landing, had been completely routed. Survivors were said to be fleeing north up the river in terror.

As the day wore on, the rumor mill cranked into full operation, with wild speculations fueling the men's unease over the disaster seemingly unfolding just south of them. Shortly before 4:00 P.M., regimental buglers sounded a hasty call to arms. Leaving all behind except their blankets and weapons, Newton and his brother infantrymen scrambled into line and prepared to board small boats headed south into the action. After they hurriedly boarded, more orders came down for them to wait until a larger relief force could be assembled. As the men sat alongside the dock, a riverboat pulled up and began unloading wounded and dead enlisted men and officers, including the bodies of the commanding officer and executive officer of the 18th Wisconsin. Newton and his men began to realize that at least some of the awful rumors had been based on fact.

About 9:00 that evening, the reinforcements arrived, and the boats finally filled up and headed south, toward Pittsburg Landing, where the broken remains of a once-proud Union army still held a foothold of ground. It had been raining since late afternoon, and Newton stepped off the boat into ankle-deep mud. In the pitch-black wilderness, he stood in the rain, waiting for the desperate fight that was only hours away; all around him, the sounds of wounded men rang in his ears. Later, Newton remarked that his only thought at the time was of how well his rubber poncho kept out the pounding rain.

A few months later, on another Sunday afternoon, another young man walked for hours along the hilly roads of western Maryland. He, too, was hoping for a boring day, but did not see any signs of one developing. Pvt. James R. Barrow of Company B, Cobb's Legion Infantry, was part of Lee's great gamble to invade the North in the fall of 1862. But he, along with his fellow legionnaires, had discovered that Marylanders—although citizens of a slave-holding, Southern-sympathizing border state— regarded them as an invading force, in much the same way as Newton's Union comrades were regarded in distant Tennessee.

About 4:00 P.M. on September 14, 1862, Barrow's unit arrived back at one of their old campsites, near Brownsville at the base of South Mountain. He promptly plopped down with the others to set about "fix-ing themselves some supper." They soon heard the sound of fighting to the south, and not long afterward, the dreaded sound of bugles calling them to duty. Running to get into line, they could not help but hear the growing sounds of combat emanating from the steep mountainsides nearby.

INFANTRYMEN

Both Newton and Barrow were infantrymen, better known as foot-soldiers, "grunts," "doughboys," "GIs," or any other of a host of names for the ordinary fighting men who have always borne the heaviest brunt of fighting and dying. The very heart, soul, and backbone of any army, at least since early medieval times, these are the men (and the occasional well-disguised woman) who carry the battle literally on their shoulders into the face of the enemy. In all periods of history, these men have been unappreciated by the unlearned, suffering under the burden of whatever wacky uniforms their generals decided were in fashion at the moment, carrying food, shelter, and other comforts in packs or slings as they trudged down one dusty road after another. Forever in movement, but always at the snail's pace of the route march, they have sometimes traveled back and forth along the same road for days on end. At other times the lowly infantryman might sit in camp for weeks or even months at a time, only to be hastily summoned by the bugle's insistent call to pack up and move out-sometimes into battle, other times only to sit in yet another camp for days, weeks, or months.

The average infantryman of the Civil War was between nineteen and twenty-one years old (although there are examples of both much younger and much, much older), single, and a farmer by trade. He had most likely never been more than 20 miles from home in his entire life. He was likely to be illiterate, or nearly so, and deeply religious, yet was given to drink and playing cards when the opportunity arose. The Confederate infantryman was, for the most part, reasonably comfortable living in the field, acceptably accurate with firearms, and almost always a volunteer. His Union counterpart tended toward these same traits, but had much more of a sprinkling of city boys, foreigners, and draftees among the ranks, along with a higher literacy rate. Despite all the eloquent speeches and patriotic rhetoric, both most likely joined for the adventure and stayed because they could not desert their friends.

Barrow's unit, Company B, the "Bowdon Volunteers" of Cobb's Legion Infantry, was recruited during the summer of 1861 from the tiny town of Bowdon, Georgia, near the Alabama state line. They reported to duty at Camp Cobb, near Richmond, Virginia, in early August. As mentioned earlier, this was at a time when the average person would never travel more than 20 miles or so away from home in his entire lifetime; doubtlessly these young men thought the several-days-long train ride was to be the highlight of their lives. They would learn differently before long.

By early September, six other companies had arrived, forming a battalion-sized infantry component of the three-service branch legion. This was a unique organization for the time, and represented Brig. Gen. Howell Cobb's vision of a self-contained, combined-arms brigade. Within this structure, infantry, artillery, and cavalry would train and work together on the battlefield to maximize each branch's strengths and minimize their weaknesses. This idea was resurrected in a limited form in World War II, but has found its greatest potential met in very modern times, with the "team" and "task force" formations used by the U.S. Army since the mid-1980s. Several officers warned Cobb that his concept was not "practicable," which proved to be quite prophetic, as the entire legion never fought in a single battle together.

Shortly after arriving in camp, the seven companies of Cobb's Legion Infantry were issued new Enfield rifles, which had arrived somehow through the Union navy's blockade. This was quite a turn of fortune, as most "irregular" scratch forces preparing in Virginia at that time were issued much lesser weapons—anything from old .69 caliber smoothbore Mexican War-era flintlocks converted to percussion cap locks, to civilian hunting rifles, down to even "refuse" guns of various calibers and makes, which would either not have all the equipment necessary to fire, or would simply fall apart and have to be reassembled after each shot. The 1853 model Enfield three-band rifles they received were of .577 caliber. They weighed about nine and a half pounds, were 55 inches long with a 38-inch barrel, and were capable of hitting targets well over 500 yards distant. This well-regarded rifle ended up being the de facto standard longarm of the Confederacy. The Union armies adopted an almost identical weapon: the 1861 Springfield rifled musket, which was .58 caliber and weighed a bit over nine pounds, with a 39-inch barrel, about 56 inches in overall length. The paper cartridge ammunition used in both weapons was interchangeable, making resupply from captured enemy ammo chests easier.

Much has been made of the incredibly high casualty rate during the war—more were killed in the single-day battle of Antietam than in all previous American wars combined (26,134 dead, wounded, and missing from both sides). But the main reason for the high number of casualties was that the majority of senior officers on both sides had trained together at West Point and learned a set of battlefield tactics that were based on the use of smoothbore, relatively inaccurate, and slow-to-reload weapons. In the 1850s this new class of weapon emerged, the rifled-barrel muzzleloader, of which both the Enfield and Springfield were shining examples. A series of lands and grooves cut in a spiral fashion down the inside of the barrel "grabbed" the bullet as it was fired, and gave it a spinning motion that helped stabilize its flight, much like a football quarterback gives a spin to the ball as he releases it. This simple change not only helped stabilize the round, increasing its accuracy, but it also helped dramatically increase its effective range. The older smoothbore weapons fired a ball that tended to tumble wildly and which was terribly inaccurate beyond a few yards, just like a quarterback throwing a football by grabbing one end of it and pushing it forward. In addition to this new rifle technology, French Army Captain Claude Minié designed a new bullet in the 1840s that was elongated, had a hollow base, and was slightly smaller than the rifle's bore diameter. This meant the bullet could be rammed down the barrel much faster, and the gases from discharge would expand the base, engaging the rifling and giving the bullet a very stable flight. The soft lead bullet, called a "minié ball," weighed 500 grains (about the same as eleven modern copper pennies), and tended to "mushroom" when it struck anything solid, depleting the entire kinetic energy of the shot onto the target. This meant that if an infantryman were struck in the shoulder, his arm would most likely be ripped off; likewise, a hit in the leg would shatter the bone into so many irreparable fragments that amputation was the only option.

Both weapons used an "angular" bayonet, which was triangular in cross-section and 18 inches long—a fearsome weapon indeed. However, it took a high degree of expertise and discipline to properly use a bayonet in combat. Imagine trying to hold a poorly balanced, eleven-pound, 6-foot stick with an off-center pointed end (the bayonet attached to the muzzle end of the weapon and was offset from the center of mass about 2 inches, so the weapon could be fired with it attached), and trying to stick it in a moving, similarly equipped, and highly motivated (to move out of the way) target—all while your hands are slick with sweat and shaking with fear and adrenaline. For these reasons, the bayonet was often either "lost" by the roadside, or put to an alternative use; they served as candleholders, were rammed into trees as coat hooks, were used as spits to roast the evening meal, or were heated and bent into hook shapes used to drag the dead bodies of their compatriots off the battlefield.

THE BOWDON BOYS

Pvt. James Barrow and the other Bowdon volunteers were in their training camp only a brief time before the war caught up with them. On September 16, 1861, they began a train and steamboat trip down the Virginia peninsula, to a squalid tent park grandiosely named Camp Washington, where they were to counter a Union attempt to seize Richmond. Instead of immediately going into action, however, the legion as a whole spent the next several months bouncing back and forth about the peninsula, setting up breastworks, investigating "shots fired" reports, and performing other general scut duties. They were eventually assigned with the 16th and 24th Georgia Infantry, the 2nd Louisiana Infantry (later reassigned), and the 15th North Carolina Infantry, along with an artillery battery, as Brig. Gen. Howell Cobb's Georgia Brigade, part of Maj. Gen. Lafayette McLaws's Division (Maj. Gen. James Longstreet's Corps, Lee's Army of Northern Virginia). They remained on the periphery of nearly every battle during Union Maj. Gen. George B. McClellan's slow campaign, known collectively as the Seven Days, without seeing action, until being ordered into the line at Malvern Hill. Five men were killed in action there, or died of disease en route. Several others were wounded and one unlucky soul, Pvt. James Hill, was captured.

At the end of the Seven Days, McClellan decided a strategic withdrawal was in order and fled back to Washington, with his army still mostly intact. Lee, seeing that McClellan would rather run than fight, decided to gamble and take the war up into Maryland and Pennsylvania. In doing so, he hoped not only to thrash thoroughly any Union army sent against him—on Yankee soil nonetheless—but also to make the locals uncomfortable enough with his army tramping about that they would demand Lincoln sue for peace. A long-shot strategy, to say the least, but considering the sort of military leadership Lincoln was able to scrounge up in those days, it was not a bad plan at all. Before long, Barrow and the Bowdon boys found themselves walking along a dirt road in western Maryland. They were hungry, tired, and listening with growing unease to the sound of fighting to their south.

THE WISCONSIN REGULARS

Pvt. James Newton's unit, the 14th Wisconsin, called the "Northwestern Regiment" or the "Wisconsin Regulars," was organized in November 1861, at Camp Wood, near Fond du Lac. By January of 1862, the original commanding officer, Col. David E. Wood, filled out the ranks with thirty-nine officers and 820 enlisted men, all from the then-frontier counties in the north part of the state. Newton's specific unit, Company F, bore the nickname of the "De Pere Rifles." Newton wrote his parents of his first military housing at the camp, in Sibley tents:

> Every tent is round and is about 18 feet in diameter at the bottom and tapers up to a point at a height of about 15 feet. There is a sheet iron stove for each tent with two lengths of stove pipe for each stove which is hardly enough as it does not reach high enough to carry all of the smoke out but after we get charcoal I think it will go a great deal better. We have good beef and potatoes, bread and butter to eat and coffee to drink and all that we want of it too.
>
> There are 18 men in the tent that I stay in. We are under Corporal Robert Beattie. We have 2 tin pails, 1 camp kettle, 2 washbowls in each tent besides a knife and fork, tin cup and tin plate for each man. Besides this we have 2 axes, 2 shovels, 2 spades and 2 hatchets for the use of each company.

The regiment was accepted into the United States Army on January 30, 1862, and departed for their first duty station, St. Louis, on March 8. Their initial assignment was to Brig. Gen. Ulysses S. Grant's Department of Cairo, which was then building up for the campaigns on the Tennessee and Cumberland Rivers. They arrived at Savannah, Tennessee, on April 28, just before their baptism of fire.

When the two armies left their home bases in 1861, both were burdened heavily by three things: inexperienced officers; gaudy, impracticable uniforms; and far too much excess baggage. The worst of the three, by far, was the officer situation. While many officers on both sides had trained at West Point, the majority either had no military training whatsoever, or just a smattering that had been picked up while drilling with their local militias. This did not necessarily mean they were bad officers or poor combat leaders. One prime example is the well-known Confederate cavalry commander, Lt. Gen. Nathan Bedford Forrest. Without the benefit of a single day of formal military training, Forrest, a wealthy pre-war businessman, raised his own regiment of cavalry, paid for their equipment out of his own pocket, and eventually became the single most feared and effective cavalry officer of the war. He only lost one major battle, at Tupelo, and was forced to surrender at the very end of the war, only due to sheer force of Union numbers. Sherman himself remarked once that he didn't care if it took ten years and broke the Federal Treasury, Forrest had to be hunted down and killed.

The real weakness in the officer corps was that, by pre-war militia tradition, most company-level and regimental commanders were elected into office by the men they were to lead. While the thought was nice— that men would more likely follow those they trusted well enough to elect—this, like all other political processes, soon turned into a popularity contest. Some men turned into capable leaders, some destroyed their own commands through sheer incompetence, and others muddled along until the forge of combat produced the real leaders. The problem here was that, while officers could either resign and go home, or be "promoted up" (e.g. Braxton Bragg after Chattanooga) or be sent packing by their superiors, the men in the line simply had to deal with whoever was assigned to lead them. This point was not lost on James Newton, who, after the Battle of Shiloh, said of his own un-beloved commanding officer, Capt. Joseph G. Lawton, that he had "behaved as brave as any of them." Not really a small thing to say about someone who received his baptism of command in that grinding hellhole, but Newton's distaste had little to do with Lawton's military prowess.

TWO ARMIES IN TENNESSEE

In early 1862, after decisive Confederate losses in Kentucky and upper Tennessee, CSA Gen. Albert Sidney Johnston pulled his forces together in northern Mississippi and, along with CSA Gen. Pierre Gustave Toutant Beauregard, began plans for a campaign to retake the lost territory. Part of the Union strategy was to divide the Confederacy in half by taking middle Tennessee and then Atlanta. The Confederate overall strategy was much more daunting: stop the Union forces when the opportunity arose, grind them up whenever possible, and simply survive until the North grew tired of the fight.

Johnston's newly organized CSA Army of Mississippi, based in the important rail center of Corinth, Mississippi, steadily built up through March of 1862. Maj. Gen. Leonidas Polk, Brig. Gen. (and former USA

Vice-President) John C. Breckinridge, and Maj. Gen. William J. Hardee brought the remnants of their corps down from Kentucky; Maj. Gen. Braxton Bragg brought most of his corps north from Pensacola, Florida; and Brig. Gen. Daniel Ruggles's Division marched east from New Orleans. Other commands around the Deep South detached individual regiments and brigades, which arrived in the northern Mississippi town throughout the last two weeks of March. By April 1, Johnston had a roughly organized, ill-trained, and mostly inexperienced force of about 45,000 officers and men under his command.

After the Union naval victories at Forts Donelson and Henry, in the north-central region of Tennessee, USA Flag Officer Andrew Hull Foote sailed his small gunboat fleet down the Tennessee River essentially unmolested all the way to Florence, Alabama—a demonstration of just how vulnerable the South was to invasion via the river systems. One of the very few attempts at a Confederate resistance to Foote's mission took place on March 1, 1862, when Gibson's Battery of the 1st Louisiana Artillery Regiment lobbed a few shells at his fleet as they passed. CSA Col. Alfred Mouton's men from the adjacent 18th Louisiana Infantry joined in, ineffectively shooting up the side of the armored gunboats. Foote returned fire and the shelling soon stopped.

Two weeks later, Union forces started moving south under the overall command of Maj. Gen. Henry Wager Halleck. They had two missions: take control of and repair roads through middle Tennessee and clear the area of any Confederate forces encountered. Once all of his forces were concentrated at Savannah, Halleck intended to move further south, into Mississippi, and destroy the rail junctions in Corinth, Jackson, Humbolt, and Iuka. To accomplish this mission, Halleck had two full armies: Maj. Gen. Ulysses S. Grant's Army of the Tennessee and Maj. Gen. Don Carlos Buell's Army of the Ohio. Combined, they had a total of just under 63,000 men on the march south.

A heavy reconnaissance force under USA Brig. Gen. Charles Ferguson Smith (promoted one week later to Major General) arrived in Savannah on March 13, charged by Halleck to seize and hold, or at least to cut, the Memphis and Charleston Railroad at Corinth. They were to accomplish this task without engaging with Confederate forces rumored to be gathering in the area. USA Brig. Gen. William Tecumseh Sherman arrived from Kentucky the next day, and Smith promptly sent him off toward Eastport, Mississippi, to see if he could cut the railroad there. As Sherman sailed south on the Tennessee River aboard Lt. William Gwin's gunboat, *Tyler*, Gwin pointed out the location of their earlier skirmish with the Confederate artillery battery. Alarmed that the enemy was so close to his intended target, Sherman sent word back to Smith that this location should be occupied in force as soon as possible. Smith agreed and immediately dispatched Brig. Gen. Stephen Hurlbut's Division to occupy the small settlement atop a high bluff, called Pittsburg Landing. It was about three miles northeast of an equally tiny settlement called Shiloh Church.

Sherman soon returned from his reconnaissance, finding the Confederates were present in force at his intended target, and joined Hurlbut at Pittsburg Landing. Scouting the area, he reported back to Smith that the area was "important" and easily defended by a relatively small force, although the ground provided a good encampment space for several thousand troops. The few settlers at the landing had fled with the arrival of Union gunboats, and the only locals remaining were small-plot farmers scattered about the county. The small Methodist meetinghouse, Shiloh Church, was described as a crude, one-room log cabin, "which would make a good corncrib for an Illinois farmer." Sherman urged Smith to relocate the majority of forces to this small landing, as it was the northernmost road link to the intended target of Corinth, Mississippi.

UNION DEPLOYMENT

Grant arrived in Savannah on March 17 to take over direct command of the Tennessee River operation from Smith, setting up his headquarters in the Cherry Mansion on Main Street. He soon deployed his force of roughly 35,000 to the west side of the river, save a small garrison in Savannah. Five divisions would join Sherman at Pittsburg Landing, and Brig. Gen. Lew Wallace's 2nd Division would occupy Crump's Landing, 6 miles north of Sherman's position.

Another major Union army, Buell's Army of the Ohio, was on its way south from Nashville with another 30,000 men (both this figure and Grant's total command size are wildly disparate in differing accounts). Grant planned to rest his men and wait for Buell's arrival before starting his operation against Corinth. Although he was aware that the Confederates were present in force just 20 miles away, he believed that they would simply entrench around Corinth and have to be forced out. An attack on Pittsburg Landing was, quite literally, the last thing he expected the Confederates to do.

It took well over a week to transport all the Union forces south to the new position. As they arrived, the divisions moved inland and encamped in a loose semicircle south of the landing and across the Corinth Road. Parts of each command, including James Newton and his mates in the 14th Wisconsin, were left scattered in small camps all around Savannah. By March 19, all six divisions were in place and comfortably making camp, believing they had several days or even weeks of preparation before they would face their next day of combat.

CONFEDERATE ADVANCE

CSA Gen. Johnston was well aware of Grant's presence to the north of his headquarters, and received a message on April 2 that Buell's force was nearby as well. Still waiting in Corinth for the last of his assigned forces to arrive, the Confederate commander decided he would have to go ahead and attack the gathering Union force before Buell's addition could make it stronger. His orders were simple: March north and engage the enemy between his encampments and the river, turning their left flank and forcing them away from their line of retreat—and up against some difficult terrain around Owl Creek on the west side of Shiloh Church—until they were forced to surrender.

CSA Gen. Beauregard planned out the tactical details of the attack, and issued orders to move out on the morning of April 3. By April 4, Confederate units across upper Mississippi and lower Tennessee were to converge at Mickey's Farmhouse, 8 miles south of Pittsburg Landing, where final preparations for the attack would begin. Hardee's and Bragg's Corps would march north from Corinth, along with one division of Polk's Corps, along the parallel Bark and Pittsburg Landing Roads. Breckinridge's Corps moved north from Burnsville and Polk's other division (Brig. Gen. Frank Cheatham's) would move southeast from Purdy, Tennessee, to join at the rendezvous farm.

The march took much longer than Beauregard had planned, due to poor preparation and a steady rain that turned the dirt roads into muddy quagmires. It was late on the evening of April 5 before everyone was in position at the junction of Corinth and Bark Roads, with Hardee's Corps arrayed in the front only a half-mile from the Union picket line. Union cavalry patrols had engaged with forward elements of each column on both April 4 and 5, leading a usually cautious Beauregard to request that Johnston call off the attack. He stated that his carefully scheduled attack plan was now "disrupted," and that given the cavalry attacks, all aspects of surprise were long gone. Johnston was adamant about continuing the attack, however, telling Beauregard, Polk, and Bragg, "Gentlemen, we shall attack at daylight to-morrow." Moments later, he remarked to one of his staff officers, "I would fight them if they were a million. They can present no greater front between these two creeks than we can, and the more men they crowd in there, the worse we can make it for them."

THE NIGHT OF APRIL 5

All through the dark, damp night, Confederate soldiers lay in the woods, listening to Union bands play patriotic tunes just yards away. Union soldiers had heard the Confederates advancing into position all evening and had sent a slew of frantic messages up the chain of command, warning of their presence. Amazingly, these warnings were ignored by Grant's staff, who believed they amounted to nothing more than reconnaissance patrols. Grant was still firmly convinced that Johnston's men were continuing to entrench heavily at Corinth. His only concern was how difficult it would be to "root them out."

To top off the Union army's lack of combat preparedness, Maj. Gen. Halleck had ordered Grant not to be pulled into a fight that would distract him from his goal of taking Corinth, and Grant followed suit by ordering no patrolling of his own forces, for fear they might engage the enemy "patrols" and create a general battle. His brigade commanders furthest south were growing increasingly nervous, passing on report after report to headquarters that their men were spotting more and more Confederate cavalry, infantry, and even artillery. Their frantic requests for reinforcement, or even for permission to mount their own scouting missions, were denied, their division commanders only reiterating Grant's orders.

Finally, as darkness fell on April 5, USA Col. Everett Peabody, encamped the furthest south of Pittsburg Landing, decided it would be better to beg forgiveness if he was wrong than to ask permission again and gave orders for a combat patrol to go out as early as possible the next morning. At 3:00 A.M., Maj. James Powell led his 25th Missouri and the 12th Michigan Infantry Regiments, with a total of 250 men, into the predawn blackness, heading south toward Corinth Road. They marched southwesterly down a narrow farm lane only about a quarter-mile before running into Confederate cavalry videttes. Both sides exchanged fire briefly before the cavalry suddenly withdrew. It was just before 5:00 A.M. Powell deployed his men into a loose line-abreast skirmish line and continued southeast, toward Fraley's Field.

THE FIRST DAY, APRIL 6, 1862:
THE BATTLE BEGINS

Powell's men moved into the cotton field and soon came under fire from CSA Maj. Aaron B. Hardcastle's 3rd Mississippi Battalion, who had observed them entering the field and waited until they closed within 90 yards to attack. The Union soldiers hit the ground and returned a heavy volume of fire. This exchange lasted until 6:30 A.M., both sides suffering moderate casualties, until Hardcastle's men suddenly disengaged and moved back into the woods. Believing they were retreating, Powell ordered his men up and prepared to move out again, when to his horror, a mile-wide mass of Confederate soldiers suddenly appeared before him— 9,000 men of Hardee's Corps on their way north.

The Confederate force was fully up and moving, their surprise attack only slightly tripped up by Powell's tiny force. Behind Hardee was Bragg's Corps, also in a near mile-wide line, followed by Polk's Corps in route–march formation (columns of brigades) on the Corinth Road. In the rear, and also in columns of brigades, was Breckinridge's Reserve Corps. The whole formation was a "T"-shaped box, almost a mile wide and more than two miles long, moving forward slowly toward the Union encampments.

Before he was killed and his small patrol force scattered, Powell managed to get word back to Peabody about the attack. Peabody immediately moved his brigade south to try and aid Powell. Hardee was having a tough time moving his large force north. The Union patrol and skirmishers delayed his general movement and the terrain was not conducive to moving such a heavy mass of troops and equipment. As the two forces moved toward each other, Union 6th Division commanding officer Brig. Gen. Benjamin Mayberry Prentiss rode up to Peabody and began berating him for sending out the patrol and "bringing this battle on." After a brief argument, Peabody set his men up in a line of battle near his original encampment, while Prentiss set his force up on the left, making ready to engage the oncoming Confederates.

The time was now 7:00 A.M., and the sun was dawning on what looked to be a beautiful, cloudless day.

HARDEE'S ASSAULT

Hardee's Corps had broken up into individual brigades while moving through the thick woods, and were now spread out to engage the Union encampments in a near 2-mile front. At Spain Field on the Eastern

Corinth Road, CSA Brig. Gen. Adley H. Gladden's Brigade burst out of the woods directly across from Prentiss's line, and the field was swept with heavy artillery fire from both sides. A galling fire came from the Union line and staggered the Confederates. Only able to stand for a few minutes, the brigade broke and retreated to the woods, dragging with them the mortally wounded Gladden, who died later that same day.

Over on the Confederate left, about the same time, CSA Brig. Gen. Sterling Wood's Brigade hit Peabody's right flank, pushing the Union infantry out of their line and back. Johnston, no longer able to stand being out of the line of fire, turned over operations in the rear to Beauregard and rushed forward to lead the battle from the front. Arriving just in time to see Wood's success and Gladden's repulse, he ordered all four brigades on the line—9,800 men—to fix bayonets and assault the Union line at the double-quick.

As Peabody's command withered under the assault, he rode forward to rally his men and was hit four times by rifle fire. Finally, in front of his own tent, watching the butternut-clad ranks close in on him from two sides, Peabody was shot from his saddle and died instantly. His command completely crumbled, followed shortly by Prentiss's own men. Even as Brig. Gen. William Wallace's and Hurlbut's brigades moved south to reinforce them, most of the Union infantry present had seen enough of this fight and retreated at a run toward Pittsburg Landing.

BRAGG'S ASSAULT

As the Union men broke and ran, the victorious Confederate infantry raced into their abandoned encampment and found piles of fresh food and good equipment left behind. Exhortations of their officers did no good, as the brigades and regiments dissolved into a rabble, pillaging the camps. Beauregard and Johnston spent several precious minutes getting the men under control and reorganized to renew their attack. The Union line, in the meantime, stopped its headlong retreat and fell in to new positions for defense.

Johnston ordered up Bragg's Corps into the growing battle, splitting his five brigades between the left and right of Hardee's men, and ordering Bragg to take command of the assault on the right flank. On the Confederate right, Brig. Gen. John K. Jackson's and Brig. Gen. James R. Chalmers's Brigades briefly joined the rout of Prentiss, while on the left Col. Preston Pond's and Brig. Gen. Patton Anderson's Brigades joined Brig. Gen. Patrick Ronayne Cleburne's Brigade, which was steadily advancing on Sherman's position at Shiloh Church. Col. Randall L. Gibson's Brigade continued straight due northeast, in between the two major assaults now ongoing, to try and break the Union center and turn Sherman's left flank. In an attempt to bring the strongest force on his right flank, and force the Ohio general's division away from the river, Johnston brought up Polk's Corps, and sent his four brigades into the line alongside Bragg. Hardee was instructed to take direct command of the left flank and hammer hard on Sherman's position.

By 9:00 A.M., thirteen Confederate brigades were fully engaged along a 3-mile front, and were steadily pushing back Union forces all along. Sherman was soon reinforced by Maj. Gen. John A. McClernand's Division, while three newly arrived divisions joined in a hastily organized line, along with what remained of Prentiss's Brigade, from Sherman's left over to the Hamburg-Savannah Road. William Wallace was particularly well positioned along a narrow wagon trace, which was concealed in an oak forest atop a low ridgeline. Before him was Duncan Field, a place in the center of Grant's defense line that is today referred to as the Sunken Road.

Sherman, wounded in the hand during his stand at the church, was forced to retreat at 10:00 in the morning, when a heavy attack by five Confederate brigades broke through to his left and threatened to envelop his position. Alongside Sherman, McClernand's Division had set up a defensive perimeter within the confines of their camp, extending the line east to the southern border of Duncan Field—directly across from William Wallace's position.

Grant had heard the cannon fire from Savannah, nearly 10 miles to the north, and had hastily traveled south via his headquarters steamship, the *Tigress*. Before leaving, he ordered Lew Wallace to march south to the growing battle. He also ordered newly arrived Brig. Gen. William "Bull" Nelson's 4th Division of Buell's Army of the Ohio to travel down the east bank of the Tennessee River to where they could be transported across to Pittsburg Landing. When Grant arrived at the landing around 9:00 A.M., it was only to find the area choked with fleeing Union soldiers. Grant painfully saddled his horse (he had been injured in a fall several days earlier, and could only walk with the aid of crutches) and rode south to assess the situation. Sherman met him in the woods just north of his new position, near the Hamburg-Purdy Road, and assured him that he could hold this new line. Grant was satisfied and returned to the landing after riding down to check his left flank.

The Union lines were seriously disrupted and unstable, but the Confederates were having their own problems. The massive, now 3-mile-long front had broken down into a series of uncoordinated attacks, due to the thickly wooded and hilly terrain, and Johnston was no longer able to control the entire line. The three corps commanders and Johnston finally decided to break up overall command into a series of sector commands; Johnston controlled the right from Prentiss's camp, Bragg took the right-center at the Eastern Corinth Road, Polk took the left-center at the Corinth Road and Shiloh Church, while Hardee moved west to Owl Creek and took control of the left flank.

A little after 10:30 A.M., just after Grant finished his visit with Sherman, Polk initiated a gigantic attack on Sherman's and McClernand's positions with ten reinforced brigades. Over two-thirds of the entire Confederate force was on the field. The Union lines reeled under the massive attack and soon broke, falling back almost three-fourths of a mile to Jones Field. Ironically, this attack produced the exact opposite of what Johnston had wanted; it drove the Union line back, but the right flank rather than the left, and ended up moving the entire Union force toward the relative safety of Pittsburg Landing.

THE HORNETS' NEST

At the same time, a smaller attack on the Union's left flank by Chalmers's and Jackson's Brigades slammed into Major Generals John McArthur's and David Stuart's Brigades, wounding both Union commanders and forcing them to retreat. By 11:00 A.M., a strong Union line was forming, centered on William Wallace's and Prentiss's position, hidden along the Sunken Road. Several Confederate attacks on this position were thrown back with heavy losses before Bragg realized what a strong force was concentrated there. As Gibson's Brigade attacked through a dense thicket just east of Duncan Field, Union artillery firing canister and infantry rifle fire raked through the brush. The way the bullets and canister balls ripped apart the leaves reminded the Confederate infantrymen of a swarm of angry hornets, and some unknown wag soon dubbed the hotly contested ground the "Hornets' Nest."

To the west of the Hornets' Nest, Bragg once again displayed his habitual impatience, and ordered attack after attack across Duncan Field on the well-positioned Union line, but each one was thrown back in turn. To add to his problem, Sherman and McClernand managed to regroup their scattered forces and counterattacked Hardee's and Polk's forces, briefly regaining their own camps. To reestablish his gains, Beauregard threw his last reserves in the lines, stopping the Union counterattack at a high cost in soldiers' lives. A fierce battle raged between the two armies in Woolf Field, near the Water Oaks Pond just north of Corinth Road. It lasted for less than two hours before the Union troops were once again thrown back to Jones Field.

THE PEACH ORCHARD

On the right of the Hornets' Nest, multiple attacks against Hurlbut and McArthur had been repulsed with heavy losses, until at last some of the Confederate soldiers refused to mount another assault. Riding forward about 2:00 P.M., Johnston announced that he would get them going, and told the battered force that he would personally lead the next attack. As he made his way down the line of infantry, he tapped on their bayonets and said, "These must do the work. Men, they are stubborn, we're going to have to use the bayonet." He then turned, and with a shouted command for them to follow, he headed toward the Union left flank. The line of infantry rose with a scream, and four brigades followed Johnston into battle.

At this same time, Stuart's Brigade, in the Union line directly where Johnston was headed, had nearly completely run out of ammunition, and Stuart ordered a retreat. With Johnston's men sweeping forward, both Hurlbut's and McArthur's flanks were exposed and caved in. Both Union brigades retreated north to the upper end of Bell's Field, near a small peach orchard. They returned a heavy volume of fire on the advancing Confederate force, and newly opened peach blossoms fell like snow on the ground as bullets and shot sprayed through the trees.

A little after 2:30 P.M., as Johnston watched the battle unfolding from the southeast corner of Bell's Field, a bullet ripped through his right leg, just below the knee. Undoubtedly fired by one of his own men (the ball came in from the rear), the wound amazingly went almost unnoticed by Johnston. Years earlier, he had been struck in the same leg during a duel, and the resulting damage to his nerves had probably numbed his leg to the point that he couldn't feel a gunshot wound. He tumbled from his horse and was caught by his aide, Tennessee Governor Isham Green Harris. His staff quickly dragged him to the safety of a nearby ravine, where Harris frantically tore open Johnston's uniform, looking for a significant wound. He dismissed the leg wound as minor. Unfortunately, the injury had opened up a major artery, bleeding down into Johnston's knee-high boots. Within minutes, the Confederate commanding officer died of blood loss.

BEAUREGARD ASSUMES COMMAND

At about 3:00 P.M., Beauregard found out that Johnston was dead and took over command of all Confederate forces in the field. Responding to the growing sounds of battle around the Hornets' Nest, he ordered most of his left flank to shift to the right to reinforce the attack there. By doing so, however, he committed two major mistakes. First, his assault that threw back Sherman's counterattack had been highly successful, pushing the Union right flank far back across the north end of Jones Field and on across the Tilghman Branch, seriously decimating their ranks. A follow-up attack could well have split the Union ranks, sending Sherman and McClernand north and west away from Pittsburg Landing, precisely as Beauregard had originally planned.

Second, the growing battle on his right flank was due to a continued hammering at a relatively small Union force, which was well positioned in the Sunken Road forest area, but isolated from retreat, resupply, or reinforcement. Bypassing this position would have undoubtedly resulted in a surrender of the entire command by nightfall, and possibly led to a successful capture of the steamboat landing itself. Instead, not only did Beauregard order a continued attack on the isolated Union position, but the shift of units from other isolated fights on the battlefield relieved pressure on other Union units, which were then able to withdraw and reestablish a line along the Hamburg-Savannah and Corinth-Pittsburg Roads—protecting Pittsburg Landing for Buell's rapidly approaching command.

BLOODY POND

Also receiving the news around 3:00 P.M. of Johnston's death, Bragg shifted over and took direct control of the Confederate right. Hurlbut had established a new Union line on the north end of the Peach Orchard just before Johnston's death, and despite having an unsupported left flank, he was making things hot for the assaulting Confederates. Just behind his position was a small, shallow pond that had the only fresh water available on this part of the battlefield. Wounded and parched infantrymen and horses alike crawled to its shores to get a cool drink; many were too badly wounded to even raise their heads once they were in the pond, and drowned in the foot-deep water. Dozens of blue-clad infantry piled up around the water, their wounds dripping and dissolving into the damp ground, until the pond was stained a deep crimson. When Confederates later advanced past the ghastly scene, someone remarked what a "bloody pond" it was; the name stuck.

About 4:00 P.M., Hurlbut's line finally caved under the intense Confederate fire, and he retreated north up the Hamburg-Savannah Road toward the riverboat landing. Jackson's and Chalmers's Brigades, supported by Col. James Clanton's Alabama Cavalry Regiment, rushed through the hole left by the collapse of Stuart and McArthur, and began advancing north on the east flank of the Hornets' Nest. About the same time, the seventh direct assault against the Hornets' Nest was hurled back, and bleeding and battered troops of Florida, Louisiana, and Texas pulled back to try and reestablish their ranks.

THE SURRENDER OF THE HORNETS' NEST

CSA Brig. Gen. Daniel Ruggles had seen enough. Gathering up as many artillery batteries and individual gun crews as he and his staff could locate, by 4:30 P.M., he had fifty-three guns parked axle to axle on the west border of Duncan Field—400 to 500 yards directly across open ground from the Hornets' Nest. This was the largest assembly of artillery ever seen at that time in the Western Hemisphere arrayed against a single target. Given the order to fire, the entire line of artillery opened up with a thunderous roar. Ruggles had ordered a mixed load of shot, shell, and canister fired as rapidly as possible. For nearly half an hour, the artillery kept up a fire that averaged three shots per second going into the Union position.

When at last the murderous fire lifted, another Confederate assault, led by Wood, charged the Union lines, this time sweeping around both flanks and meeting at the junction of the Hamburg-Savannah and Corinth Roads, north of the Hornets' Nest. As the assault came down upon them, both Wallace and Prentiss ordered a retreat, trying to break out of their position before being surrounded. While leading an Iowa brigade north to the Corinth Road, Wallace was struck in the head by a bullet and left for dead on the churned-up battlefield. His men broke and ran in panic. With the seeming death of Wallace (he actually died in his wife's arms a week later, in Savannah) and the impossibility of the situation painfully obvious, Prentiss finally surrendered what was left of the two brigades a little after 5:30 P.M. It was the largest surrender to that date in the war: 2,250 men.

GRANT'S LAST LINE OF DEFENSE

While the remainder of his forces were slowly dissolving away to the west and south, Grant hurriedly brought up as much artillery and as many men as he could scrape together to guard the critically important landing. By the time the last survivors of the Hornets' Nest surrendered, Grant had about seventy cannons and 20,000 infantrymen in line for defense. His 1½-mile long, last-ditch defense line started at Dill Branch on the left flank. From there, it entered the Tennessee River just south of the landing, ran due west to the Hamburg-Savannah Road, then turned north along the road to just beyond Perry Field. The majority of artillery was placed below the crest of one of the low, rolling hills above the landing, obviously intended to be used for point defense should an evacuation prove necessary.

As the last artillery batteries were pulling into position, the vanguard of Buell's Army of the Ohio, Nelson's 4th Division, finally appeared across the river from the landing. Hastily transported across the river, they had to force their way through thousands of panicked Union soldiers who were desperately trying to flee the battlefield. As they fell into place, a last Confederate charge came up the hill at them.

THE LAST CHARGE OF APRIL 6

About 6:00 P.M., Jackson's and Chalmers's Brigades moved through the Dill Branch ravine, aiming straight at the hill above Pittsburg Landing. The mass of Union artillery opened fire on them, joined by the gunboats *Lexington* and *Tyler* with their eight-inch guns. As these two brigades struggled through the flooded branch and rugged ravine, the remnants of Anderson's, Stephens's, and Wood's Brigades joined in the attack, without coordination—a mere 8,000 Confederates attacking without artillery support, reserves, or reinforcements. They moved uphill and across rugged terrain, into a strongly fortified Union position that was manned by at least 10,000 infantry, studded with nearly forty-inch-range artillery pieces, and had thousands more reinforcements hustling down the road to join in.

Within minutes the Confederate assault petered out, the butternut-clad infantry slipping away in squads and companies to find safer shelter as the early spring sun set on the horizon. Only Chalmers's and Jackson's infantrymen managed to briefly get within rifle range of the Union line, and most of them were out of ammunition by that point, intent on closing in and using the bayonet.

At 9:00 P.M., Beauregard sent word to his commanders to suspend the attack for the night, and pull back to the captured Union encampments. One by one, guns fell silent as the Confederates moved south and west, out of range. Units were in serious disarray on both sides, and the long night would be needed just to restore some semblance of order. Some Confederate units had not slept, other than the occasional nap, in two days, and most had not eaten since the day before. Although warned that Buell was nearby, Beauregard disregarded the threat and decided along with Bragg, Polk, and Hardee that the best plan was to rest and wait until daylight to get the army back into proper organization to renew the assault. All felt that the only task remaining was to sweep up Grant's line and force him to retire north, a task that should not take more than a few hours.

Losses on both sides were very high in the day-long battle, with both sides suffering near identical casualties—almost 8,500 dead, wounded, and missing. The critical factor in these losses, however, was that Grant had reinforcements on the way, while Beauregard was on his own, without hope of relief.

THE NIGHT OF APRIL 6–7, 1862

Just as the fighting on April 6 was ending for the day, Lew Wallace's Division finally arrived on the battlefield. Only 6 miles away when they were sent for at 11:00 A.M., a march that should have taken about two hours had taken over seven. Grant was livid, but mistakes in navigation had simply tied up the men all day, and they had wandered around muddy country roads north of the battlefield, trying to find the right one that led to Sherman's support. Later, Grant used Lew Wallace's tardiness as a scapegoat for some of the Union army's disaster of April 6; but if he had shown up on time, his division would have entered the brunt of the fighting around Shiloh Church, and most likely been routed as Sherman and McClernand had been. Lew Wallace, the future author of *Ben Hur*, lived with this series of mistakes, and the knowledge of Grant's misplaced blame, the rest of his life, and died with the thought on his mind that his errors had needlessly killed Union soldiers.

As the two battered armies settled down for a fitful rest, clouds gathered and a heavy, cold rain started to fall shortly after 10:00 P.M. Grant wandered around his headquarters, reluctant to enter; the building had been converted to a hospital, and the shrieks of the wounded and the charnel-house atmosphere were simply unendurable. Sherman, wounded again in the shoulder during the afternoon, finally found Grant under a large oak tree, holding a lantern and smoking one of his ever-present cigars. "Well, Grant, we've had the devil's own day, haven't we?" remarked the fiery Ohioan. Grant, far from demoralized, replied simply, "Yes. Lick 'em tomorrow, though."

Grant ordered the gunboats stationed on the Tennessee River to keep up a steady bombardment all night, but their shells burst mainly among the Union wounded who were still left out in the killing fields. The Confederates had pulled back to the former Union encampments, and were comfortably housed in the enemy's tents while they feasted on the abundant supplies. Cleburne, sitting in a tent and watching the shells burst around the bodies of the Union dead and wounded, later remarked, "History records few instances of more reckless inhumanity than this."

As the night wore on, Buell's Army of the Ohio traveled south from Savannah and crossed over into Grant's line. By 8:00 A.M. on April 7, over 13,000 fresh, well-equipped troops stood ready to renew the fight. Beauregard had no reinforcements, but remained optimistic. Upon hearing a false report that Buell's force was moving on Decatur, Alabama, he fired off a report to Richmond that he had "won a complete victory" that day, and would finish off Grant's force in the morning.

As morning approached, Grant had about 45,000 men ready for an assault on the Confederate positions, most of them well-rested and spoiling for a fight. Beauregard, on the other hand, could only field about 28,000 tired men (some accounts say 20,000), not yet reformed into their brigades or resupplied. Most of the battle-weary Confederate infantrymen had simply eaten what they could find for supper, then dropped into a fitful sleep without refilling their musette bags or cartridge boxes.

Newton and his comrades of the 14th Wisconsin stood in the pouring rain through the night of April 6, 1862. The hellishly black skies were only broken by the occasional flashes of lightning, or the more frequent booming naval cannons coming from the Union gunboats on the nearby Tennessee River, as they blindly blasted parts of the battlefield thought to house the Rebel army. He remarked later that daylight "was an awful long time coming," but once it did, the battle heated up again quickly. The 14th Wisconsin had been thrown together with three other regiments as part of a "provisional" brigade assigned to Brig. Gen. Thomas L. Crittenden's 5th Division of Buell's Army of the Ohio. They had the task of defending the extreme left of the Union line, and keeping the Confederates away from the critical port at Pittsburg Landing. As soon as it was light enough to see, skirmishes and pickets from both sides began shooting at each other.

6:00 A.M., APRIL 7, 1862

Just before dawn on Monday morning, April 7, 1862, Grant ordered his combined armies to move out. Buell's fresh troops moved south, toward Hardee's and Breckinridge's lines, while Grant's resupplied and reinforced army moved southwest in two lines of battle toward Bragg's and Polk's lines. Led by heavy artillery fire from the massed Union guns, the sudden dawn attack caught their Confederate opponents completely by surprise, turning the tables from the day before.

No organization existed. The Confederate infantry had simply dropped in place the night before at whatever camp was handy, and few had bothered to resupply their depleted cartridge boxes from the piles of Union ammunition boxes scattered literally everywhere. Most of them likely believed that, if Grant were smart, he would leave the field during the night rather than suffer another "lickin'."

To top off Beauregard's problems, Polk had withdrawn his corps nearly 4 miles to the south, to the site of his previous night's encampment, and it took nearly two hours after the Union's initial attack to locate him and get his corps moving. Once in the line, none of the four corps commanders actually commanded his entire corps; the units intermingled and were confusingly arrayed in the haste to mount a defense.

As part of the Union's general advance, orders came for Crittenden's scratch force to move forward and drive the Confederates out of his part of the battlefield. This was a tall order, since this area featured a very steep and heavily overgrown ravine, with Col. Preston Pond's able and capable 3rd Brigade (Maj. Gen. Daniel Ruggles 1st Division of Bragg's 2nd Corps) manning the top of the adjacent hillside, backed up by Capt. William H. Ketchum's Battery Alabama Artillery. Most of the surviving Confederates staring out across that short, deadly space at Crittenden's men that early morning were from two exceptional Louisiana units: the Crescent Regiment and the Orleans Guards Battalion. They were backed up by three other Louisiana and Tennessee infantry regiments. These men had helped lead the previous day's plunging battle through literally miles of bloody Union resistance, and were not exactly in the mood to give it back without a fight.

As Newton's line of battle moved out on Crittenden's command, the Confederate battery opened fire on their ranks, but misjudged the range and their deadly bolts flew harmlessly overhead. Before the Rebel cannoneers could adjust their range, Newton and the rest of the Union assault lines were ordered to lie down on the slope below the crest of the hill, so subsequent shots would bound harmlessly past them. For an hour and a half, they lay on the muddy ground, enduring a blistering bombardment, until a slackening of incoming fire and an earthshaking Rebel yell announced the Confederate infantry was heading their way. The 14th rose as a single unit, and delivered an effective volley, smashing the charge as it came up the hill toward them. Rapidly reloading, Newton and other Union soldiers poured volley after volley into the mass of gray uniforms until the Confederates were forced to quit the attack and withdraw to the other side of the ravine. As they pulled away, Crittenden ordered a full-scale assault on the fractured Confederate line. Newton began running down the hill into the brush while his captain, Joseph Lawton, was seen by other men of the 14th breaking away from the charge and running back up the hill toward the river, away from the hot battle.

With great effort, the four Confederate corps commanders managed to form a meandering defense line in the face of the Union attack, roughly running northwest to southeast. It stretched from Jones Field, across Duncan Field just south of the Hornets' Nest, to about the place of Johnston's death the day before, on the Hamburg-Savannah Road. They managed to hold this line under great pressure until about 11:00 A.M., when a general pullback in order was called. The line moved back, intact, about half a mile on the left and extended another half a mile on the right to counter increased pressure from Buell's forces.

Like other parts of the Shiloh battle line, the fight for the ravine soon became a confused tangle, with charges met by counter-charges, both Union and Confederate reinforcements coming up to try for one more punch that would break the other's line, and the capture and re-capture of the Rebel artillery battery no less than three times. After one successful capture of the battery, Newton and others set fire to the gun carriages and caissons, while Lieutenant Staley of Company D and Sergeant Blackett of Company K hastily spiked one of the guns before another Confederate charge drove them away yet again.

By noon the Confederate line had again pulled back under pressure to a position centered on Shiloh Church. Union units all along the line kept up a steady artillery and infantry fire; Grant's plan was simply to roll south using his fresh troops to grind up the tired Confederate infantry. The plan worked quite well. Several counterattacks by Hardee, Breckinridge, and Bragg were absorbed and thrown back with heavy casualties.

However, by 1:00 P.M., it was obvious to Beauregard that not only were they going to lose this battle, but he was in danger of being swept in pieces from the field. He hesitated for nearly an hour before finally passing orders down the line for his commands to break contact and retreat to Corinth. Several Confederate artillery batteries positioned at Shiloh Church, along with Col. Winfield S. Statham's and Col. Robert P. Trabue's Brigades of Breckinridge's Corps were to act as a heavy rear guard.

Cavalrymen were ordered to hastily destroy all Union equipment and supplies that the retreating infantry were unable to carry off. As the piles of broken tents and wagons blazed in the stormy afternoon, Breckinridge broke off contact and withdrew in good order at the rear of the long Confederate column.

All told, the 14th Division stayed under fire for more than ten continuous hours, until the Confederate lines finally broke as evening approached, and the gallant Alabama Battery fell into the Wisconsin men's hands for good. Newton later asked his parents in a letter to send him any newspaper descriptions of the battle, as "All we know about the battle is what we saw & that wasn't much, so I would like to see a paper if possible to see what we did."

What Newton and the 14th Wisconsin did that spring afternoon was break a strong, reinforced Confederate assault, one which had aimed to finish the job they had started the previous morning: dividing the Union force in two, driving them away from the safety of the river and reinforcements, and then cutting them to ribbons in detail. Instead, the shattered ranks of the Confederates limped back south to Corinth, minus their commanding general, Albert Sidney Johnston, who had accidentally been killed the previous afternoon by his own men. They were also missing almost half their men. As darkness fell, the men of the 14th broke off their day-long attack, turned around, and marched back to the riverside, mourning the loss of two dead and five seriously injured in their own ranks. Despite the savage fighting and total exhaustion that sapped them all, Newton complained, "the worst of it was that we couldn't get any thing to eat but hard bread [hardtack] and not much of that."

Grant had won a magnificent victory, but at a heavy price. Of his and Buell's 65,000-man combined army, 1,754 were killed, 8,408 were wounded, and 2,885 were captured or missing in action—a fifth of his whole command. The tattered remnants of his proud regiments were too shot up and exhausted after two solid days of combat to pursue the retreating Confederates, who made it back into Mississippi without resistance.

Beauregard suffered worse. In addition to losing the beloved commander, Albert Sidney Johnston, he reported losses of 1,728 killed, 8,012 wounded, and 959 missing or captured. This loss of 10,699 soldiers constituted nearly a fourth of all the men he had brought into the campaign. Once back in Corinth, he ordered the town prepared for defense against an attack by Grant, and set about turning nearly the entire small community into one vast hospital for his thousands of wounded.

The cannon spiked by Lieutenant Staley and Sergeant Blackett was captured at the end of the battle and afterwards sent back to Wisconsin as a war trophy. The men of the 14th had fought so gallantly during the long afternoon that other units dubbed them with the high-praise name, "Wisconsin Regulars." As the 14th arrived at Pittsburg Landing, they were called back into ranks and the roll was called. Every man was present or accounted for as killed or wounded, without a single man listed as missing or made prisoner—a most unusual event for that time in the war.

Newton wrote home after the battle,

> As for myself I came off with out a scratch and I am sure I don't know why it was for I stood as good a chance as any of them to get hurt. A good many of the boys came to the conclusion after the battle that the Secesh shot awful careless with their guns, and I guess all the Co are perfectly satisfied as to what war is & they would be willing to have the war brought to an end so they could be discharged and sent home.

Unfortunately, Newton would see much more of "what war is" before his own trip home finally came. James Barrow's war, however, was about to come to an abrupt end, many miles to the east and a few months later.

SOUTH MOUNTAIN

After McClellan's failed Peninsular Campaign, and the spectacular Confederate victory at 2nd Manassas (2nd Bull Run to the Confederates), Lee decided that the Union armies were weak enough, at least in their top leadership, to risk a change in the overall Southern strategy. Formerly, Lee had been a proponent of the plan to fight a purely defensive war against the numerically superior Union military, forcing the North to expend its energy and men against strongly held Southern cities and positions until they tired of the fight and gave up. McClellan's timidity and the failure of his successors caused Lee and other Southern strategists to adopt the belief that the war could be considerably shortened by a strong show of Confederate military prowess in Union territory. In addition, Lee believed that the Union armies were in disarray, taking considerable time to regroup and would be forced to expend most of their strength in defending Washington against an always-threatened Confederate attack. Lastly, Lee thought that a strong show by Confederate armies might bring increased support for the South from "fence-sitting" Marylanders (if any were actually left by this time is another question!); or that Confederate victories might finally gain the fledgling nation diplomatic recognition, as well as military support, from France and Great Britain. Less than a week after 2nd Manassas, he ordered the Army of Northern Virginia to march north, heading for Maryland and Pennsylvania.

James Barrow and the Bowdon Volunteers had been rushed up from Richmond during the second battle at Manassas Junction the week before, but even after a three-day forced march, with men falling by the wayside and dying of heat and exhaustion, they arrived only in time to view the post-battle carnage. They camped near the battlefield only briefly, before marching north again to rejoin the rest of Lee's army. Together, they arrived on the banks of the Potomac River at White's Ford on September 5. The next morning, stripped to the skin and balancing their uniforms atop their heads, they waded across the river into Union territory. A regimental band on the opposite bank played "Maryland, My Maryland" to cheer them along.

The uniforms they carried that day were an improvement over the ones issued and purchased by other units in the early days of the war. Most antebellum commanders were mightily impressed with the European, and specifically French, methods of handsomely outfitting their armies, leading to some very interesting ideas about what men should wear into combat. This was based almost exclusively on the theories of the Swiss military philosopher, Antoine-Henri de Jomini, who had served as one of Napoleon's officers. A very influential antebellum theorist, Jomini held that war was a "grand stage for heroes," and that an army in the field must dress and comport itself as the representative of the proud and correct state that it was. (Presumably, then, an army representing an incorrect state could dress any old way they wanted to!) His theories were widely read and very influential on American military thought in the 1850s; the future Confederate general, William J. Hardee, wrote a series of books on organization and strategy based largely on Jomini's theories, the core of which became the standard field reference manuals for both sides during the war.

One telling example of the devotion to Jomini's theories was the adoption by both sides of so-called "Zouave" units, inspired by a troop of the French Algerian soldiers who had traveled the pre-war U.S., giving displays of their precision marching to standing-room-only crowds. The Zouave uniform consisted of white leggings or gaiters, brightly colored pantaloons (very baggy, knicker-length pants), usually red or brilliant blue, white shirts under what were then fashionable red or blue "Arab-style" velvet or wool vests, darker colored shell jackets, usually decorated with brass or gold trim and buttons, and sometimes a short blue or red cape. Finally, the whole affair was topped off with a fez or turban. These units were noted for their esprit de corps and their drilling abilities, but their gaudy uniforms made them stand out far too distinctly on the battlefield. Most units soon abandoned these outfits in favor of more standard uniforms, but a handful wore them throughout the war, most notably Wheat's Tigers out of New Orleans and Duryee's Zouaves out of New York.

The standard infantry uniform in both armies (after all the pre-war glamour had faded) was a wool shell or sack coat, worn over a three-button white or natural-colored cotton shirt, with wool trousers held up by cotton or leather suspenders, usually with the pants stuffed into the top of tall wool socks, and topped off by either a cowboy-style "slouch" hat or short-brimmed kepi. Shoes were usually pegged-soled "Jefferson" bootees-high-topped brogans made on a straight last, meaning there was not a distinct right or left shoe. A waist belt fastened with a lead-filled buckle held a cap box on the right front and a bayonet scabbard on the left hip. A cartridge box filled with a standard load of sixty rounds was slung over the left shoulder, resting on the right hip. A canteen and a canvas haversack were slung over the right shoulder (resting on the left hip). The haversack was about the size of a large purse, sometimes tarred black for waterproofing, and it contained rations and small personal items.

The differences in the two armies were reflected in two things: the color of their uniforms and equipment and the way they carried their bedrolls and personal supplies. By 1863, the Union army almost universally wore dark blue coats and jackets over sky-blue pants, usually trimmed with brass buttons bearing letters designating their branch of service—"I" for infantry, "A" for artillery, and so on. Their belts and other leather gear were usually black, and most infantrymen carried black-colored canvas or leather knapsacks, with their bedroll tied on top. Their Confederate counterparts wore uniforms that were by regulation "Richmond gray," but that ranged in hue from a gray so dark it was almost black all the way to barely dyed examples that soon turned white in the sun. The late-war usual Confederate color, "butternut," came from the use of plant dyes that could not truly replicate the designated gray colors, and soon turned into shades of light to medium brown. As an unintended consequence, this provided a sort of unofficial camouflage. Confederate buttons ranged from brightly polished brass decorated with state seals, to stolen Union buttons, down to ones made of wood or bone.

Confederate leather gear was by regulation brown in color, although equipment shortages and the ensuing use of captured Union equipment meant that many men had mixtures of black and brown leather gear. Unlike their Union counterparts, Confederate cartridge boxes rarely had lead-filled plates attached, and almost never had polished brass cartridge breast strap-plates attached. The fancy, lead-filled, brass belt buckles were replaced in the Western Theater by "Georgia frame" buckles, which are very similar to today's minimalist belt buckles. An interesting and creative use of captured Union gear was to simply turn a standard "U.S." belt buckle upside down, and the resourceful Rebel could then claim it stood for "Southern Nation."

Toward the end of the war, shortages in leather led to the use of brown or black painted canvas for belts and straps. Confederate-issued canteens tended toward the thick, round, heavier, wooden type, but the Union tin "bullseye" pattern canteens were very popular and scavenged from the dead on battlefields whenever possible.

Rather than using uncomfortable knapsacks, most Confederate infantrymen placed what little they carried—an extra pair of socks, a "wiper" to clean their weapon, a "housewife" containing sewing supplies, a tobacco tin, occasionally a wallet, maybe a small *Bible*, and a photograph of their loved ones or a letter—inside their single blanket, rolled it up, fastened the ends together with a thick rubber band or piece of rope, and slung it over their right shoulder.

INTO MARYLAND

Once safely across the river, Barrow, the Bowdon Volunteers, and the rest of the great Southern army suited back up and, at a leisurely pace, marched off to Frederick, Maryland, only 40 miles northwest of Washington, D.C. There, Lee divided his forces. Maj. Gen. Jonathan "Stonewall" Jackson's Corps was sent southwest to seize Harper's Ferry. McLaws's Division, including Cobb's Legion, was deployed due west to take and hold Maryland Heights, overlooking Harper's Ferry and protecting Jackson's eastern flank. The main body of Lee's army would travel due west, across South Mountain and Elk Ridge, then turn north to strike at Pennsylvania.

All the elements of Lee's army moved at a slow pace, Jackson swinging to the south to approach Harper's Ferry, while other commands infiltrated through passes on South Mountain, taking up positions on the heights surrounding the river town, and even bringing up and emplacing artillery, all without any real opposition. McLaws followed his orders to pass through Burkettsville, then crossed Brownsville Pass on South Mountain and entered Pleasant Valley before heading up onto South Mountain. This valley lay just to the north of Jackson's operations at Harper's Ferry, and east of Lee's main force on the other side of Elk Ridge, near Sharpsburg, Maryland. McLaws was given a large responsibility for a single division. He was to support Jackson to the south, guard the passes over South Mountain to the east, and seize Sandy Hook, just downriver from Harper's Ferry, cutting off the only remaining avenue of escape for the Union garrison there. Gen. Joseph Brevard Kershaw's and Gen. William Barksdale's Brigades were sent to link up with Lee's main force at Elk Ridge, while Gen. Paul Jones Semmes's Brigade was posted atop South Mountain at Brownsville Pass, to guard against the seemingly unlikely event of a Union flanking attack there. Brig. Gen. Howell Cobb marched his brigade, including the boys from Bowdon, south to take Sandy Hook. They succeeded in their task without any serious opposition on September 13.

Lee's long column snaked through the valleys and mountain passes into Hagerstown, again without any real opposition from the Yankee garrisons in the area. It seemed as if Lee had so thoroughly cowed McClellan in the Seven Days and 2nd Manassas battles that the "Little Napoleon" would not come out to fight again. While some element of truth was there, an opportunity arose that finally propelled the reluctant Union army commander into action.

By early September, word that Lee's army occupied Frederick and had cut off lines of communication to the Union garrisons at Harper's Ferry and Martinsburg caused a general panic in Washington and Baltimore. McClellan, spurred into action at last by the great consternation of the President, for once moved with near blinding speed. Within a week, he not only had reorganized his shattered army, but forward deployed them to both protect the two cities and to move west and uncover Lee's objective. He divided his army into three great columns: Gen. Ambrose Burnside, with the I and IX Corps, moved north to Leesborough and Brookville; Maj. Gen. Edwin V. Sumner, with the II and XII Corps, moved west toward Rockville; and Maj. Gen. William Franklin took the VI and IV Corps westward along the Potomac River through the southwestern Maryland countryside.

On Saturday, September 13, the 27th Indiana Infantry Regiment, the vanguard of the XII Corps, crossed the shallow Monocacy River and cautiously entered the railroad crossroads of Monocacy Junction, one of the military campsites just south of Frederick, which had very recently been abandoned by Lee's forces. In front, scouting for any danger, were Company B's skirmishers, led by USA 1st Sgt. John M. Bloss. While stopping for a brief rest in a field that had been used as a Confederate encampment only days before, Bloss noticed a dropped roll of cigars wrapped up in a piece of paper. Picking them up to enjoy a hit of good Virginia tobacco, Bloss removed the paper and glanced at it before tossing it away. What he saw printed on the paper gave him pause, however, as the name of one of the Confederate generals was listed as the sender. Unbelievably, a copy of "Special Order No. 191," written on behalf of Lee by Asst. Adj. Gen. R. H. Chilton, and addressed to Maj. Gen. Daniel Harvey Hill, the marching orders detailing Lee's entire plan for this part of his campaign, had been found by the enemy.

By noon, the "lost orders" had been forwarded to McClellan, and within the hour, he issued new orders and set his ponderous army moving toward where he now knew Lee was positioning his divided forces. McClellan's habitual overconfidence returning in spades, he informed Lincoln that he had in his possession "a paper with which I shall whip Bobby Lee."

The next day, Sunday, September 14, back on South Mountain, the vanguard of Franklin's VI Corps was observed moving toward the scattered Confederate commands, along a road no one had thought to guard, over Crampton's Gap. McLaws hastily ordered Col. Thomas Munford's Cavalry Brigade to seal off the road over the pass at the base of the mountain, in order to buy some time while he recalled Cobb's Brigade to reinforce Semmes's Brigade in the process of partly repositioning atop the pass. James Barrow and the other boys from Bowdon marched for hours northward from Sandy Hook to the base of South Mountain near Brownsville, before plopping down, intent on fixing something to eat. Less than an hour later, a runner brought orders to Cobb to send his command in relief of Munford's Cavalry, now being hard pressed on the other side of the hill. Cobb's Legion and the 15th North Carolina Infantry immediately threw on their equipment, formed up, and started up the mountain at a rapid pace, soon followed by Cobb himself leading his other two regiments, the 16th and 24th Georgia. Cobb's orders were to hold as long as possible, in order to allow Jackson the time he needed to overwhelm the Union garrison at Harper's Ferry. This only added fuel to the aggressive fire of his troops.

The road over Crampton's Gap is very steep on the western side of the mountain, and it took over a half-hour for the first of Cobb's men to reach the top. As they approached, they could not help but hear the sounds of a desperate fight at the eastern base of the pass, where over 6,500 Union infantrymen were attacking Munford's reinforced cavalry force of less than 1,000. Cobb's men reached the top at last—Barrow later told his son that they had run the last few hundred yards—and Munford fell back to join them on the crest. Franklin pushed his Union infantry force on, telling his men to push through the seemingly weak Confederate line of defense and press on to Brownsville before darkness set in. It was about 6:00 P.M. when all three forces met atop the pass, and dusk was fast approaching.

As Munford's men reached the top of the pass, they turned and stood for only a volley or two of fire before resuming their retreat down the western side of the hill. Franklin's men pressed on, hard on the heels of the fleeing cavalrymen, who nearly ran over Cobb's men as they pounded over the top of the pass. Instead of stopping and joining together with Cobb's men, Munford continued to pull his men away from the surging Union assault. Cobb's men, now led by Lt. Col. Jefferson Lamar, raised a Rebel yell and raced forward in attack, charging down the eastern side of the mountain into the very face of the onrushing Union troops.

In front was the 1st New Jersey Brigade, commanded by Col. Alfred T.A. Torbert. As the Rebel infantry charged down the mountain, Torbert's command wheeled to envelop them, soon bringing down fire on three sides of the Georgia men. Lamar ordered his men to halt, form a deeply bowed line of battle under fire, and return same. Twenty minutes of desperate fighting later, 72 percent of Cobb's entire brigade was dead, wounded, or captured, but as darkness fell around them, they had bought just enough time for the two-gun Troup Artillery battery to haul up and unlimber on the road above them. The guns, firing canister and double-canister at attacking Union forces, kept the road clear long enough for the remaining Confederates to evacuate the mountain safely. As the Union attack petered out after dark, the mostly unscathed artillerymen withdrew, leaving one of their guns behind after a lucky Union counter-battery shot broke its axle.

Cobb's Legion was deeply hurt, and the ranks of the Bowdon Volunteers were shattered. James Barrow had been hit twice, in the left ankle and in the lower leg, but was picked up by Union stretcher-bearers later that night and taken to a field hospital. He lay atop a hospital table late that night, not yet eighteen years old, while the torn remains of his left leg were amputated just below his knee. Fourteen of his friends in Company B were killed or mortally wounded in the brief battle, including Colonel Lamar. Seventeen others were captured along with Barrow, and almost half the remains of the small company suffered non-lethal wounds. James Barrow's war was over.

The three battles for South Mountain (the other two were fought the same day at Fox's Gap and Turner's Gap, to the north of Crampton's Gap) were overshadowed by events of the following week. Lee, warned of the Federal army's approach by the running fights atop South Mountain, rearranged his forces in and around Sharpsburg, partly along the meandering Antietam Creek. The subsequent battle fought there on September 17, while technically a draw, prompted Lee to abandon his plans to invade the North for a while and withdraw back south into Virginia. The "Bloodiest Day in American Military History," with over 26,000 dead, wounded, and missing on both sides, was also close enough to a Union victory to allow Lincoln to issue his long-delayed "Emancipation Proclamation." Although it only "freed" the enslaved people in Confederate-held territories, not those owned by Union army officers or Northern citizens, it did have the effect of changing the Union's reasons for fighting, from one of preserving the Union to a crusade to free enslaved people—a cause many Union soldiers saw as actually worth dying for.

JAMES K. NEWTON

James K. Newton remained in the line after Shiloh, and fought at Corinth, where he was captured and later paroled. Keeping strictly to the letter and spirit of his parole, Newton stayed put in St. Louis until he was "exchanged" for a captured Confederate soldier, then promptly joined the ranks again in time to participate in the long campaign for Vicksburg. Assigned to the Vicksburg garrison force after the fall of the beleaguered city, Newton and the rest of the 14th Wisconsin were later reassigned to Maj. Gen. Nathaniel "Commissary" Banks's Department of the Gulf, and followed the unfortunate (and some would say incompetent) Massachusetts general on his ill-fated Red River Campaign.

Newton was no more impressed with Banks than most soldiers and on his return to Vicksburg wrote, "The famous 'Red River Expedition' is over at last & we are out of Banks' Dep't. I hope we may never go near it again."

In December 1864, Newton and the 14th Wisconsin were reassigned to the Federal depot at Nashville, arriving just in time to join in the utter rout of the Confederate Army of Tennessee. Two months later they were moved back to Vicksburg yet again, before Newton participated in his last battle actions at Mobile. In July of 1865, he was commissioned as a lieutenant, sent to Alabama, and tasked with the job of administering the amnesty oath to returning Confederate veterans.

He mustered out of the ranks on October 9, 1865, and shortly afterward enrolled at Ripon Academy in Wisconsin. He wrote to his parents, "This life beats army life 'all hollow.' To tell the truth I like it a great deal better too. I wish now, I could spend the same length of time at study that I did in the army. I think I could make it of some use to me, don't you?"

Newton enrolled the following year at Oberlin College in Ohio, where he eventually gained a faculty position as a professor of German and French. He married a widow and former Oberlin student, Francis Woodrow, in 1870, and retired from the college in 1888. He later moved to Nordhoof, California, and died on June 26, 1892. He is buried in Ojai, California.

By the end of the 14th Wisconsin's war in Mobile, they had gained a total of 1,212 men by recruitment and reenlistment and suffered the loss of 827 men throughout the war (including transfers, discharges, 97 desertions, and 287 combat deaths). In the last unit muster back in Wisconsin, a total of 1,355 officers and men answered the roll. Amazingly, with all the serious combat they saw during the war, only thirteen men were listed as "missing."

JAMES R. BARROW

James Reeves "Jimmy" Barrow was born on October 3, 1844, in Bowdon, Georgia, a small town close to the Alabama state line. His grandfather, Moses Barrow, had fought in the Revolutionary War with a North Carolina unit. James left an academic career at Bowdon Collegiate Institute to enlist for the Cause as one of the original members of Company B, Cobb's Legion, mustering in on July 30, 1861.

His military career ended a bit over a year later, on September 14, 1862, during the running battle atop Crampton's Gap on South Mountain, Maryland, where he was wounded, captured, and had his left leg amputated by Union surgeons. After recovering, he spent several months in Union prisons, was eventually exchanged, and possibly served to the end of the war in Atlanta's Invalid Corps (about the only place he could have served, with his wounds).

Cobb's Legion reformed after South Mountain/Sharpsburg (which many historians consider a single extended battle). They fought in Virginia most of the rest of the war, leaving Virginia's battlefields only to go with Longstreet's Corps to Georgia and Tennessee during the Chickamauga–Chattanooga–Knoxville Campaigns, and were present at the Army of Northern Virginia's surrender at Appomattox Courthouse. Only fifty-five men stood by the Legion's colors that day, including a single corporal and three privates who composed the remnants of Company B.

After the war, Barrow became a mill owner and respected businessman in Bowdon, soon marrying Martha Holmes. Their union produced one son, John William Barrow. James died on June 11, 1880, of tuberculosis contracted in prison during the war, and was buried in the Bowdon Baptist Church Cemetery.

James had two older brothers who also served in the war. John Turner Barrow was a sergeant in Company B, Georgia Volunteer Infantry

Regiment, and died of smallpox in an Atlanta hospital, possibly during the great campaign for that fair city. His other brother, William Henry Bowdon, fought alongside James in Company B, until he was wounded, captured, and later exchanged at Cold Harbor, June 1864.

2

Thunder on the Battlefield: The Artillery

Capt. Francis DeGress, 1st Illinois Light Artillery, Battery H
Capt. Thomas J. Key, Arkansas Battery, Hotchkiss's Battalion

Two obscure western states officers. Two artillery batteries. Two battles near Atlanta, separated by less than 35 miles in distance and two months in time. One officer earns widespread acclaim, newspaper headlines, a personal review by the President, and the thanks of a grateful nation, despite his battery having lost its guns in the midst of a critical battle. The other officer vanishes into the mist of history, although his battery divided its guns in the face of a multiple-front enemy threat and saved the day through superior gunnery skills.

Thomas Jefferson Key of Arkansas was a prominent newspaperman and slavery defender before the war, but did not enlist to fight until shortly after the Battle of Shiloh. He was over thirty years old at a time when the average infantryman was less than twenty. He rapidly rose through the ranks, becoming a lieutenant in short order and was soon reassigned to the artillery. Eventually, he was given command of the Helena Battery of the Arkansas Light Artillery, which was soon renamed "Key's Battery" in the fashion of the day.

The pre-war life of Francis DeGress, sometimes referred to simply as "Frank," is not as well documented. He was born in Cape Girardeau, Missouri, and mustered in as a second lieutenant with the 1st Illinois Light Artillery on February 20, 1862. He rose to the rank of captain, and was given command of Battery H, 1st Illinois Light Artillery, which, in turn, was soon renamed "DeGress's Battery." In that era's fashion, this battery was also known as "Silversparre's Battery" and "Hart's Battery," in honor of earlier commanders.

The name "light artillery" refers to units that possess cannons that are only "light" compared to fixed-fortification "heavy" guns. Both of these units dragged four guns from one side of the Western Confederacy to the other, with each one weighing 1,500 to 1,800 pounds—and that is just the weight of the tube alone! Add the weight of the gun carriage, caissons, accruements, and various bits and pieces of tackle and tack, and it becomes clear that "light" artillery was somewhat of a misnomer. No soldier who grunted under the load of pushing and shoving these bronze and iron beasts mile after mile along rutted, muddy roads would ever agree that they were "light" under any circumstance.

Key's Battery, part of a larger organization known as Hotchkiss's Battalion (usually assigned as part of Maj. Gen. Patrick R. Cleburne's divisional artillery), had a number of different configurations, but ended up at the time of the Atlanta Campaign with four smoothbore howitzers, probably M1841 12-pounder field howitzers. Key also had overall command of the other two units in his artillery battalion through parts of this campaign. Goldthwaite's Alabama Battery had a four-gun battery of M1857 12-pounder "Napoleon" smoothbore howitzers, and Sweet's Mississippi Battery had a four-gun battery of M1861 10-pounder Parrott rifles.

DeGress's Battery, which was officially known as Company (sometimes Battery) H of the 1st Illinois Light Artillery, started the war with a number of different cannons, including Napoleon howitzers and nearly obsolete M1841 6-pounder smoothbore howitzers, but by the time it went into battlefield service, it was equipped with four deadly and effective 20-pounder Parrott rifles.

All of these specifics may seem as if they should mean a lot to the artillerymen of that day, or even historians of the period, but the truth is that the subject of Civil War artillery has so many oddities and inconsistencies that it could (and has) encompass whole books in and of itself. From an ancient tradition of a branch of military service used primarily for harassment and minor support of the more dashing infantry and cavalry branches, the science of artillery had undergone a renaissance in the post-Napoleonic antebellum years. Along with the field of military engineering, artillery became the branch of choice for some of the brightest minds emerging from West Point in the 1830s and 1840s—including Confederate Gen. Pierre Gustave Toutant Beauregard and his old friend,

West Point instructor and opponent at Fort Sumter, USA Maj. Robert Anderson—and had evolved into a central part of planning for both defense and offense. During the war, the use of artillery further developed in two disparate directions. "Flying" batteries (horse-drawn, relatively light, and very mobile) were used to support rapidly moving cavalry operations, and, in static situations, heavy siege guns were used as the primary offense weapon, as in the case of Atlanta.

Basically put, "artillery" is both the organizational designation and use of heavy cannons designed to toss a solid or explosive round, for distances varying from point-blank to over 10,000 yards (just under 6 miles). Artillery weapons came in three basic types:

1. Rifled guns, which were long-barreled, heavy cannons designed to fire heavy solid shot great distances at high velocities and with flat trajectories, in order to hit distant targets or batter down masonry structure;

2. Smoothbore, relatively short-barreled howitzers, which were originally designed to shoot explosive shells using less of a powder charge and were used for more rapid and direct fire, and which also had the advantage of having a shorter and lighter tube than the rifled guns, making them easier to transport and set up;

3. Mortars, which were very short, thick, and heavy-barreled weapons used to shoot large explosive shells at very high trajectories, so they were able to drop their charges in almost vertically. Mortars were primarily used in situations where the enemy force was dug in trenches, or behind walls or redoubts, where flat-trajectory ordnance would simply bounce off the glacis (forward slope of the fortification) or sail overhead.

Each of these three basic types came in several varieties and in a wide range of sizes, measured by their "caliber" (internal diameter of the tube), or by the weight of the ammunition itself. However, to make this subject as confusing as humanly possible, there was never a universal standard for the naming of cannons. In antebellum days, it was customary to designate cannons based on the weight of the solid-shot ammunition, e.g., a cannon that fired a solid-round shot weighing six pounds would have a caliber of 3.67 inches, and would be designated a "6-pounder." The advent of rifled cannons caused this system to collapse, as they fired oblong rather than round shot, and therefore had no standard weight; the longer the round, the heavier it would be, depending on whether it was solid shot or explosive shell. For example, one of the most common and notorious artillery pieces, the 10-pounder Parrott rifle, fired a range of ammunition that weighed between a 9-pound shell to an 11.5-pound case shot, and the tube itself had a caliber varying from 2.9 inches (1861 model) to 3.0 inches (1863 model). Larger models of the Parrott rifle, the so-called 200-pounder and 300-pounder, actually fired shells weighing 175 and 250 pounds respectively. Confused? You're not alone. Even experts in the field of Civil War artillery sometimes have a hard time keeping up with the whole mess.

Cannon ammunition, also known as "shot," "ordnance," (which really refers to the entire system or grouping of weapons), or "rounds," commonly fell into three categories: solid shot, exploding shells, or canister. Solid shot was exactly what it sounds like: solid round balls or oblong bolts. Originally designed to tear through the hull and rigging of sailing ships, it was mostly useful to physically blow through enemy defenses. Exploding shells came in several varieties (including the very common "case shot"), and had some form of fuse that ignited on firing. The timing of the fuse was adjustable in many cases, so it could explode after the round had traveled a certain distance. This was why artillery had attracted so many of the best and brightest before the war, as the math needed to determine the time of flight to a set distance was daunting at best. The third type of ammunition was canister, which also came in several varieties, such as "grape shot." These consisted of many smaller iron or lead balls packed into some sort of housing (classic "canister" shot looked much like a modern coffee can), that would explode out of the barrel exactly like a gigantic shotgun. This type of round did not have much of a range, but was deadly effective against close-in charging infantry.

Just like their infantry counterparts, artillery weapons were almost all muzzleloaders. They required a team of six to eight men to set up, load, aim, and fire the weapon. A well-drilled team could fire two shots per minute, "by the book," but in the heat of combat sometimes shortcuts were undertaken that increased this rate to an average of three or even four shots a minute. A well-trained battery could keep up a sustained fire of one shot every five to ten seconds, and larger assemblies of cannon could put out amazing rates of fire. At Shiloh, CSA Brig. Gen. Daniel Ruggles gathered up as many artillery batteries and individual gun crews as he and his staff could locate, and ended up with fifty-three guns parked axle to axle on the west border of Duncan Field, 400 to 500 yards directly across open ground from the Union position in the Hornets' Nest. This was the largest assembly of artillery ever seen at that time in the Western Hemisphere arrayed against a single target. Ruggles ordered a mixed load of shot, shell, and canister fired as rapidly as possible. For nearly one-half hour, the assembled artillery kept up a fire that averaged three shots per second going into the Union position.

Union batteries usually had four or six guns, almost always of the same type and size. Confederate batteries were almost invariably four guns, and very frequently had two or sometimes even three different types and sizes of weapons within them, making supply and logistics a nightmare. As per the usual in artillery, even this basic setup was not universally standard. During the Atlanta Campaign, the Union armies had one five-gun, 22 six-gun, and 29 four-gun batteries. Their Confederate counterparts, on the other hand, had 44 four-gun batteries, all organized into 3 twelve-gun battalions (which maintained their four-gun battery designations and internal command system), and 2 four-gun batteries (which were independently assigned). A battery was usually commanded by a captain, called the Battery Commander. Early in the war batteries were typically assigned to infantry brigades, and the captain would answer directly to the general commanding the brigade. Later in the war both sides gradually moved away from this system into one where the artillery was organized into independent artillery battalions (Confederates) or brigades (Union). They were headed by divisional "Chiefs of Artillery," usually a colonel, and they were composed of three to five individual batteries.

Obviously, with all this variation in command structure, it is impossible to set a precise figure on how many men each battery contained, but on average, a four-gun battery would have about 70 men and 45 horses, while the largest batteries might have over 170 men and 100 horses. Organizational structure within the battery itself was remarkably similar on both sides. A lieutenant "Section Chief" would command two guns, with each individual gun commanded by a sergeant "Chief of the Piece"; two corporals were the "Gunners" in charge of the firing operation; and the "Chief of Caisson" was in charge of supply and reloading operations. Six privates rounded out the individual gun crew, all with very specialized and specific tasks to perform during a firing operation. Other assigned personnel were the First Sergeant (sometimes known as the Orderly Sergeant), who assisted the captain in administrative matters and served as a second-in-command of the battery; a Quartermaster

Sergeant, who was responsible for the logistics and supply of the battery; drivers, teamsters, and wagoneers of the horse teams, usually privates; an Artificer (blacksmith) and Farrier (who kept the horses and mules shod); Musicians, usually just one or two buglers; and a Guidon, who carried the battery's colors and was usually the most trusted and reliable man.

Because hauling the heavy cannons across rough roads and open fields wore out the horses at an alarming rate, cannoneers usually walked alongside their rig, riding on the horses or caisson only when very rapid movement was necessary. The "flying batteries" attached to the cavalry doubled the number of horses assigned to the battery, and tended to use the lighter howitzers, so everyone could habitually ride and keep up with the fast pace.

Key and DeGress would cross paths, and find their greatest fame, during the four-month-long Atlanta Campaign, which started in May 1864. DeGress, with his heavier guns, tended not to get engaged in the swifter-moving early May battles, showing up for the fight first during the Dallas Line battles at the end of the month. Ironically, this is where Key made his greatest stand.

APPROACH TO DALLAS

Sherman kicked off his Atlanta Campaign in early May 1864, with assaults on the towns of Dalton and Resaca, both of which were successful in forcing Confederate commander Gen. Joseph Eggleston Johnston into a gradual retreat toward Atlanta. Within three weeks, Sherman had forced his way south nearly a hundred miles, fighting an almost continuous series of pitched battles, skirmishes, ambushes, counter-ambushes, and raids, until he finally stood just north of the rocky Gibraltar marking the entrance into Marietta, and ultimately, Atlanta. Here, he had a serious problem, as he needed to stay close to the Western and Atlantic Railroad line, his lifeline back to the Union supply depots at Chattanooga and Nashville—but a lifeline that hampered any attempt at widespread maneuvering.

Before the war, Sherman had ridden around Kennesaw Mountain and Allatoona extensively as a young Army officer assigned to Marietta. He was courting (ultimately, unsuccessfully) a certain young Cecilia Stovall, who lived in Etowah Heights near the railroad line at Altoona, and spent a considerable amount of time riding the low hills between his station at Marietta and her home. From this possibly painful memory of hopeful rides through the countryside years earlier, he recognized the potential for making the terrain into natural fortresses. Changing his usual frontal assault tactics, he took a chance at marching overland with limited supplies, and abandoned his line of approach straight down the railroad to move westward down the Kennesaw Due West and Acworth-Dallas Roads, toward the small town of Dallas. It is not clear whether he was trying to pull CSA Gen. Joseph E. Johnston's Army of Tennessee behind him into more open terrain, though this is doubtful, or whether he was trying to take a more western approach into Atlanta. The real danger for Sherman was, despite his superior manpower and available supplies, that by abandoning the railroad, he was lengthening his critical supply column, making it more vulnerable to hit-and-run attacks by Johnston's troops and cavalry.

Ordered up and out by buglers on the morning of May 22, the three grand Union armies moved out of camp at Cassville and Kingston in their usual three columns. Maj. Gen. George H. Thomas's Army of the Cumberland and Maj. Gen. John M. Schofield's Army of the Ohio moved nearly due south, while Maj. Gen. James B. McPherson's Army of the Tennessee swung far to the right, in order to eventually turn and approach Dallas from the due west. The huge columns of massed Union infantry in a front nearly 20 miles wide were hard to conceal, and scouts from CSA Maj. Gen. Joseph Wheeler's Cavalry Corps soon discovered the westward movement.

By the afternoon of May 23, Johnston ordered CSA Lt. Gen. William J. Hardee to move his corps to a good defensive ground just east of Dallas and CSA Maj. Gen. Leonidas K. Polk's position west of Kennesaw Mountain—to what had been the left of the Confederate line there—astride a tiny crossroads nearby called New Hope (some maps label it New Hope Church). CSA Lt. Gen. John Bell Hood's Corps remained entrenched at Altoona Gap overnight, in case Sherman's move proved to be a feint, and was then ordered to New Hope once Johnston realized that all the Union forces were headed toward Dallas. Polk was ordered to move his corps rapidly toward Dallas itself, slightly to the west of New Hope, where he could join in with Hardee and form a strong defensive line nearly 4 miles long. The line ran from a point directly south of Dallas to a mile east of New Hope, their right flank hanging in the air in the vicinity of a small community called Pickett's Mill.

Hood settled into line just before the forward Union skirmishers and scouts came into view. Other Confederate divisions took their positions around the small log building that was New Hope Church. Maj. Gen. Carter L. Stevenson's Division set up on the right, Maj. Gen. Thomas C. Hindman's Division deployed in the slightly higher ground on the left, and Maj. Gen. Alexander P. Stewart's Division deployed directly in front of the church. Just before 10:00 A.M. on May 25, skirmishers about a mile in front of their own lines encountered the forward elements of USA Maj. Gen. Joseph Hooker's XX Corps, the vanguard of Thomas's Army of the Cumberland, who were rapidly marching toward New Hope. The Confederates attempted to burn a bridge over Pumpkinvine Creek to set up a delaying action, but were quickly overrun by USA Brig. Gen. John W. Geary's 2nd Division.

Warned that action was imminent, Stewart deployed his men in line astride the crossroads, ordering them to dig in as rapidly as possible. Brig. Gen. Marcellus A. Stovall's Georgia Brigade was positioned on an open hilltop in the midst of the church's graveyard and was unable or unwilling to dig in at all, but Brig. Gen. Henry D. Clayton's and Brig. Gen. Alpheus Baker's Alabama Brigades, in the center and right of the line, threw up hasty but strong works of felled trees and earthen embankments. Sixteen guns from Capt. McDonald Oliver's Eufaula, Alabama Battery and Capt. Charles E. Fenner's Louisiana Battery were amassed within Stewart's roughly half-mile front, and ordered to load with double-canister. Both battery commanders knew instinctively that the looming action would be up close and personal.

Advised that some resistance had been unexpectedly encountered, Sherman rode forward and personally ordered Hooker to push through what he believed was a small force and to march directly to Dallas, irritably remarking, "There haven't been twenty rebels there today" to the front of him. Just before 4:00 P.M., a severe thunderstorm started to blow in over the battleground. Marching steadily on through the mounting wind and pounding thunder came USA Brig. Gen. John W. Geary's 2nd Division, with Maj. Gen. Daniel Butterfield's 3rd Division to his left and Brig. Gen. Alpheus S. Williams's 1st Division on his right. They were spread across a one-half-mile front, in heavy-brigade column formation, and they were bearing down directly on the unseen massed Confederate front of Stewart's Division. The natural earth and timber works, combined with the very thick underbrush, served to conceal the strength of the Confederate line from the Union attackers.

Just after 5:00 P.M., as Geary's skirmishers drove back Hood's, Union buglers sounded the call to go forward at the double-quick. Stumbling and falling through the thick brush and unable to see what lay ahead, the men from Ohio, Pennsylvania, and New York hoped to sweep straight through what they believed was a weak line of Confederate militiamen and detached infantry brigades. Just as the monsoon-force rains began, Williams's men broke out of the thickest part of the woods and rushed uphill, straight for the Confederate line.

Stewart had wisely ordered the artillery to load with double-canister, and had positioned his 4,000 men nearly shoulder to shoulder on a very tight front, anticipating quite accurately that Hooker's men would be packed in these heavy infantry formations. As lightning crackled all around and sheets of rain poured down, the shouting mass of over 16,000 blue-coated infantry burst into sight less than one hundred feet in front of Stewart's lines. Immediately, the Confederate line opened up and disappeared again just as quickly behind a thick cloud of bluish-gray rifle and cannon smoke. Williams's men took the brunt of the concentrated fire. Most of his more than 800 casualties were lost in the first ten minutes of battle.

For over three hours, this one-sided slaughter continued, into the dark and stormy evening. Geary, Butterfield, and Williams all ordered assault after assault, trying to break through what was increasingly obvious was the main Confederate army line; but each time, they were thrown back by murderous artillery and rifle fire. Stewart's Confederate forces started running out of ammunition, the sixty-round-per-man standard issue being depleted in as few as thirty minutes in some cases. Stewart brought his reserve forces into the line primarily for their ammunition supply, and runners began searching the wounded and dead for any extra cartridges. Hooker finally admitted defeat about 7:30 P.M., pulling his men back a short distance to dig in for the night, while Rebel yells and rude catcalls greeted their retreat.

Throughout the long night, as Union men dug in with shovels, bayonets, tin cups, or bare hands, sporadic rifle and artillery fire broke out, killing and wounding even more men, but no further full-scale assaults by either side were mounted. Hooker's command lost more than 1,600 men in the short fight, while Confederate losses amounted to "between 300 and 400," as reported by Stewart. One bitter Union infantryman later remarked that Hooker had sent them into a "hell hole." The name stuck and became a common reference to the brutal fight that took place there and at Pickett's Mill.

PICKETT'S MILL

After the pasting he received at New Hope Church, Sherman returned to his standard backup tactic of rapid-flanking maneuvers. He ordered three divisions under the direct command of IV Corps Commander Maj. Gen. Oliver O. Howard to the far left in an attempt to turn the Confederate right. It was very difficult, however, to keep the movement of massed, jangling infantry a secret in those days, and Johnston soon learned of the flanking attempt. He ordered two divisions to shift to the right of Hood's line, covering the probable Union line of attack. To the far right of the newly extended Confederate line was one of Johnston's best, Maj. Gen. Patrick R. Cleburne's Division, who took up position on a hilltop overlooking Pickett's Mill.

Although his scouts reported fresh earthworks and Howard himself rode forward and observed gray-uniformed troops reinforcing them, the Union commander was somehow convinced that he had reached the flank or rear of the Confederate line of battle, and possibly believed that what he had observed was only a small picket outpost. His uncertainty is obvious in a message sent about 3:30 P.M.: "I am now turning the enemy's right flank, I think." Just after noon on May 27, Howard brought his three divisions in line of attack on a hilltop just north of the small mill community, again forming the men into the same narrow, deep, heavy infantry formations that had failed so miserably two days earlier at New Hope Church.

At this point, the Confederate line curved to the east, following the ridgeline atop a low hill that overlooked a steep, densely overgrown ravine. As the battle unfolded, two brigades of Cleburne's force were shifted to the far right of the line, refusing at right angles to the line, so as to prevent any possibility of being flanked.

At 4:30 P.M., the Union line stepped off into the thick, entangling underbrush, or at least most of them did. There were some very serious communications and land navigation problems, and one brigade ended up marching completely away from the growing sounds of battle, "to get rations." That particular brigade's commander, Brig. Gen. Nathaniel McLean of Kentucky, was a political enemy of Howard, and on this day chose a particularly poor way of demonstrating his contempt.

Howard's leading brigade, ably commanded by Brig. Gen. William B. Hazen's 2nd Brigade, easily drove away the Confederate pickets and moved into the steep-sided ravine. The undergrowth was so thick that the colors had to be encased to prevent them from being torn to pieces, and Hazen was forced to resort to his compass to stay moving in the right direction. Emerging suddenly in an open field, his troops first encountered a weak skirmish line of about 1,000 dismounted cavalrymen from CSA Brig. Gen. John Kelly's and CSA Brig. Gen. William Hume's Divisions, who they mistook as unentrenched infantry. Steadily overpowering the cavalrymen, Hazen's men rushed cheering across the open ground, upward to what they thought was an undefended rocky ridgeline. Just before they reached the heights, however, CSA Brig. Gen. Hiram M. Granbury's Texas Brigade suddenly appeared in view at the very top, and began pouring a galling fire into the face of the onrushing Union line.

Hazen's men kept up the pressure, despite suffering appalling casualties from a two-gun battery that had suddenly appeared to their right at the point of the ravine. Captain Key had set up his four guns far to the left of the Confederate line atop the ridgeline, along with Sweet's Mississippi Battery, at the point thought to be in most danger of a frontal infantry attack. As the Union infantry began their assault, Key and half his men rolled two of their howitzers to the far right of the original Confederate line, amid the rush of Granbury's redeploying Texans, setting up just to their left. Key could easily see that his half-battery had a clear field of fire and soon began sweeping the field with case shot and canister. Key's other two guns, now commanded by one of his section chiefs, and Sweet's four 10-pounder Parrott rifles commenced a hot bombardment of Howard's rear and reserve elements, about a half-mile to their front.

Two more Confederate regiments quickly rushed in to support Granbury: Col. George Baucum's 8th/19th Arkansas Consolidated Regiment moved in to his left, and Brig. Gen. Mark P. Lowrey's Alabama-Mississippi Brigade took position to his right. Hazen managed to stay in the fight for about fifty minutes before being forced to withdraw, leaving over 500 wounded and dead in place in the open ravine. Key kept up rapid fire from his two guns until no more live Union troops could be seen moving in the open field.

As Hazen withdrew, USA Col. William H. Gibson's 1st Brigade advanced over nearly the same ground and met the same fate. Far from hitting a weakened Confederate line, as 3rd Division commander USA

Brig. Gen. Thomas J. Wood had hoped, Gibson's troops advanced as far as the Confederate line before being thrown violently back. Roughly an hour of combat resulted in nothing more than an additional 687 Union casualties.

Johnston wrote after the war of the bravery of Gibson's men:

> *When the leading Federal troops paused in their advance, a color-bearer came on and planted his colors eight or ten feet in front of his regiment, but was killed in the act. A soldier who sprang forward to hold up or bear off the colors was shot dead as he seized the staff. Two others who followed successively fourth bore back the noble emblem.*

Another brigade, USA Col. Frederick Knefler's 3rd, was sent in about 6:30 P.M. in order to cover Gibson's retreat and to recover as many wounded as possible. They too were subjected to intense, nearly point-blank fire from the Confederate positions and Key's guns as soon as they entered the ravine, and were forced to withdraw in short order, without accomplishing their mission.

The Union assaults ended by 7:00 P.M., but occasional firefights erupted until 10:00 that night, when Granbury was ordered to "clear his front." The Texans fixed bayonets and with wild Rebel yells, charged forward into the darkened ravine, killing or capturing many of the Union troops. The remaining Union troops either "skedaddled" or "retreated in good order, with no pursuit [by the Texans] even being attempted," depending on whose account, or post-war excuse, you read. After the firing died down around 11:00 P.M., both sides encamped in place for the night, their attention still fixed on the body-strewn battleground, which was eerily lit up by blazing pine trees set afire during the hot exchange.

Key's two guns fired a total of 187 rounds of canister and spherical case shot during the two-and-a-half-hour Union assault. While they were not solely responsible for stopping the attack, they crippled the bluecoats to such a point that they could not carry the field. Both Union and Confederate reports and memoirs remarked on Key's deadly accurate gunnery skills, and most gave primary credit for the Confederate victory there to his battery.

Total Union losses for the day's action totaled 1,689 killed, wounded, captured, or missing. This failed action apparently so upset Sherman that he completely "forgot" to mention it in both his official report and his postwar memoirs. Cleburne had a much happier report to relate:

> My casualties in this battle were few. I had 85 killed, 363 wounded, carrying into the engagement 4,683 muskets. The enemy's losses were very heavy. The lowest estimate which can be made of his dead is 500. We captured 160 prisoners, who were sent to army headquarters, exclusive of 72 of his wounded carried to my field hospital. He could not have lost in all less than 3,000 killed and wounded. I took upward of 1,200 small-arms.

The following day, May 28, 1864, Sherman finally decided that this westward flanking movement was getting him nowhere quick. He was short on rations, and his resources were stretched nearly to the breaking point trying to hold their entire 5-mile line of battle, as well as the lines of communication necessary to protect their supply line back to the railroad north of Altoona. He ordered a gradual shifting of the line back east toward Kennesaw and Marietta and sent his cavalry to capture Altoona Gap itself. Johnston soon learned of this movement and ordered an attack on the Union right, straight toward Dallas, but his men were repulsed with no positive effects on the Union movement, and at the cost of over 600 casualties.

Captain DeGress's Battery was in the right of the line at Dallas, firing with effect on CSA Brig. Gen. Thomas B. Smith's onrushing brigade, but he found his own critical position to be in another, later battle for Atlanta.

Sherman moved back east and reluctantly attempted a frontal, nearly suicidal attack on Kennesaw Mountain itself, which failed just as he had feared. Returning yet again to his rapid flanking movements, he sent his three armies skirting around the western side of the mountain, pushing Johnston's scattered forces out of Marietta and Smyrna, and then back behind the wide, shallow Chattahoochee River. Finding unexpectedly effective resistance at the crossing spot of choice, Nickajack Creek, Sherman sent his cavalry out to find a safer place to cross. On the morning of July 9, he found a suitable spot at Sope Creek, which was defended only by a tiny picket outpost.

By nightfall one entire Union division had crossed the creek. With the news of additional Union troops on the south bank, and with few other natural barriers between the fortifications of Atlanta and Sherman's new positions, Johnston decided his only recourse was to once again retreat. Abandoning the river line to Sherman, Johnston pulled his forces back to south of Peachtree Creek, on the very doorstep of Atlanta itself. In a little over sixty days, the hardened Rebel force had been forced back from no less than eight strongly prepared defensive lines by Sherman's flanking movements and had been forced to surrender all of northern Georgia.

Without further resistance to his river crossing, Sherman paused only long enough to rebuild pontoon and railroad bridges before striking south again. On July 11, McPherson was sent eastward toward Decatur and Stone Mountain, with orders to cut the railway between Atlanta and Augusta. Sherman's greatest fear at this point was that Johnston would receive reinforcements by rail from Lee's Army of Northern Virginia. Thomas was sent south toward Peachtree Creek, with Schofield marching just to his right, headed toward Buckhead.

Johnston carefully noted the Union approach, and planned to wait until close contact was established, then attack the gap between Thomas and Schofield before they were deployed for the fight. Before he could carry out this attack, Jefferson Davis carried out one of the most bone-headed decisions made during the war and fired Johnston. Late in the afternoon of July 17, Hood was promoted to General and given command of the entire Army of Tennessee. Just thirty-three years old and considered a hot-headed, division-level commander out of his league at the corps level, the move delighted no one more than Sherman. In his postwar memoirs he noted, "I was always anxious with Johnston at my front." He knew Hood was rash and prone to ordering ill-timed and poorly planned movements and was anxious for him to do so before Atlanta. It would be much better to destroy the Confederate forces in the field and then take the vital transportation and supply center than to be forced to assault its heavily fortified defenses.

Least happy of all were the Confederate soldiers, who had loved Johnston for his humane treatment of them, and who feared Hood would kill them all off in ill-considered battles. Confederate Pvt. Sam Watkins of the 1st Tennessee Infantry said Johnston's removal was "like the successful gambler, flushed with continual winnings, who staked his all and lost. It was like the end of the Southern Confederacy." Captain Key remarked in his diary that evening:

> *Every man looked sad and disheartened at this information, and felt that evil would result from the removal of Johnston, whom they esteem and love above any previous commander. His address touched every heart, and every man thought that his favorite General had been grievously wronged. The cause for this procedure on the part of the President at this eventful moment when the enemy is pressing us we have been unable to conjecture.*

ADVANCE TO PEACHTREE CREEK

The day after Hood took command, Union infantrymen of Maj. Gen. John McCauley Palmer's XIV Army Corps advanced through heavy resistance by Wheeler's Cavalry to the northern banks of Peachtree Creek, near Howell Mill Road. At just about the same time, Brig. Gen. Kenner Garrad's Cavalry, supported by McPherson's infantry, reached the Georgia Railroad and captured the railroad depot at Stone Mountain, 15 miles east of Atlanta. On July 19, three brigades of Palmer's XIV Army Corps forced a crossing of Peachtree Creek toward Moore's Mill, followed by other crossings under fire by elements of Howard's IV Army Corps and Hooker's XX Army Corps. By nightfall the Union forces formed a solid line of blue-coated infantry on the south banks of Peachtree Creek. They faced due south toward the Confederate line, arranged atop low hills about one-half mile away.

THE BATTLE

Pleased with the progress of his subordinates, Sherman ordered Thomas to cross Peachtree Creek and engage Hood, Schofield to capture Decatur, and McPherson to advance toward Atlanta, tearing up the railroad tracks along the way. Obsessed with detail, Sherman sent word on exactly how he wanted the tracks torn up: "Pile the ties into shape for a bonfire, put the rails across and when red hot in the middle, let a man at each end twist the bar so that its surface becomes spiral."

Hood had a reputation as a battlefield brawler, and he wasted little time going on the offensive. A general attack was ordered at about 1:00 P.M. on

July 20, intended to drive the dug-in Union infantry back across the creek and as far as the banks of the Chattahoochee River. Before the attack could commence, Hood ordered the entire line to shift a little under a mile to the east, to protect his right flank from counterattack. Despite the fact that this movement threw the whole line into disarray and caused a general confusion as to exactly where they were to advance, he ordered the attack to begin at 4:00 P.M.

At about 2:45 P.M., CSA Maj. Gen. William W. Loring's Division of Stewart's Corps stepped off, almost immediately encountering Union infantry and mistakenly initiating battle action in the center of the line. CSA Maj. Gen. William B. Bate's Division of Hardee's Corps, ordered to begin the general assault on the extreme right of the Confederate lines, didn't actually move out until nearly one-half hour later. As a result of the uneven terrain and thick underbrush, the rest of the 2-mile-long line followed in piecemeal, advancing in small groups and masses rather than well-formed lines.

The only real success of the entire assault was made by CSA Brig. Gen. Thomas M. Scott's Brigade of mostly Alabama troops, who advanced through the Tanyard Branch and Collier Road vicinity, attacked, drove off, and captured the flag of USA Col. Patrick H. Jones's 33rd New Jersey Infantry Regiment, as well as a four-gun artillery battery. Scott's men were soon forced to withdraw, however, as no other unit was able to break through to support them on either flank.

No other unit met with even a modest success, and the entire attack was over, with all units back in their original positions by 6:00 that evening. The well-positioned Union forces had handed the advancing Confederates quite a mauling. Although the numbers engaged were fairly even (21,450 Union vs. 18,450 Confederate), casualties were much more one-sided: Union losses totaled 1,780, while Confederate losses reached an estimated 4,800. Hood's first outing as an army commander was an unqualified disaster.

To add insult to injury, shortly before noon on July 20, Captain DeGress set up his four 20-pounder Parrott rifles on a small hilltop, two-and-a-half miles east of the city, and in short order began firing the first of thousands of artillery shells into the Gate City itself. The very first shell exploded at the intersection of Ivy and East Ellis Streets, killing a young girl who had been walking with her parents past Frank P. Rice's lumber dealership on the northwest corner. Shelling from DeGress's Battery and other specially procured siege artillery batteries continued for several weeks at the average rate of one round every fifteen minutes, more as a harassment and reminder of the siege conditions than as a real destruction attempt. The DeGress Battery itself would soon be the very object and center of fighting for the city.

THE BATTLE OF ATLANTA

Before the fighting even died down at Peachtree Creek, Sherman was massing his forces for the next assault. McPherson's three corps were set in motion down the Georgia Railroad to attack Atlanta from the east, while Thomas and Schofield were ordered to close up and keep as much pressure on the Confederates as possible. By late in the day on July 20, forward elements of USA Maj. Gen. Frank P. Blair's XVII Army Corps engaged Wheeler's dismounted cavalry on a small hilltop 2 miles to the east of Atlanta—close to where DeGress's Battery was pounding out its lethal tattoo. Heavy combat erupted as the two lines collided, until the Southern cavalrymen were overwhelmed and withdrew about midnight.

THE NIGHT MARCH THROUGH ATLANTA

Hood had no intention of pursuing the same sort of well planned, plodding, and slow-retreat defense that Johnston had utilized and thought he saw an opportunity for offensive action against McPherson. Withdrawing Stewart's corps and the Georgia Militia to the strongly fortified positions in the outer ring of defenses around Atlanta, he ordered Hardee's Corps southward on an all-night forced march. Moving due south down Peachtree Street through the middle of town (and panicking the civilians, who believed their entire army was deserting them), they swung east toward Decatur, attempting to get behind Blair's Corps' lines, before moving north into the planned line of battle. Cleburne's Division withdrew with some difficulty from a fight just east of the city and joined Hardee's march. At the same time, two divisions of Wheeler's Cavalry were sent around the Union left flank, to attempt a strike at their supply wagons in Decatur.

To the lowly infantryman, this brilliant plan must have lost some of its luster. Having been in action off and on for over two months, they pulled back time after time only to spend hours of back-breaking labor digging in and reinforcing when they arrived at new positions, for "spades is trumps," as the men said. Then, after doing this again and again without adequate rest and with dwindling supplies, they were ordered up on the line of battle and into the assault on July 20—only to be violently thrown back with heavy losses. Within hours, the order was once more given to withdraw and then go immediately into an all-night march. Without a doubt this was nearly more than the poorly supplied, hungry, and thirsty men could endure.

CSA Brig. Gen. Daniel C. Govan of Cleburne's Division was equally unimpressed and deathly worried that "the loss of another night's rest was a heavy tax upon their powers of endurance." Hundreds of soldiers simply plopped down on the side of the road, unable to go any further, until at last a two-hour rest was called. Hood intended for the attack to begin at daylight, but it became apparent that any possible attack could be launched no earlier than noon.

Unknown to the Confederates, McPherson was worried that they would attempt this exact movement and ordered his lines extended and turned to the south. Maj. Gen. Grenville Mellen Dodge's XVI Army Corps was ordered in to Blair's left, facing southeast. At McPherson's urging, Blair's men heavily entrenched and blocked lanes of approach before them.

By the morning of July 22, Hardee's men had trudged down the McDonough Road south of Atlanta, and then turned to the northeast on the Fayetteville Road toward Decatur. Still trying to make up time lost on rest stops, Hardee ordered Cleburne's and Brig. Gen. George E. Maney's Divisions to begin deploying to the left when they reached Bouldercrest Road, while Bate's and Maj. Gen. William H. T. Walker's Divisions were to continue on up the road and turn left on Wilkinson Drive. Both of these moves into line were short of their original goals.

Running into a large millpond their guides had repeatedly warned them about, Walker's and Bate's Divisions wandered around through the thick forest for nearly an hour trying to get into line of battle. As Walker roundly cursed their guides, grumbling that they must be "traitors" to allow him to get himself in such a fix, he raised his field glasses to try and figure out his next move. A nearby Union picket spotted Walker and killed him with a single well-aimed shot.

FIGHTING IN EAST ATLANTA

Walker's place was taken over by Brig. Gen. Hugh W. Mercer, and the planned dawn attack finally commenced, after further confusion and shifting troops, at about 12:15 P.M. On advancing to the planned line of departure, the Confederates discovered to their horror that, far from being in the Union rear, they were advancing straight into a heavily invested front-line position. Pressing forward under intense fire from Brig. Gen. Thomas William Sweeney's 2nd Division of Dodge's XVI Army Corps, their ranks were immediately raked by fire from two artillery positions. One of them was a six-gun Napoleon battery (Lt. Andrew T. Blodgett's 1st Missouri Light Battery), and one was a six-gun, three-inch ordnance rifle battery (Capt. Jerome M. Burrows's 14th Ohio Light Battery).

About thirty minutes later, Cleburne's and Maney's Divisions launched their attack to the left of the ongoing fight, straight into the "bend" of the Union line held by Brig. Gen. Giles Alexander Smith's 4th Division of Blair's XVII Army Corps. This attack was much more successful, driving the Union line all the way north to Leggett's Hill and capturing an entire infantry regiment (Lt. Col. Addison H. Sanders's 16th Iowa), along with eight artillery pieces.

McPherson had been eating lunch with his staff and corps commanders less than a mile away when he heard the sudden crash of artillery fire. He hastily mounted his horse and rode south with a small group of officers to check on the situation, pausing atop a nearby hill. From there, he could see that Sweeney's Division was holding up well, but he could not see the situation on the other end of the line. Striking out immediately for the spot between the two Confederate assaults, he realized that his line was not continuous in that area, and quickly ordered up more troops to fill the gap. Riding through the unmanned gap toward Giles Smith's position, he and his party suddenly burst out of the heavy forest into a clearing, where they came face to face with the advancing 5th Confederate Regiment (Capt. Richard Beard's Tennessee). The Confederates called on him to surrender, but in an attempt to escape, he wheeled his horse around, raised his hat in salute, and galloped off toward the tree line. A single shot fired by CSA Cpl. Robert F. Coleman tore through McPherson's lungs, killing him instantly.

Hood finally realized that he had engaged the Union left flank, not the enemy's rear as planned, and ordered Maj. Gen. Benjamin Franklin "Frank" Cheatham's Corps out of the east Atlanta defense line and in to assault the entrenched Union main line. At the same time, Maney's Division was ordered to break off and move to Cleburne's left, where they could support Cheatham's attack. Maney's Division started their assault at about 3:30 P.M. Cheatham's Corps moved out a half hour later, possibly due to a confusion over orders. Once again Leggett's Hill was in the center of much of the action, but the repeated Confederate assaults failed to regain control of it.

The general assault found a weak spot at the position held by USA Brig. Gen. Joseph Lightburn's 2nd Brigade. CSA Brig. Gen. Arthur M. Manigault's Brigade, of Cheatham's Corps, led the assault, pushing through the railroad cut capturing Captain DeGress's Battery, and attempting to prepare them for withdrawal into the Confederate lines. Leading Manigault's assault, and first into the artillery redoubt, were the Blue Ridge Rangers, Company D of the Georgia State Line's 1st Regiment, led by their recently appointed captain, William Jasper Worley.

Manigault's order was foiled from the start by DeGress's instructions to shoot all of their draft horses before retreating, making removal of the one-ton guns nearly impossible. Frustrated, Manigault ordered his men to continue their assault to the left of DeGress's battery emplacement, flanking and scattering four Ohio regiments (the 47th, 54th, 37th and 53rd, in turn). More Confederate units poured through the opening, capturing another two-gun artillery battery, and forcing a total of four Union brigades to retreat from a now nearly half-mile wide break-through. DeGress led his artillerymen back under heavy fire toward a small hill to the north, the location of Sherman's headquarters.

Sherman, observing from the Augustus Hurt House atop that hill, turned and ordered Schofield to amass all his available artillery (twenty guns at that point) at the Confederate breach. He then ordered Logan to collect up eight brigades of infantry to fill in the breach and retake their original positions. Between the massed artillery and Logan's strong counterattack, the Confederates were soon forced back into their original positions, at a heavy loss. Sherman later remarked about DeGress's loss that day in his memoirs:

> Poor Captain de Gress came to me in tears, lamenting the loss of his favorite guns; when they were regained he had only a few men left, and not a single horse. He asked an order for a reequipment, but I told him he must beg and borrow of others till he could restore his battery, now reduced to three guns. How he did so I do not know, but in a short time he did get horses, men, and finally another gun, of the same special pattern, and served them with splendid effect till the very close of the war.

Wheeler's cavalry struck at Decatur during the fight in east Atlanta, meeting with somewhat more success. His cavalrymen drove back two regiments of infantry and captured 225 prisoners and an artillery piece, but were ordered back west to support Hardee before Wheeler could capture or destroy the Union supply train, which had been his main goal.

The day was another unqualified disaster for the Confederate Army of Tennessee. Total casualties ran over 5,000 (Sherman claimed over 8,000, but this was no doubt exaggerated), for no gain other than a few briefly captured artillery pieces, which could not even be withdrawn in the subsequent retreat. The Union Army of the Tennessee fared little better, giving up no territory in the end, but finishing the battle with 3,722 killed, wounded, or missing.

JOURNEYS OF DEGRESS'S BATTERY

Battery H of the 1st Illinois Light Artillery was raised in and about Chicago during the first few months of 1862, by the original commanding officer, Capt. Axel Silversparre. In the spring of 1862, after the usual initial fumbling about and poor equipage, it was sent to St. Louis, where the battery received their four 20-pounder Parrott rifles. "Silversparre's Battery" was immediately reassigned to Ulysses S. Grant's Department of Cairo, which was then building up for the campaigns on the Tennessee and Cumberland Rivers. They arrived at Savannah, Tennessee, in late March, moved downriver with Grant's corps-sized department to Pittsburg Landing on April 5, and were in the line of battle the next day when a strong Confederate force swept down upon the ill-prepared Union army, centered on Shiloh Church. At nightfall on April 6, this battery was placed in the center of the line of artillery that demolished the last Confederate charge of the day. After Shiloh, the battery was assigned to the 2nd Division of the XV Corps, where they remained for the rest of the war.

Moving west with the rest of XV Corps, Captain Silversparre was made Chief of Artillery at Fort Pickering during the Memphis Campaign, but was captured during one of the last battles for the river city, and never rejoined his battery. Command was transferred to Silversparre's most able lieutenant, Francis DeGress, who subsequently was commissioned Captain, and who made the battery one of Sherman's personal favorites. DeGress and his men soon earned a reputation as fast and accurate gunners. They participated in Grant's extensive Vicksburg

Campaign before moving east with Sherman's command to Chattanooga and Ringgold.

DeGress commanded his battery throughout the fights for Chattanooga and Missionary Ridge, Tunnel Hill, the Atlanta Campaign, the Georgia Campaign (also known as "The March to the Sea"), and through the long march north through the Carolinas. DeGress's final military post was leading his men as they marched in review before President Lincoln in Washington, and on March 13, 1865, Lincoln personally promoted DeGress to Brevet Major. Despite their central presence in so many bitterly contested battles, his battery lost only one officer and six enlisted men, with an additional twenty-seven, who died of disease.

Very little is documented about DeGress's postwar life as well, but it is known that he became an arms dealer with the import–export firm of Wexel and DeGress, primarily selling guns to Mexico and other Central and South American nations. While engaged in arms sales in the region, he became caught up in the speculation surrounding the building of a canal across either Nicaragua or Panama. He corresponded with his old friend, Sherman, back in Washington, who was by then Secretary of War, and sought the help of the Grant administration in funding such a venture.

In the end, DeGress apparently found the climate of Mexico agreeable over his old home soil. He lived there until he died on January 4, 1883, and is buried with fellow Union (and a few Confederate) veterans in the small U.S. Civil War Veteran's section of the Mexico City National Cemetery.

Thomas Key and the Helena Artillery (Key's Battery)

The Helena Artillery was organized at Helena, in Phillips County, Arkansas, on April 27, 1861, and the officers and men mustered in for three months of state service on April 29. At that time, few entertained any notion that the war would last much longer than that, and it was considered highly doubtful that far-western units, like the Helena Artillery, would play any role in it at all. Capt. A.W. Clarkson was appointed as the first commander, and on July 6, 1861, the battery was mustered into Confederate service for twelve months in Memphis, Tennessee. This period, like nearly every other time-limited mustering in both armies, was later extended to the duration of the war. The battery was originally organized as Company C, 20th Alabama Artillery Battalion, based around a single originally assigned unit, Waddell's Alabama Artillery Battery, and assigned as the artillery component of Brig. William J. Hardee's Brigade.

The battery crossed the Mississippi River with Hardee's Brigade in the fall of 1861 and never returned to Arkansas. Captain Clarkson soon resigned and was succeeded by Capt. John H. Calvert on July 2, 1862. Later that year, charges of public drunkenness and lewdness were lodged against Captain Calvert, and the provost marshal jailed him. As part of his pleadings, he promised not to turn to drink again during the war, under threat of forced resignation—a deadly insult of the day. However, Calvert was observed to be quite drunk on the battlefield at Murfreesboro, Tennessee, on December 31, 1862, and subsequently he was forced to tender his resignation. He was succeeded in command by Capt. Thomas Jefferson Key, who had been promoted out of the 15th Arkansas Infantry the previous summer. Key's Battery fought in the Kentucky Campaign of 1862, as well as the Battle of Shiloh. After Shiloh, the battery was reassigned as one of three batteries in Maj. Thomas R. Hotchkiss's Battalion, Hardee's Corps Artillery, under the direct command of Brig. Gen. Francis A. Shoup, the Army of Tennessee's Artillery Commander.

Going east with the great Army of Tennessee, Key's Battery was center-stage at Murfreesboro and Chickamauga, before entering the Atlanta Campaign. Key's colors were captured at Jonesboro on the last day of the campaign, September 1, 1864, as his position was overrun and his guns were captured by men from Company E of the 52nd Regiment Ohio Volunteer Infantry.

Although a superbly capable battery commander, with excellent gunners in his ranks, Key could not control every aspect of his task. The low quality of Confederate-made ordnance sometimes resulted in less than desirable results. Col. Allen L. Fahnestock, commanding the 86th Illinois Volunteer Infantry, noted one such incident in a May 7, 1864, diary entry, at Tunnel Hill, where Key was in charge of all the Confederate artillery batteries:

> The rebel Battery on Tunnell Hill fired a shott at our Battery one shell went into the ground and did not explode. Sgt. McDonald of our Battery dug it up and saw it was the same caliber as his gun. He cut the fuse and loaded it in his cannon and

fired it back at the rebel battery and it exploded. The rebels retreated.

Two members of Key's Battery, Pvts. James McCourtney and George McMillon, were listed on the Battle of Chickamauga Roll of Honor, the only Confederate award ever actually presented, for heroism they displayed amid the great slaughter. Three generals each cited Key in their after-action reports for his gallantry on those two days of hard fighting. Key himself had a reputation as a daring and heroic battery commander, sometimes to the point of being considered suicidal by fellow officers. He often ran his guns up close to the enemy, out in front of the infantry, while his crews poured out a rapid and accurate fire. Many reports and letters mention the incredibly fast loading and dead-on accurate firing that characterized his crews. At the end of the war, the battery was divided into two sections. One group, under Captain Key, surrendered at Macon, Georgia, on April 20, 1865. The other group, under 1st Sgt. D.G. Johnson, surrendered at Selma, Alabama, on May 4, 1865.

Key himself had been born in Bolivar, Tennessee, on January 17, 1831. His father, Chesley Daniel Key, had grown up on a plantation in Virginia, where one of his neighbors was Thomas Jefferson. The family moved to Mississippi while Key was still a boy, settling in Tishomingo County. Key began work in the newspaper business while still a young teenager, attending school through his sophomore year at LaGrange College, then leaving the academic world behind to buy and publish a newspaper, the *Day Book*, also known as the *Franklin County Democrat*, in 1852. In the midst of the great slavery debate, Key moved with a group of Alabama slave owners to Kansas Territory, to help defend the right of slavery there. In direct opposition to the large number of abolitionists pouring into the territory, Key started up the *Kansas Constitutionalist*, a militantly pro-slavery newspaper, in 1856.

"Bleeding Kansas" was not exactly a welcoming place for pro-slavery men, as John Brown proved that same year, and Key and his presses were thrown in nearby rivers on more than one occasion. Giving up after the pro-slavery Lecompton Constitution was rejected, Key moved to Helena, Arkansas, started another Democratic political newspaper, and was elected to the state legislature. There, on May 6, 1861, he voted with the majority for secession.

Key was not considered prime material for military service, at first. He was thirty years old, married with three children, and was an established businessman and politician to boot, with not a day's military train-ing behind him. However, after traveling to Shiloh after the battle to recover the body of his cousin, Capt. Robert Lambert (commanding offi-cer of Co. A, 13th [Josey's] Regiment, Arkansas Infantry), who had died of wounds suffered during that great battle, Key soon enlisted in Company G of the same regiment as a private. In short order, he was pro-moted to First Lieutenant, and found himself reassigned to the artillery (no doubt in consideration of his advanced age—advanced for a foot infantryman, that is!). He was soon given command of the Helena Battery.

Key took the oath of allegiance to the United States in May 1865, in Nashville, where he had been transported with a trainload of new POWs. He returned to Helena briefly after the war, before moving to Corinth, Mississippi, in 1869, to start up yet another newspaper. This time, instead of a fiery political journal, he started up a small farm journal given the name of the *Southern Agriculturist*. Obviously restless, he moved both his family and his newspaper from city to city across the war-ravaged South, finally settling in Nashville in 1897. The little farm journal ended up becoming a rather large success, reaching over one million subscribers during the depths of the Great Depression. He died at his home in Nashville on April 5, 1908, the forty-sixth anniversary of the battle that had taken his cousin's life and propelled him onto that great stage of war.

The last entry in Key's war diary serves well as his epitaph:

> *O the young cannon was my bride,*
> *Her orange is wreathed with bay,*
> *And on the blood-red battlefield,*
> *I have celebrated my wedding day.*

3

Chivalry and Sabers: The Cavalry

Sgt. James Larson, Co. H, 4th U.S. Cavalry
Pvt. Benjamin Wortham, Co. H, 12th Georgia Cavalry Regiment

Nashville and North Carolina

O N THE COLD, FOGGY MORNING OF DECEMBER 15, 1864, UNION SGT.
James Larson of Company H, 4th United States Cavalry, rode
among nearly 12,000 other Union cavalrymen, all part of Maj. Gen.
James Wilson's Cavalry Corps, on a sweeping trot out of the western
defenses of Nashville, and headed south over some low hills along the
Charlotte Pike Road. Larson had only just arrived in Nashville with the
relatively few remaining in the 4th Cavalry, after many months of skirmishes and battles with Confederate forces in Mississippi and Georgia.
Sherman had already left on his great march out of the burned ruins of
Atlanta, and was headed to the Georgia coast, while his defeated foe,
Confederate Lt. Gen. John Bell Hood, was actually leading his battered
army north, away from Sherman, with the intent to invade the North
and seize Cincinnati. Just two weeks earlier, Hood had nearly completely destroyed his army at Franklin. But now, unbelievably, those few
remaining in his ranks were dug in atop a low series of hills southeast of
the city, supposedly threatening to assault the Union's main supply
depot, which was guarded by no less than 72,000 well-equipped and quite
comfortable men. Hood could claim only about 23,000—on paper at
least—and all of them were numbed from months of fighting and the
hellish carnage at Franklin; they were cold, nearly starving, and many

were without anything resembling a real uniform or even proper clothing for the freezing weather. Today was the date set for their utter destruction, with almost every Union cavalryman and infantryman on the move, their artillery batteries moving out of the city's defenses right behind them.

Four months later, early in the morning of March 10, 1865, in the dark pine woods of North Carolina, Confederate Pvt. Benjamin Wortham of Company H, 12th Georgia Cavalry, sat in his saddle amid 6,000 other troopers of Lt. Gen. Joseph Wheeler's Cavalry Corps, near the tiny settlement of Monroe's Crossroads, waiting for the signal to advance. His unit was also battered and road-weary, with many months of hard fighting in the Atlanta and Georgia Campaigns under their belts. Now, it was getting close to the end, and everyone knew it. After almost completely destroying his own army after the Atlanta Campaign, Hood had quietly resigned, allowing his old nemesis, and the common soldier's best friend, Gen. Joseph E. Johnston, to resume command of the Army of Tennessee. Wortham's own unit, originally the 4th (Avery's) Georgia Cavalry, had been refitted, reorganized, redesignated, and put on the road north toward the Carolinas to try and help stop Sherman's howling juggernaut. So far they had not been successful at even slowing down the 60,000 bluecoats, but this morning they were planning to take out at least a few. Just to the east, across a small clearing, were the neatly arranged tents of Maj. Gen. Hugh J. Kilpatrick's 3rd Cavalry Division, with 4,438 cavalrymen and their mounts encamped along a quarter-mile of Blue's Rosin Road, to the far left of the scouts and cavalrymen screening Sherman's main body. At 6:00 in the morning, the rain that had fallen all night was replaced by a heavy, thick fog, and the order to move out at the trot was given. The largest all-cavalry battle of the entire Civil War had just commenced.

CAVALRY

The simplest definition of "cavalry" is the use of armed soldiers mounted on horseback. Starting at about the time of Darius I of Persia's invasion of western Asia and the Greek city-states (c. 500 B.C.), mounted soldiers began developing into the preeminent force on the battlefield. While infantry was certainly still used, and was an important part of military tactical deployment, the cavalry became the fighting element that all military planning revolved around. This situation continued into the early medieval period in Europe, finally fading out in favor of a concentration on infantry combat, around the period bookended by the battles of Stirling Bridge, Scotland (A.D. 1198) and Agincourt, France (A.D. 1415), both of which demonstrated the complete failure of heavy cavalry formations in breaking up an infantry position.

The U.S. Army had cavalry organizations of various sizes since its 1775 inception, and by the beginning of the war in 1861, it had several mounted units. In the early 1850s the 1st United States Cavalry was formed, the first regiment in the Army that was intended from the start to fight from the saddle. Earlier formations, known as Dragoons, used their horses simply to carry them rapidly from one place to another, and fought dismounted. The 1st Cavalry, a "light" cavalry force, was primarily intended for use as scouts and videttes, or for mounted sentries or pickets, used to screen the flanks of an army in the field. With the new concept came new weapons. Cavalry-model pistols were designed with rings in the butt that attached to lanyards looped around the trooper's neck—modern military troops call these lanyards "dummy cords," for obvious reasons. A lighter-weight steel saber, intended for use from horseback, was also specially designed for the cavalry.

After Fort Sumter, the Army reorganized its cavalry forces, spreading them out among the various theaters. The 1st Cavalry was redesignated as the 4th U.S. Cavalry and was assigned to the Western Theater, encompassing Tennessee, Georgia, Alabama, and Mississippi. These newly constituted cavalry regiments were soon relegated to the tasks of scouting and forward patrolling, guarding railroads, and providing keen-looking escorts to politicians and generals. During combat actions, they were primarily used as "first strike" attackers, charging at full tilt toward the enemy line, firing pistols and screaming as loudly as possible—a tactic designed to either scare off the enemy or at least blow a hole in his lines that could then be exploited by follow-up infantry attacks. At the beginning of the war, cavalrymen bore the brunt of sometimes mean-spirited ridicule from the infantry, who regarded them as dandies at best, and shirking cowards at worst. A frequent jibe, admittedly hard to translate into today's culture, was an infantryman's cry of, "Mister! Here's your mule!" when he saw a line of cavalry approaching. That was a real knee-slapper back in 1862.

By 1863 things had started to change across the board in military thought, including the role and use of cavalry in combat. Still maintaining their primary role as advance scouts and videttes, the cavalry on both sides began being used for dedicated attacks on enemy flanks and marching columns, even when unsupported by infantry. That same year, cavalry-on-cavalry battles became more common, peaking with the cavalry-only battle at Brandy Station, Virginia, which was the opening fight of the Gettysburg Campaign. This rapidly escalated into the use of regular army cavalry in roles that had been reserved for the disdained guerilla and "partisan ranger" units (who were seen as roughly on the same level as murderous mercenaries): raids into enemy camps, supply depots, and even cities. The end result of this expansion in the use of cavalry was that garrison units had to be equally expanded and changed from those staffed by the sick, lame, and lazy, into combat-ready units that had to be able to respond to a lightning-fast attack by a raiding cavalry unit.

The relatively small cavalry units, especially the Confederate regiments led by Lieutenant General Forrest and Major General Wheeler, had an impact on grand campaigns far beyond what their small size would suggest. During the 1863 Union approach to Vicksburg, Major General Grant was forced to abandon his initial overland movement across Mississippi, after Forrest's raids on his supply lines in southern and western Tennessee threatened to cut his men off from ammunition and food. Later that same year, Wheeler led a raid through central Tennessee that cut off the besieged Union garrison at Chattanooga from desperately needed supplies, routed Union supply columns, and caused havoc with the central Union command structure in the area. It could have resulted in a collapse of the entire Union control of the area, if CSA Gen. Braxton Bragg, then the local commander, could have bothered to rouse himself enough to follow up on the advantages Wheeler had practically handed him on a silver platter.

Despite the enmity of the infantry, the life of a cavalryman was far from glamorous or safe. As the fastest moving military force in the field at the time, a cavalryman could be in the midst of battle literally at a moment's notice. The swift movement of his nature of combat meant that near instantaneous decisions and lightning-quick reflexes were an absolute necessity in order to live to tell about it. Individual weapons used by cavalrymen changed as rapidly as their tactics, with the early-war, drawn-saber charges giving way to pistols, and eventually rapid-fire, breech-loading carbines.

One similarity to the infantry, however, was the grossly overloaded manner in which the cavalryman left home. In his monumental work, *The Life of Johnny Reb*, eminent historian Bell Irvin Wiley described a typical load carried by one Texas cavalryman with the "W.P. Lane Rangers":

> . . . saddle, bridle, saddle-blanket, curry comb, horse brush, coffee pot, tin cup, 20 lbs. ham, 200 biscuit, 5 lbs. ground coffee, 5 lbs. sugar, one large pound cake presented to me by Mrs. C.E. Talley, 6 shirts, 6 prs. socks, 3 prs. drawers, 2 prs. pants, 2 jackets, 1 pr. heavy mud boots, one Colt's revolver, one small dirk, four blankets, sixty feet of rope with a twelve inch iron pin attached . . . and divers and sundry little momentoes from friends.

Also similar to their infantry counterparts, carried equipment rapidly downgraded, until the typical load consisted of a light steel saber (rarely used after 1863, and abandoned completely in Forrest's and some other Southern commands), one or two .36 or .44 caliber, six-shot pistols, a short-barreled carbine, a saddle and other horse-related necessities, a shelter half, blanket, poncho, sometimes a change of clothes and socks, and a saddle bag that held coffee, food, and other absolute necessities.

One element of the cavalry that never completely died out during the war was their dash and élan, perceived or real as it was. Largely promoted by the dashing personality of CSA Maj. Gen. James Ewell Brown Stuart, the image of the cavalryman developed into one of the gallant cavalier, forever prancing about the battlefield in a rather hyperactive sort of way, or swooping down into an unprotected Northern town—where the women would be romanced, the men would be respectably placed out of the line of danger, and some random supplies would be gathered up to take back to the unglamorous, starving infantry. Dressed in a fancy, yellow-trimmed uniform, tall polished boots, a gleaming saber buckled over a yellow silk sash, topped with a slouch hat trimmed with a large ostrich feather, and his own personal band in tow (literally), the rather weak-chinned and somewhat homely Stuart somehow proved irresistible to Southern (and some Northern) women. He was even more irresistible, apparently, after he hid his shortcomings behind a thick and usually immaculately groomed beard. The popular perception of his cavalry, promoted in newspapers both North and South, was that his war was a sort of grand adventure, fought in a gentlemanly manner and treated by friend and foe alike as a great lark, in which both sides could not wipe the grins off their faces from the pure joy of it all. This was helped in no small part by a popular song of the day, said to be Stuart's favorite:

JINE THE CAVALRY
(by Sam Sweeney, one of Stuart's musicians)

CHORUS:
If you want to have a good time, jine the cavalry!
Jine the cavalry! Jine the cavalry!
If you want to catch the Devil, if you want to have fun,
If you want to smell Hell, jine the cavalry!

We're the boys who went around McClellian,
Went around McClellian, went around around McClellian!
We're the boys who went around McClellian,
Bully boys, hey! Bully boys, ho!

CHORUS
We're the boys who crossed the Potomicum,
Crossed the Potomicum, crossed the Potomicum!
We're the boys who crossed the Potomicum,
Bully boys, hey! Bully boys, ho!

CHORUS
Then we went into Pennsylvania,
Into Pennsylvania, into Pennsylvania!
Then we went into Pennsylvania,
Bully boys, hey! Bully boys, ho!

CHORUS
The big fat Dutch gals hand around the breadium,
Hand around the breadium, hand around the breadium!
The big fat Dutch gals hand around the breadium,
Bully boys, hey! Bully boys, ho!

CHORUS
Ol' Joe Hooker, won't you come out of The Wilderness?
Come out of The Wilderness, come out of The Wilderness?
Ol' Joe Hooker, won't you come out of The Wilderness?
Bully boys, hey! Bully boys, ho!

CHORUS

The truth, of course, is not anywhere even close to this romantic fantasy, but as in so many other situations, image won out over substance. The sight of a dirty, nasty cavalry trooper mounted atop an unbathed, rather fragrant horse, could set the heart of a Southern belle all aflutter, while the sight of an equally dirty, unkempt foot infantrymen would usually make her wonder if she had adequately hidden all the silverware. The media of the day, and many latter days, kept up this romantic hogwash; images of saber-drawn cavalry at a gallop toward lines of a faceless enemy remained popular well into the twentieth century.

4TH UNITED STATES CAVALRY

The pre-war 1st Cavalry was assigned to Fort Riley, Kansas, and charged with protecting the frontier from Indian attacks. Their commander on the eve of the war was none other than then-Major John Sedgwick, who would later gain fame, albeit posthumously, as the Major General who remarked contemptuously of his Confederate foes at Spotsylvania, "Why, they couldn't hit an elephant at this distance!"

With the secession of South Carolina, followed by the first shots at Forts Barrancas and Sumter, the 1st Cavalry, along with the rest of the regular U.S. Army, was hit by a wave of resignations and outright desertions from Southern-sympathizing troopers and officers. Adding to the headache was the fact that the reduced-strength Cavalry regiments had to maintain their western posts to guard against continued Indian raids, and those same Indians had started choosing up sides, with the majority supporting the rebellious Confederacy. In addition, the Union army was rapidly ramping up for major, sustained operations, and requesting as many cavalry regiments, or even individual companies, as could be spared from the frontier. Setting a precedent that would last the remainder of the war, newly appointed commanding officer Lieutenant-Colonel Emory divided the 1st Cavalry, sending his companies individually to the Eastern Theater armies, and keeping just two companies on the frontier. In early August 1861, the regiment and its scattered companies were all redesignated as the 4th United States Cavalry, in a reorganization scheme that had been, ironically enough, suggested by then-Secretary of War and new President of the Confederacy, Jefferson Davis.

Based on his rank during the final campaigns of the war, James Larson was probably either a pre-war cavalry trooper or he joined up early in the war. However, like so many faces on so many undocumented, faded pictures, all we really know for a fact is that he was present in the regiment when it fought through Georgia and Tennessee. He is found listed on the roster for Company H during these campaigns, but it was very common at the time for enlisted men and sergeants to be reassigned, formally or informally, to any of the companies in a regiment on a frequent and routine basis.

Two companies, A and E, fought with noted gallantry at the 1st Manassas (Bull Run) in Virginia, the first major land battle of the war. At the same time four other companies (B, C, D, and L) were engaged with Confederate "bushwhackers" in Missouri. At Wilson's Creek in Springfield, Missouri, Company D and I each suffered four casualties while trying to protect the rest of the Union force fleeing the field, and were noted for bringing some small measure of triumph to what was euphemistically referred to as a "mixture of glory, disgrace, and disaster" in the after-action reports. "Spin," as one may note from this example, is not a modern invention.

During McClellan's Peninsular Campaign, in the spring of 1862, two companies of the 4th Cavalry (A and E) served as the diminutive general's personal escort, while Company I participated in the Battle of Shiloh. Companies F and H stayed out west at Fort Laramie, Nebraska, while six companies (B, C, D, G, I, and K) reunited for the short campaign around Corinth, Mississippi. Later that year, all the companies were pulled off the frontier and out of the Eastern Theater armies, and were reassigned to the Western Theater armies. They were still assigned out as individual companies, but at least they were all fighting in or around the same battlefields.

In the long battles for middle Tennessee in late 1863 to early 1864, and during Sherman's 1864 Atlanta Campaign, the regiment was noted repeatedly for their cool heads under fire and for their willingness to charge far superior numbers of Confederate cavalry, usually with great success. Late in October 1864, while in Atlanta, the regiment was pulled out of the line and ordered to Nashville, where they were to join as a full regiment the new cavalry corps being formed by Maj. Gen. James Wilson. The timing could not have been better, as Hood was en route to the same city, with what remained of his once-formidable Army of Tennessee. However, the 4th Cavalry was not in the greatest shape, either; long months of hard campaigning had reduced its strength to only 175 men and officers.

FRANKLIN/NASHVILLE

In a short list of all the bone-headed maneuvers during the Civil War, Hood's invasion of Tennessee in late 1864 without a doubt ranks at or near the very top. Possibly influenced by his reported use of large doses of laudanum, as a pain reliever for injuries sustained at Gettysburg and Chickamauga, Hood concocted this plan after being thoroughly trounced by Sherman's three grand armies around Atlanta in the late summer of 1864.

Maintaining to his death that the only way to defeat Sherman was to draw him into battle on terrain of his own choosing (which was possibly true), Hood decided to take what was left of his Army of Tennessee and march north out of the Atlanta area, hoping to "force" Sherman to follow so that Hood could defeat him by parts as the Union armies marched after him. Jefferson Davis encouraged Hood to attack Sherman and recapture the city, but that overwhelming task daunted even the "attack at all costs" Texan. Instead, he proposed to march north of the city, striking and cutting Sherman's supply line from Chattanooga, which, hopefully, would force the Union army out of the city and north in pursuit. Although neither Hood nor Johnston had yet defeated Sherman in a major pitched battle the entire campaign, with the Southern army intact, he now convinced the Confederate president that by choosing his defensive terrain carefully, he could defeat a well-armed, equipped, and relatively fresh force four times his size. Amazingly, Davis bought the idea and approved the plan.

HOOD MOVES NORTH

With three corps in his command, Hood moved out of his last Atlanta base of Lovejoy on September 18, swinging wide around the western flank of the Atlanta defenses, and headed north. Sherman had anticipated Hood would do exactly this, and had already sent Brig. Gen. George Henry Thomas, the "Rock of Chickamauga," with three infantry divisions back to Chattanooga to prepare.

Hood moved relatively slowly. Crossing the Chattahoochee River near Campbellton on October 1, he continued north for two days, and finally encamped near Hiram. Stewart was ordered to move east and attack and cut the Western and Atlantic Railroad line at Big Shanty (now Kennesaw), Acworth, and Allatoona.

THE ATTACK AT ALLATOONA PASS

Stewart's men surprised and captured about 170 Union troops at Big Shanty on October 4, then quickly moved north and captured a larger garrison at Acworth. Flushed with these easy successes, Hood personally ordered Maj. Gen. Samuel G. French to take his division on up the tracks, to capture and destroy the bridge and railroad cut at Allatoona Pass. Hood was under the impression that the pass was only lightly held, as the two previous rail stops had been. However, Sherman had made the tiny settlement on the south side of the deep railway cut into a central base of logistical operations. It was heavily fortified, and he ordered another division under Brig. Gen. John M. Corse forward to garrison it. On both peaks over the ninety-feet-deep railroad cut, heavily reinforced emplacements had been built. The westernmost set of peak defenses was dubbed the Star Fort because of the arrangement of railroad ties surrounding it.

French divided his force and approached Allatoona from the north, west, and south. Once all were in position, he rather arrogantly sent Corse a terse message:

> Sir: I have the forces under my command in such positions that you are now surrounded, and, to avoid a needless effusion of blood, I call upon you to surrender your forces at once, and unconditionally. Five minutes will be allowed for you to decide. Should you accede to this, you will be treated in the most honorable manner as prisoners of war.

Corse was somewhat less than impressed. Fifteen minutes later he replied, "Your communication demanding surrender of my command, I acknowledge receipt of, and respectfully reply, that we are prepared for the 'needless effusion of blood' whenever it is agreeable with you."

French wasted no time, sending Brig. Gen. Francis M. Cockrell's Missouri Brigade and Brig. Gen. William H. Young's Brigade assaulting from the west. Both pushed through the first line of defenses, then the second, then through a third line of defense, all the while fighting hand-to-hand with clubbed rifles and bayonets. Advancing to within a few feet of the Star Fort, the fighting rapidly intensified, with the Confederate advance being stopped before it could overrun the fort. Finally, with warnings coming from outposts that a Union force had been spotted moving rapidly toward the battle area, French disengaged and marched his depleted force west to rejoin Hood.

All through the day-long battle, a Union signal post at Kennesaw Mountain sent a message to Corse: "General Sherman says hold fast; we are coming." This message, which popularized the expression, "hold the fort," was nothing more than a moral booster, for Sherman did not order any additional infantry to the area until the next day, and none actually arrived until two days later. The forces spotted by the Confederate side were apparently just cavalry on a scouting mission.

Casualties in the brief battle were exceptionally high, with Corse reporting 706 dead and wounded, and French also reporting 706 (including seventy officers)—about 30 percent of either side's total force. Young himself was wounded just outside the fort and captured shortly afterward. Corse reported that he, too, had been wounded. In a message to Sherman, he said, "I am short a cheek bone and an ear but am able to lick all hell yet!" When Sherman came up later, he was unimpressed with the severity of the brigadier general's wounds, "Corse, they came damn near missing you, didn't they?"

THE ARMIES ADVANCE IN OPPOSITE DIRECTIONS

Following the decisive loss at Allatoona Pass, Hood elected to continue north, moving west around Rome through Cedartown, Cave Springs, and Coosaville, while Sherman followed after him with a force of 40,000 men (55,000 by some accounts)—a partial vindication of Hood's audacious plan. Wheeler's Cavalry joined the campaign at this point, screening his movement from Sherman's force, while Jackson's Cavalry stayed below Rome near the Coosa River. Attacks at Resaca on October 12 and 13 were failures, but Lee's and Cheatham's Corps were able to capture the railroad north of Resaca the next day. In one of the only real Confederate successes in north Georgia, the 2,000-strong Union garrison at Dalton was forced to surrender, but with Sherman hot on his heels, Hood was unable to hold the city or take any prisoners with him.

Hood moved west again, toward northwestern Georgia near the Alabama state line, and set up a line of battle near Lafayette on October 15. Hood's strategy here is uncertain, as he was moving away from the mountainous terrain he had claimed would be to his advantage. There are mountains near Lafayette, and rugged ones at that, but this was the same area in which Sherman had already demonstrated an ability to operate successfully. The northeastern mountains were not specified in Hood's plans, but were most likely his original destination. If his plan was to keep Sherman bottled up in northern Georgia, it both succeeded and failed.

When Hood slipped away after the Union troops deployed for battle at Lafayette on October 17, Sherman remarked that Hood's tactics were "inexplicable by any common-sense theory . . . I could not guess his movements as I could those of Johnston." After three weeks of chasing the now fast-moving CSA Army of Tennessee, Sherman ordered his forces to return to Atlanta and prepare for a march to the south.

Warned by Grant that Hood was taking his army north into Tennessee and was threatening his supply lines, Sherman remarked, "No single force can catch Hood, and I am convinced that the best results will follow from our defeating Jeff Davis's cherished plan of making me leave Georgia by maneuvering."

At the same time, Davis was begging Hood "not to abandon Georgia to Sherman but defeat him in detail before marching into Tennessee." Hood replied back that it was his intent to "draw out Sherman where he can be dealt with north of Atlanta." In his postwar memoirs, Hood clung to this unrealistic strategy for defeating both Sherman and Thomas's powerful force in Tennessee:

> I conceived the plan of marching into Tennessee . . . to move upon Thomas and Schofield and capture their army before it could reach Nashville and afterward march northeast, past the Cumberland River in that position I could threaten Cincinnati from Kentucky and Tennessee . . . if blessed with a victory [over Sherman coming north after him], to send reinforcements to Lee, in Virginia, or to march through gaps in the Cumberland Mountains and attack Grant in the rear.

It was whispered by not a few members of the CSA Army of Tennessee that Hood was half-mad from his injuries. He had been shot in the arm at Gettysburg and had a leg shot off at Chickamauga the year before. Widely viewed as a gallant fighter, in the sense that a lot of his own men were killed as a result of his tactics, his leadership did not impress those under him. Pvt. Sam Watkins said, "As a soldier, he was brave, good, noble, and gallant, and fought with the ferociousness of the wounded tiger, and with the everlasting grit of the bull-dog; but as a general he was a failure in every particular."

Hood continued his march north, and Sherman, upon hearing the news, couldn't have been happier. "If he will go to the Ohio River, I will give him rations." He sent Schofield's Army of the Ohio, consisting of Maj. Gen. David F. Stanley's IV Corps and Brig. Gen. Jacob D. Cox's XXIII Corps, to defend Tennessee and turned his attention on his March to the Sea.

HOOD IN ALABAMA

The CSA Army of Tennessee reached Decatur, Alabama, on October 26, where it met CSA General Beauregard, commander of the Division of the West. Beauregard approved Hood's plan to invade Tennessee, but made him give up Wheeler's Cavalry, which was sorely needed in the coming campaign against Sherman in southern Georgia. In exchange, Major General Forrest's Cavalry Corps was moving down from eastern Tennessee to provide coverage.

While he waited for Forrest to arrive, Hood moved his force west, retaking and fortifying Florence, Alabama, and Corinth, Mississippi, and repairing the railroad line between the cities to shuttle his supplies as needed. Forrest took nearly three weeks to arrive, finally appearing on the seventeenth of November.

To counter Hood's move west, Thomas sent Stanley's Corps, reinforced with one division from Cox's Corps, to Pulaski, Tennessee, directly astride the Nashville and Decatur Railroad, where he expected Hood to advance. On November 14, Schofield arrived in Pulaski to establish his headquarters and detail the defense against Hood's army. At that time Schofield commanded an army of 25,000 infantry and 5,000 cavalry, while Thomas had another 40,000 troops scattered between Nashville and north Georgia, nearly all of them relatively fresh and well-supplied. With Forrest's arrival, Hood had about 33,000 infantry and 6,000 cavalrymen—all tired, battle-weary, and poorly supplied.

HOOD MARCHES NORTH

On November 19, Hood at long last moved out on his great campaign, led by Forrest's Cavalry and Lee's Corps. Rather than following the railroad as Schofield expected, Hood moved along three parallel roads to the west of Pulaski, heading toward Columbia, some 31 miles to the north. The weather was wretched. A cold rain mixed with snow and sleet turned the muddy roads to ice, which cut and burned the bare feet of most of the tattered infantrymen.

Schofield recognized the danger of his flank being turned and hustled all but one brigade of his army to Columbia, arriving and fortifying the bridges over the Duck River by November 24. Hood's army closed in on the town on the morning of November 26. That night he outlined yet another strategy to his three corps commanders. He told them that Nashville was an "open city" and a ripe prize to be easily taken. To do so, they had to move fast toward the capital city, bypassing any Union forces they could and overwhelming those they could not.

Once again, it is difficult to comprehend Hood's overall intent. Originally moving north to draw Sherman out of Atlanta, he succeeded, but then ran into Alabama rather than finding suitable terrain for fighting. Once in Alabama, he ignored Davis's pleas not to abandon Georgia completely and convinced Beauregard that he could defeat Thomas's forces in Tennessee piecemeal, recover the state for the Confederacy, and either help reinforce Lee's army in Virginia or invade Ohio. To do either he had to eliminate any Union threat from his own base of support by defeating Thomas, or at the very least, forcing him to retire from Tennessee. Yet, when literally given the opportunity to challenge parts of the Union armies with a superior force, at Pulaski and now at Columbia, he chose to outflank them and continue north.

SPRING HILL

Realizing early on that Hood had no intent of a direct assault at Columbia and might possibly try to envelop him to the north, Schofield sent Stanley's Corps, reinforced with additional infantry and artillery, to Spring Hill. The Union corps arrived at Spring Hill about 2:00 P.M. Hood had sent Forrest to bypass the Union defenses north of Columbia, and his men arrived at Spring Hill at nearly the same time Stanley did. Both sides skirmished to no real gain, until just before dark. Lee's Corps had stayed outside Columbia to 'make a racket,' distracting the bluebellies while Hood moved Cheatham's and Stewart's Corps east to Davis Ford on the Duck River. Overnight, the two corps crossed through pastures, woods, and creeks before reemerging on Rally Hill (Franklin) Turnpike toward Spring Hill just at dark on November 29, neatly flanking Schofield in the maneuver.

Arriving just at dark, part of Cheatham's Corps came up and helped push the Union force back into town. Stanley managed to hold the town and keep the road to Columbia open. Hood's army was exhausted by the rough march and the combat action, however, and nearly immediately lay down in the mud on either side of the road to catch some badly needed sleep.

As the Confederate infantry slept, Schofield slipped out of Columbia and passed through a mere 200-yard-wide gap between the two Southern corps without being detected, making it to Spring Hill without incident. When Hood found out, he blamed Cheatham for the escape, and a huge fight erupted between the two. Hood then requested that Richmond send a replacement, while Cheatham complained he had not been specifically ordered to take and cut the road. Other Southern generals joined in the fun and argued through the night, and in the meantime, Schofield and the rest of his corps moved out of Spring Hill and on toward Franklin, reaching the outer defenses by dawn on November 30. Once there, Schofield discovered he would not be able to move his men and heavy supply trains into the city until his engineers rebuilt the bridges and fords destroyed by Forrest's raids. He ordered his men to hastily throw up earthwork defenses on the south edge of town, in case Hood was following too closely. He planned on withdrawing back across the river after dark, and then moving up to Nashville during the night. To help ensure Schofield's safety, Wilson sent part of his cavalry corps, including part of the 4th Cavalry, south to Franklin, to screen the flanks and scout for Hood's army.

FRANKLIN

Hood was indeed following closely. After withdrawing his request for Cheatham's replacement and making a few last rude comments, he got his army moving north again, chasing after Schofield. The vanguard of the Southern force arrived atop a low range of hills just south of Franklin around 3:00 P.M., and Hood immediately gave orders to attack the Union lines they could see being constructed. The three corps commanders were incredulous. Dusk wasn't far off, the army was still in column road-march formation with parts of it still hours away, and the Union troops clearly had a superior and fortified position that was well protected by artillery batteries.

This is when Hood threw another one of his fits. He habitually considered anyone who disagreed with him as an enemy, and was loath to change his plan, even in the face of overwhelming evidence that it was a poor one. In addition, he had often remarked since taking command that the men and officers loyal to former commander Johnston were "soft" and prone to retreating in the face of the enemy. He insisted that they were to march right down there and take those works, even at the cost of their own lives—almost as a punishment for daring to disagree with him.

THE BATTLE OF FRANKLIN

After 3:00 P.M., the two Confederate corps present started forming in line of battle, with Cheatham's Corps on the left and Stewart's Corps on the right. At the same time, the bridge and ford work had been completed, and Schofield was getting ready to pull his Union forces back north across the river. At 3:30 the signal trumpets blew, and a mass of butternut-clad infantry charged across the open ground toward the Union emplacements. CSA Maj. Gen. John Calvin Brown's and CSA Major General Cleburne's Divisions briefly overran USA Brig. Gen. George B. Wagner's Division, which was left out on the pike road south of the main defense belt.

Mounting a strong counter-attack, USA Col. Emerson Opdyke's First Brigade of Wagner's Division, who had been the rear guard all day and was taking a well-deserved rest at the river, leapt back over the defense wall and charged at Cleburne's men. A furious fight erupted, with point-blank shots and hand-to-hand combat all along the line. One of Opdyke's officers, Maj. Arthur MacArthur, father of the WWII hero Douglas MacArthur, managed to slash a Confederate regiment's color bearer with his sword and take the prize, despite being shot three times in the process.

Individual regiments and brigades eventually reached the second Union line of defense, but none were able to pierce it. The field behind them now raked by constant canister and shot from the Union batteries, there was no place left to retreat, either. Both sides stood just yards apart for hours, pouring musket and artillery fire into each other's ranks, without either side giving way.

The slaughter finally stopped about 9:00 P.M., well after dark, when gun by gun, the firing slowly petered out. Surviving Confederate regiments literally crawled back across the body-strewn field to the safety of their original positions. Schofield promptly abandoned the field as well, leaving his dead and wounded behind, and, with his cavalry formed a rear-guard, immediately marched back to Nashville. He arrived about noon on the first of December.

Hood's casualties were almost unreal. Of the 26,000 he had sent in battle, 5,550 were dead or wounded, with another 702 missing. Thirty-two regimental and brigade battle flags had been taken. No less than fifty-four regimental commanders were killed, wounded, or missing. The worst loss was that of six generals, including Cleburne Brig. Gen. Hiram Bronson Granbury. Of the other six generals on the battlefield, one had been captured and only two were left unwounded and fit for service (sixteen other generals were with Hood's army, but were not on the battlefield that day).

Schofield's casualties, although heavy, were still lighter than Hood's. Of the 28,000 men he had on the line that afternoon, 1,222 were killed or wounded, while 1,104 were captured or missing.

THE MARCH TO NASHVILLE

Hood's army was in no shape to fight anymore, after the beating at Franklin, but nothing would deter Hood from his determination to take the Tennessee capital back. Schofield's forces had quit the field at Franklin immediately after the battle, and Hood followed suit. Ordering his men up and at 'em, the depleted Army of Tennessee stood outside the defenses of Nashville by December 2, 1864.

Once again, we face the question of what Hood was planning to do. After the war, he admitted that he knew his army was too depleted to assault the Nashville emplacements, and that Schofield was well placed, well supplied, and had reinforcements on the way. It takes nearly a suspension of belief to follow his plan, as outlined in his postwar memoirs, *Advance and Retreat*. His strategy was to wait outside for Thomas's combined army to come out and attack his own fortifications, and hope that promised reinforcements of his own (which probably did not even exist) could manage to travel from Texas in time to help him.

Thomas, on the other hand, was quite comfortable and in no mood to hurry into a fight. USA Maj. Gen. Andrew Jackson Smith arrived with his three divisions of XVI Corps by the time Schofield came in from Franklin, and USA Maj. Gen. James Blair Steedman brought up a division of 5,200 men detached from Sherman's command the next day. By December 4, Thomas had a total of 49,773 men under his command, some of whom were well rested and had not seen combat recently. Hood, by comparison, could muster (on paper) only 23,207 tired, cold, and demoralized troops. This figure did not take into consideration the large number of desertions of battle-hardened veterans the Army of Tennessee was beginning to experience.

THE BATTLE OF NASHVILLE

Under growing pressure from Grant to move into action, Thomas made preparations to defeat the weaker Confederate army and gain "such a splendid and decisive victory as to hush censure for all time." Finally, at 6:00 A.M. on the foggy morning of December 15, his army moved out. Thomas planned to hit both of Hood's flanks with a coordinated attack that would destroy his lines of battle in a matter of minutes. Thomas had no desire to simply push Hood away from Nashville; he was determined to destroy that Confederate army once and for all.

At 8:00 in the morning, Steedman started the attack on Hood's right, the coordinated plan falling apart immediately due to the poor weather and bad roads. Two hours later Smith's Corps hit Hood's left flank, along with about a third of Wilson's Cavalry, followed by Wood and Schofield over the next few hours. Hood was steadily pushed back, but his lines held fast and pulled together to form a tight, straight line of battle. By nightfall, Hood had been pushed back about a mile, where he formed a new line of battle that stretched between Shy's Hill and Overton Hill.

At dawn on December 17, Thomas's forces started probing the new Confederate line for weakness. At 3:00 P.M., a strong attack was made against the defense atop Overton Hill, followed a half hour later by initial actions against Shy's Hill. Within an hour the attack on Hood's right had been repulsed with heavy losses, but the attack on Shy's Hill succeeded in routing the Confederate defenders, and effectively bringing the battle to an end. Part of Wilson's Cavalry had dismounted just as the battle began, sweeping up the hill on foot and charging into the very face of the Confederate defenders. Thomas, observing from his headquarters, mentioned their charge in his after-action report:

> *Whilst slightly swinging to the left, [the cavalry] came upon a redoubt containing four guns, which was splendidly carried by assault, at 1 p.m., by a portion of Hatch's division, dismounted, and the captured guns turned upon the enemy. A second redoubt, stronger than the first, was next assailed and carried by the same troops that carried the first position, taking four more guns and about three hundred prisoners. The infantry, McArthur's division, on the left of the cavalry, . . . participated in both of the assaults; and, indeed, the dismounted cavalry*

seemed to vie with the infantry who should first gain the works; as they reached the position nearly simultaneously, both lay claim to the artillery and prisoners captured.

The Army of Tennessee was at long last broken. All semblance of order broke down as many soldiers either ran for the rear or allowed themselves to be taken prisoner. Many more simply dropped their rifles and returned home, too defeated to fight anymore. Hood pulled what was left of his force south out of Nashville and marched through a brutal winter landscape all the way back to Tupelo, Mississippi. Once there, Hood quietly asked to be relieved of command.

During Hood's long retreat, Wilson stayed right on his heels, attacking whenever the exhausted Confederates paused for too long in one place. One incident, on December 24, featured one officer of the 4th Cavalry, Lt. Joseph Hedges, leading a charge straight into a battery of Confederate artillery, driving them off the line of battle and ultimately capturing the entire battery after a short running fight. Wilson recalled this incident after the war:

> *Late in the evening, apparently exhausted with a rapid marching, the enemy took up a strong position in the open field about a mile north of the West Harpeth. It was then so dark from fog and approaching night that the men of Hatch's division who had become somewhat intermingled with the sullen and taciturn Confederate stragglers, began to doubt that the ranks which were now looming up in their front were really those of the enemy's rear-guard. The momentary hesitation caused by this doubt gave Forrest an opportunity to straighten his lines and to push his single remaining battery in position so as to sweep the turnpike. Hatch on the left and Knipe on the right were at once ordered to charge the enemy's flanks, while the Fourth Regular Cavalry, under Lieut. Hedges, was directed straight against his centre. Seeing what was about to burst upon him, the battery commander opened with canister at short range, but had hardly emptied his guns before the storm broke upon him. Forrest did his best to hold his ground, but it was impossible. Hedges rode headlong over the battery and captured a part of his guns.*

Lieutenant Hedges, outstripping his men, was captured three different times, but throwing his hat away and raising the cry, 'The Yankees are coming, run for your lives,' succeeded in getting away.

Hood insisted that his losses were "very small," but he was not the sort to admit defeat or desertion of his own men. Various sources give wildly disparate figures, but a rough guess is that there were about 1,500 killed and wounded in the battle, with another 4,500 captured. He lost a grand total of nearly 20,000 men in the whole failed campaign. Thomas, on the other hand, reported losses of 387 killed, 2,562 wounded, and 112 missing in the battle.

Larson and his fellow troopers did well, with the physical proof of their daring, close-in fighting provided by the list of "spoils" taken during the running battle:

> During and after the battle of Nashville, and including prisoners taken in the hospitals at Franklin, the Union cavalry captured 2 strong redoubts, 32 field guns, 11 caissons, 12 colors, 3,232 prisoners (including 1 general officer), 1 bridge train of 80 pontoons, and 125 wagons. Its own losses were 122 officers and men killed, 1 field-gun, 521 wounded, and 259 missing.

Even after this shattering defeat, the end of this great army was not yet at hand. Reorganizing yet again, the Army of Tennessee was reunited with their beloved commander, Gen. Johnston and moved back east to confront Sherman one more time, this time in his march through the Carolinas.

Sgt. James Larson and the 4th U.S. Cavalry were not through with the war, either. Resting briefly from the fights at Franklin and Nashville, they joined the rest of Wilson's Corps at Gravelly Springs, Alabama, and rode in the last great campaign of the war, through Alabama and Georgia, as the Confederate armies individually surrendered and lay down their arms. Wilson rebuilt his force into a 13,500-man command, all mounted, based out of Gravelly Springs. In late March 1865, he led his command south to Selma, taking and destroying the essential Confederate arsenal there, and routing most of Forrest's command in the process, before turning toward Georgia. For the next six weeks, his command ranged all through central Alabama and central and southern Georgia, destroying warehouses and manufacturing facilities, and capturing scores of local militias and independent commands, almost without opposition. Finally, on May 10, near Irwinville, Georgia, an element of his command captured the fleeing Confederate president himself, Jefferson Davis.

12TH GEORGIA CAVALRY

While Sergeant Larson and the 4th U.S. Cavalry were resting and refitting at Gravelly Springs, Pvt. Benjamin Wortham and his fellow cavalrymen were doing exactly the same thing in Georgia. Wortham had fought under CSA Col. Isaac W. Avery with the 4th Georgia Cavalry, all through the Chickamauga and Chattanooga Campaigns, and the hundred-mile rolling battle against Sherman advancing on Atlanta. Wortham was near Avery when he was shot through the stomach during the vicious brawl at New Hope Church. Avery not only survived the wound, but continued to lead his regiment through the rest of the Atlanta Campaign and up through eastern Tennessee, assigned to one of Wheeler's innumerable raids. He manned the ramparts of Savannah as Sherman's forces pounded down its defenses. Now, with that great city fallen as well, Avery's troopers reformed their shattered ranks early in January 1865. They were redesignated as the 12th Georgia Cavalry, a part of Johnston's reconstituted Army of Tennessee, and they prepared to try a last-ditch defense of the Carolinas against Sherman's coming onslaught.

As with Union Sgt. James Larson, little is known about Wortham, other than the few physical artifacts he left behind, safely encased at the Atlanta History Center, where his saddle is helpfully marked with his regiment's number. Civil War cavalrymen were the special-operations troops of their day, their ranks filled with men who were more action-oriented than literary, their minimal postwar output of memoirs and reminiscences complicated by the fact that so many cavalry records were lost or deliberately destroyed in the closing weeks of the war. Many "raids" were actions that could be considered, in the cool calm of military courtroom proceedings, just short of outright thievery and highwaymen assault, and they were often against civilians as well as uniformed enemy formations. Few cavalrymen wanted anything left behind that could possibly be used against them later by a vengeful, reunited nation.

SOUTH CAROLINA

After the fall of Savannah in December 1864, Sherman wasted little time in turning his attention northward. Entering South Carolina with 63,000 men arranged in four great columns in late January 1865, almost no Confederate force was available to stand up against him. A single division under CSA Maj. Gen. Lafayette McLaws did their best at the Salkehatchie River Bridge east of Allendale, but all they managed to do was hold up one Union corps for a single day, at the cost of 170 men killed or wounded.

As Sherman's "bummers" ravaged the middle of the state, CSA Lieutenant General Hardee, now in command of forces around Charleston, determined that he would have to immediately evacuate his troops or risk having them cut off and trapped between Sherman and the Union Navy. On the night of February 17, 1865, with the bulk of Union forces entering and burning the undefended capital city of Columbia, Hardee ordered Fort Sumter abandoned and marched out of the city. He headed for Cheraw, to join Johnston, who was now ahead of Sherman's great army at the North Carolina border town and was preparing for last-ditch defenses. Surprising almost everyone, Sherman never moved toward Charleston, instead moving his army northeast toward North Carolina, meeting almost no resistance along the way.

THE LAST OF THE ARMY OF TENNESSEE

As Charleston was abandoned without firing another shot, the Union campaign to take Wilmington wound to a close in early February 1865. Combined Confederate operations in the Deep South were rapidly coming together near the eastern North Carolina town of Goldsboro. CSA Gen. Braxton Bragg's defeated force was withdrawing to Wilmington to regroup and perhaps for its commander to figure out who to blame for his latest disaster. Sherman was pounding through South Carolina, driving what was left of the Army of Tennessee and various attached militias toward Goldsboro. Newly appointed USA Department of North Carolina commander, Major General Schofield, had been directed to move in from New Bern and take Goldsboro under Union control.

Desperately seeking some way out of the disaster looming before him, Davis finally came to a long-overdue decision and appointed Robert E. Lee as General-in-Chief of all the combined Confederate armies. One of Lee's first acts was to place all the combined Confederate forces in the Western Theater with Johnston as commander of the Army of Tennessee and almost incidentally as commander of the CSA Department of the Carolinas—with an aggregate total of about 45,000 men of widely varying skills and training levels. Bragg was reduced to command of a division under Johnston, not even a corps. It was a move that no doubt humiliated him but delighted his many political enemies. Lee had also dispatched Lt. Gen. Wade Hampton from his defenses at Petersburg to help Johnston, who placed him in overall command of Wheeler's Cavalry Corps and Maj. Gen. Matthew C. Butler's Cavalry Division.

Johnston promptly ordered most of his command to concentrate with him in the central portion of the state, to make a stand against Sherman's oncoming force. From reports filtering up from South Carolina, where Sherman was advancing without any real resistance, he knew that the Union commander was arrayed in a column four corps abreast, in an almost 60-mile-wide front. Johnston planned to concentrate his forces so as to hit Sherman from one flank, then attack each corps' flank and defeat each in turn.

THE BATTLE OF WYSE FORK

As Wilmington had been effectively, if hastily, abandoned by Bragg's troops, Schofield found no wagons or trains there to move his troops rapidly inland. Undeterred, he ordered Cox's forces in the base at New Bern to also move inland, and by late February, two great Union columns were moving inland. Bragg had pulled some of his troops safely out of Wilmington, and now had about 8,500 men under Maj. Gen. Robert Frederick Hoke near Kinston to protect his headquarters at Goldsboro. Johnston had sent a few green troops under Maj. Gen. Daniel Harvey Hill to reinforce Hoke's line, including a unit known as the "North Carolina Junior Reserves," which largely consisted of completely untrained teenage boys.

On the morning of March 8, as Cox rather casually moved up the Kinston Road toward Southwest Creek, Hoke and Hill moved out of the trench line in a well-timed attack and assaulted the Union column on both flanks. Several thousand surprised and horrified Union soldiers either ran or surrendered on the spot, while Cox hastily ordered the remainder to dig in and fight back. Sporadic fighting lasted the rest of the day and into the next, while some Union reinforcements came up to replace the scattered force. By nightfall on March 9, Cox had about 12,000 men in his trench line.

At dawn on March 10, Hoke swung around and hit the Union left flank while Hill struck the right flank, forcing a few troops to pull back or run, but both Confederate commands were forced to withdraw after a relatively short fight.

Seriously weakened by the three-day battle, Hoke and Hill were forced to withdraw back into Kinston, then almost immediately pull out as Cox's stronger force approached. Cox entered the city on March 14, as Bragg pulled what was left of his forces back into Goldsboro.

SHERMAN'S ADVANCE

Sherman had stormed through South Carolina without any real resistance and by the first of March he was approaching Cheraw, near the North Carolina border. After evacuating Charleston, also without a fight, Beauregard had directed Lieutenant General Hardee to take his corps (with two divisions and 8,000 men) to Cheraw and delay Sherman's advance, while everyone else got into some kind of order. Johnston determined that he should concentrate his forces near Fayetteville in order to best strike at Sherman's flank, no matter if he went south toward Goldsboro or north toward Raleigh.

Schofield and Sherman agreed that they would link up their respective commands at Goldsboro before moving on Raleigh to cut the main Confederate supply line there; Johnston was determined to strike hard at Sherman's column and was maneuvering his forces to hit before that linkup could be produced.

Hardee wisely pulled his infantry steadily back from Sherman's advance, leaving most of the fighting up to Wheeler's Cavalry Corps, who kept up a running battle with Sherman's cavalry chief, Brig. Gen. Judson Kilpatrick, most of the way to Fayetteville. Warned that his choice of "Kill-Cavalry" (as his own overworked cavalrymen called him behind his back) to lead the approach to Fayetteville was one that might lead to disaster, Sherman simply remarked, "I know Kilpatrick's a hell of a damned fool, but that's just the kind of man I want to lead my cavalry on this expedition."

MONROE'S CROSSROADS

On March 10, with Sherman's force still two days shy of Fayetteville, Wheeler laid a trap for his hated opponent, "Kill-Cavalry." The weather had turned cold and rainy, and the dirt roads were little better than slick mud-bogs, slowing down men and horses alike. Kilpatrick's Cavalry was strung out for miles along the Morganton Road, and he called for a halt to regroup after his scouts found a favorable spot, a tiny settlement called Monroe's Crossroads. Two of his four brigades arrived around 9:00 P.M. on March 9, along with a single battery from the 10th Wisconsin Light Artillery. Two other brigades were slowly approaching the site, with Kilpatrick and his escorts in between.

An advance guard from CSA Major General Butler's Cavalry Division, working alongside Wheeler's Cavalry in the Carolinas, moved up to Morganton Road at that same time, just after dusk, with light fading fast. They noted prints and tracks in the muddy road, indicating a brigade-sized force had just passed through, and stopped to plan where to scout next. As they sat in their saddles, Kilpatrick's own advance guard trotted up out of the gloom. Expecting to see soldiers from their own brigade, they were undoubtedly shocked and confused when the Confederates pulled their pistols and quietly took them all prisoner. Kilpatrick himself, a short distance behind on the road, saw the capture and quickly disappeared into the piney woods on the south side of the road before he and his men, too, became captives. As his advance scouts and videttes had not raised an alarm, Kilpatrick believed they had simply encountered a local militia patrol by chance, and spent the next couple of hours getting his forces rearranged and back together in camp. At the same time, three more divisions of Sherman's infantry moved into position on Plank Road, to the south through thick woods.

Distracted by both the seeming end of the war and fatigue from moving around in the hostile, wet terrain, Kilpatrick and his senior officers failed to post sufficient pickets, in every possible avenue of approach, before retiring with their consorts to a local house. Unbelievably, these seasoned Union cavalry officers were actually campaigning through enemy territory, in bad weather, with Confederate troops operating in the area, with female "escorts" in tow to provide for their comforts. Calvary pickets were posted to the east, toward their target of Fayetteville, but none were posted to the north, where Butler's and Wheeler's Cavalries were even then making their stealthy approach.

Captain Shannon, of Wheeler's Corps, led his small company of scouts all around the Federal campsite, noting carefully the lack of proper guards, and quietly "removing" the westernmost set of pickets, before returning to post his findings. A small group of his scouts even entered the Union camp at one point, and boldly led several of their mounts away to their own camp. On receiving Shannon's report, overall

Confederate cavalry commanding officer, Lt. Gen. Wade Hampton, realized that he might be able to pull off a successful raid if he could get his cavalry close in to the camp while remaining undetected. As the thick, piney woods were blackened further by the moonless night and the rain, Hampton came to the conclusion that his cavalry could pull it off, especially since Kilpatrick now had no pickets in two directions from his camp.

This was not just a Stuart-style cavalry jaunt Hampton was considering; there were some very serious reasons to hit Kilpatrick hard and delay his move north. First, Confederate forces in Fayetteville needed time to withdraw across the Cape Fear River and rejoin Johnston's army, which was moving into a blocking position to their north. The Union cavalrymen in this camp constituted two brigades, at most, with the closest reinforcements some distance to the south, and not in a position to provide any timely relief. Lastly, inside the Union camp was an undetermined number of Confederate prisoners, captured in the previous few days of skirmishing, who might also be freed. Even though neither Wheeler's nor Butler's forces were fully up and in position, Hampton decided to attack the Union camp at first light. Butler's Division was to approach from the north, Wheeler's Division was to come from the northwest, and Brigadier General Hume, of Wheeler's Corps, was to lead his division in from the west.

The orders were quickly passed from trooper to trooper, who then moved out in total darkness. Leading their mounts on foot and ordered not to talk above a whisper, they settled into their assault positions outside Kilpatrick's camp. The Union forces at Monroe's Crossroads consisted of a total of two cavalry brigades, with somewhere in the neighborhood of 1,500 men.

Just as dawn broke, Wheeler's bugler sounded a shrill call to action. Wheeler turned to his men and ordered, "The walk!" as Butler turned to his own men and shouted, "Troops from Virginia, follow me!" After just a few seconds came the second expected order from both commanders, "Charge!" The three divisions of cavalrymen soon swept through the camp, scattering the just-awakening Union cavalrymen, and cutting them down by the dozens as they swept past. The Confederate prisoners, deserted by the guards, ran toward Wheeler's men in delight, only to have some of their own number shot down in the confusion. Butler's men galloped up to the house Kilpatrick and his officers were occupying, just as the man himself ran out onto the porch in his nightshirt. Sabers and pistols pointed at the near-naked general's head, the Confederate troopers demanded to know where Kilpatrick was. His wits still about him, Kilpatrick turned and pointed to one of his rapidly skedaddling officers, just then leaping onto a saddle and making haste for parts south, "There he goes right now!" The ruse worked, just long enough for Kilpatrick to beat feet over the railing and head south into the swampy bog near Plank Road, where many of his command were even then cowering from the sudden attack.

As Hume slammed in to the western part of the Union camp, he encountered an intact and fully prepared unit, the 1st Alabama Cavalry (the only recorded full regiment raised from that dear Southern state to fight for the Union). The Confederate attack was soon blunted by both unexpectedly hostile terrain and heavy, accurate fire from the Union Alabamians. In the camp, Wheeler's and Butler's Divisions were soon engaged in close-quarter, hand-to-hand fighting with the Union troopers who had refused to flee. Buoyed by both their compatriots' stand, and heartened (or at least amused) by the sight of their underdressed commander urging them on, most of the troopers hiding in the swamp soon ran back toward their camp in a rough counter-attack. Most already had their weapons—grabbed even as they ran in terror—and soon put the same to good use.

As the close-quarter combat reached its peak, USA Lt. Ebenezer Stetson, the commander of a two-gun, 3-inch Ordnance Rifle battery, ran alone to his guns, now surrounded by hundreds of Confederate cavalrymen. The guns had been preloaded with canister rounds, and he was able to prime and lanyard one gun without being noticed. The subsequent blast tore through the tightly packed cavalry troops, scattering pieces of horses and men for yards around. Lt. Col. Barrington King, eldest son of a wealthy Roswell, Georgia family and then-commander of Cobb's Georgia Legion, was struck in the forehead with a chunk of shot, and bled to death within minutes.

As Stetson attempted to load another round into the piece, some of his own men ran up to support him, while Wheeler's troopers turned on them with a renewed fury. Amazingly, Stetson and his men were able to escape, again without injury, but ended up losing the guns, ten artillery horses, and some of their ammunition supply without being able to return even one more shot for all their effort.

The attack was now well over an hour in progress, and Hampton was terribly worried that the three Union infantry divisions might even then be en route to reinforce Kilpatrick so he ordered the attack to cease.

Firing as they withdrew, the Confederate cavalrymen galloped off to the north, taking around a hundred Union prisoners with them. Their main mission, to slow down Kilpatrick's advance, was accomplished.

Kilpatrick, presumably fully dressed again, reported the attack to Sherman, and claimed a total victory, in that he had driven off the reinforced Confederate cavalry corps, killing as many as eighty men and capturing thirty more. He said his total loses amounted to 19 dead, 68 wounded, and 103 missing. Wheeler reported to Hampton that his was a total victory, as well, scattering Kilpatrick's camp and taking "at least 350" Union prisoners, while freeing all their own men from the POW camp without losing any additional men, and at the same time inflicting "heavy casualties" in the Union camp. Confederate after-action reports have varying figures for the total losses in the brief fight, but were most likely in the 100–200 range for deaths, with another 500–600 probably wounded in action.

Now wary of the very real possibility of further cavalry raids, Sherman's infantry moved slowly forward, highly alert pickets and videttes deployed, reaching Fayetteville on March 12. There, Sherman's great army rested for three days before starting out again.

The Battle of Averasborough

As he had in Georgia and South Carolina, Sherman arranged his force of four corps into two great columns covering a 60-mile front. On the left were the XIV and the XX Corps, collectively referred to as the Army of Georgia, under Maj. Gen. Henry Warner Slocum. On the right were the XVII and XV Corps, under one-armed Major General Howard, collectively referred to as the Army of the Tennessee. On March 15, the great Union army marched northeast out of Fayetteville, toward Goldsboro and an expected linkup with Schofield's army.

Hardee had pulled back to a strong defensive position near the tiny settlement of Averasborough, on the Raleigh Road atop a ridgeline between a swamp and the Cape Fear River. On the afternoon of March 15, not long after leaving Fayetteville, Kilpatrick's Cavalry Corps, attached to Slocum's Corps, ran into the line of Confederate defenses, and immediately tried to ram their way through them. Hardee's men held fast, forcing Kilpatrick to withdraw and request infantry support. Slocum deployed his men during the night, and at dawn on March 16, they assaulted Hardee's line.

Hardee's only task was to delay the Union force, and he did an outstanding job here. Alternately pulling back and counterattacking, Hardee's army of less than 6,000 men forced Slocum to deploy his entire XX Corps, and then order up the XIV Corps for reinforcements late in the afternoon. By nightfall, well over 25,000 Union soldiers were engaged or deployed for battle, while Sherman's lines were starting to become unstrung, just as Johnston had hoped. Rather than turn and support Slocum's fight, for some unknown reason, Howard's right wing kept moving forward, separating the two armies by more than a day's march by the morning of March 17.

As darkness fell, Hardee broke contact and moved his small force rapidly back toward Johnston's line outside Goldsboro, no doubt pleased that his actions had delayed the Union left wing by at least two days. About 600 Union soldiers were killed or wounded, while Hardee reported a loss of about 450.

THE BATTLE OF BENTONVILLE: DAY ONE, MARCH 19, 1865

Unknown to Sherman and Slocum, Johnston was amassing his available forces just 20 miles north, outside the tiny village of Bentonville, and was hidden in the woods on the north side of the Goldsboro Road. Howard's right wing was advancing down the New Goldsboro Road about 4 miles to the southeast and was well on down the road by the time Slocum's troops were reorganized and on the road again. Sherman was convinced that Johnston, the defensive genius, was entrenching around Raleigh at that very moment. With Hardee's Corps still advancing up the road from Averasborough, the Confederate commander could muster about 21,000 men, as opposed to the 30,000 in Slocum's command alone.

As USA Brig. Gen. William Passmore Carlin's 1st Division, the lead elements of Slocum's XIV Corps, moved up the Goldsboro Road early on the morning of March 19, his skirmishers started engaging what they thought were local militia. Instead, they were running straight into Hoke's newly reinforced command arrayed across the road, fresh up from the battles around Wilmington. Slocum ordered an envelopment movement to his left, which instead had his men running straight into the middle of Johnston's main line of battle.

As the battle started unfolding, CSA Major General McLaws's Division, the vanguard of Hardee's command, finally arrived. Johnston, responding to panicked requests for reinforcements from Bragg, sent the road-march-weary soldiers over to the far left of his lines to join Hoke, but when they arrived, it was only to see the Union troops retreating in disarray. Johnston's tactical plan had been to stop and break up the Union column and then spring a strong attack into their flank from his wooded position. Thanks to Bragg's continued ineptness as a battlefield commander, the chance to do this with McLaws's troops was lost.

While the rest of Hardee's command moved into position, and Johnston prepared to attack, Slocum had his men hastily dig in, and sent word for his XX Corps to move up as soon as possible. The Union commander also sent word to Sherman that he had found Johnston's army, and requested Howard's army be moved north into the rapidly growing battle.

Just before 3:00 P.M., with all his forces now in place and ready, Johnston gave the order to start what became the last major Confederate offensive of the war. Led by Hardee, Johnston's combined force swept out of the woods and thundered down on Carlin's seriously outnumbered division. In minutes the Union line fell apart, and Johnston's screaming men ran down the road toward the next Union division coming into the line, Brig. Gen. James Dada Morgan's 2nd Division.

Morgan had ordered his men to quickly construct a log breastwork soon after encountering Hoke's men, and this hastily built barricade broke up the Confederate assault. Under heavy attack, Hardee's men hit the ground and returned fire, while Hoke was ordered out of his trench line into the assault. Soon, every reserve Johnston could muster was thrown into the fight, while Slocum's XX Corps made it into the line in time to withstand the assault. As darkness fell, Johnston ordered his men to break contact and pull back to a strong defensive position near Mill Creek. Sherman ordered Howard's entire Army of the Tennessee north into battle.

THE BATTLE OF BENTONVILLE:
DAYS TWO AND THREE, MARCH 20–21, 1865

Very little fighting occurred during the day of March 20, with Johnston strengthening his position around Mill Creek and Howard's two corps moving into the line of battle. As day dawned on March 21, both armies stood static in their defensive lines. Johnston was trying to keep his force intact, and Sherman simply wondered when his Confederate opponent would withdraw and allow him to proceed to his rendezvous with Terry and Cox at Goldsboro.

By the middle of the afternoon, hotheaded USA Maj. Gen. Joseph Anthony Mower grew impatient and ordered his division to advance, totally without orders from either Slocum or Sherman. Moving west along a narrow path by Mill Creek, Mower's men blew past pickets set up in the rear of Johnston's line, and soon advanced to within 600 feet of Johnston's headquarters. Commanding a hastily assembled counterattack, Hardee personally led a Texas cavalry unit into Mower's left flank, followed in short order by cavalry and infantry attacks on every flank of the Union command. Mower was soon forced out of the Confederate lines with heavy losses, but managed to inflict the ultimate blow to Hardee. CSA Pvt. Willie Hardee, his son, was a member of the Texas cavalry brigade the general had led into battle and was mortally wounded in the heavy exchange of fire.

Johnston had enough, and during the night of March 21, he pulled the remnants of his command out of the line and headed back toward Raleigh. The ill-conceived stance had cost him 2,606 men killed, wounded, captured, or missing, while Sherman's forces suffered a loss of 1,646. The only objective Johnston managed was the delay of Sherman's march for a few days, while nearly destroying his own army in the attempt. With hindsight, it is clear that even if Johnston had somehow managed to total destroy Slocum's Army of Georgia, he would have still faced the 30,000-plus Army of the Tennessee shortly thereafter.

LAST OF THE ARMY OF TENNESSEE

Johnston had once commanded a powerful, relatively well-equipped, and extremely well trained Army of Tennessee. His army had been 42,000 strong, before Sherman's grinding "total war" tactics had reduced it to a pitiful shell of its former glory. CSA Cpl. Sam Watkins, of the Maury Grays, 1st Tennessee Infantry Regiment, who had marched as part of this great army since the very beginning, remarked in his postwar memoirs that after the battle of Bentonville, his regiment—which had once numbered as high as 1,250 men, and which had received about 200 replacements and had joined with other regiments throughout the war, to a grand total of about 3,200 men—was reduced to just sixty-five officers and men.

Sherman rather half-heartedly moved on to Goldsboro, where he met up with Terry's and Cox's commands, newly arrived from the coast. He then moved north to take the abandoned city of Raleigh. There, he received word on April 16 that Johnston wanted to discuss surrender terms. The two generals met at Bennett Place, between Durham and Hillsborough, where very generous terms were offered to the courtly Confederate general after two days of talks. Both generals had just learned of Lincoln's assassination on April 14, which no doubt added some haste to their efforts to end the fighting.

Grant traveled south to tell his old friend Sherman that these terms were not acceptable to the new administration in Washington, and that he would have to insist the Confederates accept the same terms offered to and accepted by Lee on April 9. Jefferson Davis, newly arrived in Goldsboro in flight from the Union armies, rudely ordered his political enemy to break away from Sherman's armies and join him in flight to the south. Johnston quietly ignored him, and as Davis continued his escape attempt southward, he met again with Sherman to discuss the surrender. After agreeing to the new, harsher terms, Johnston surrendered his once-great army on April 26, 1865.

While we know Pvt. Benjamin Wortham, with the 12th Georgia Cavalry, was present in the last few battles of the war, we do not know where he was on the battlefield, nor do we know what he saw and did. The answers to those questions, along with Wortham's personal insights on battles and commanders, died with him. He did survive the war, with his saddle and blanket as fond souvenirs, but as with Sgt. James Larson, his own exploits were lost to the grander story of the war. General Wheeler, following the surrender of Johnston's Army of Tennessee at Durham Station, bid farewell to his beloved cavalrymen, in a touching epithet:

> During four years of struggle for liberty you have exhibited courage, fortitude, and devotion. You are the sole survivors of more than two hundred severely contested fields; you have participated in more than a thousand successful conflicts of arms. You are heroes, veterans, patriots . . . In bidding you adieu, I desire to tender my thanks for your gallantry in battle, your fortitude under suffering, and your devotion at all times to the holy cause you have done so much to maintain. I desire also to express my gratitude for the kind feeling you have seen fit to extend toward myself and to invoke on you the blessing of our heavenly Father, to whom we must always look in the hour of distress. Pilgrims in the cause of freedom, comrades in arms, I bid you farewell.

4

WOOD AND IRON:
THE NAVIES

Seaman William Burke, USS Cairo
Seaman James A. Wicks, CSS H. L. Hunley

The seaman of Confederate fame
Startled the wondering world,
For braver fight was never fought.
And fairer flag was never furled.

—Miss Janie Watts, dedication of Confederate Navy Memorial;
Montgomery, Alabama, December 7, 1897

Shortly before 7:00 a.m. on the cold morning of December 12, 1862, Seaman William Burke scrambled to his station. The drummer was pounding out a call to quarters, gun crews were raising their armored port hatches and running out their guns, while firemen in the engine room were carefully raising the steam pressure in the USS *Cairo's* five 24-foot-long boilers. The thirteen-gun, 175-foot "City" class ironclad gunboat stirred to life, smoke billowing out of her twin 28-foot chimneys, as Burke and the rest of the 158-man crew readied for another dangerous day's journey, down the Mississippi and up the Yazoo River, toward the very heart of the Confederate stronghold of Vicksburg, Mississippi.

Cairo's commanding officer, Lt. Comdr. Thomas O. Selfridge Jr., had received orders the previous afternoon to escort a small fleet of "tinclads" (small river steamers that were "armored" with wooden bulwarks) and other armored riverboats up the Yazoo toward Chickasaw Bluff and to clear it of Confederate defenses. This was in preparation for bringing a larger fleet southward to support the Union assault on the beleaguered city. A smaller force sent out the day before had run into a series of sniper posts, artillery batteries, and floating mines—a new kind of warfare device called "torpedoes." Selfridge, who had assumed command of the ironclad only three months earlier, already had a reputation for being plagued with bad luck. He was an able and combat-experienced officer, credited with heroic actions during the loss of the Norfolk Naval Yard at the very beginning of the war. But a year before taking charge of the *Cairo*, Selfridge had been blamed for the failure of the Navy's first attempt at an attack submarine, the USS *Alligator*. Furthermore, he was an officer aboard the USS *Cumberland* during her terminal engagement with the Confederate ironclad CSS *Virginia* (the ex-USS *Merrimac*), in March of 1862. The *Cairo*'s sailors were anything but happy about their new commander's presence. They were a superstitious lot even in the best of times, and Selfridge's reputation prompted one sailor to remark, "He doomed our vessel the minute he stepped onboard."

Casting off shortly after 8:00 A.M., the *Cairo* moved into position to support the tinclads, whose primary mission was to find, haul out of the river, and neutralize the Confederate torpedoes and other obstacles. Leading the small flotilla were the 190-ton, stern-wheel tinclad river gunboats *Marmora* and *Signal*, followed by the 406-ton, side-wheel ram *Queen of the West*, and finally, the twin "Pook turtles," 512-ton ironclad river gunboats *Cairo* and *Pittsburg*. After pausing briefly to bombard an isolated Confederate outpost, the flotilla turned to port, into the mouth of the Yazoo, and began sailing north up the shallow, debris-choked, muddy brown river. Burke, Selfridge, and the *Cairo* were just hours away from meeting with one of the Confederacy's most lethal "secret weapons."

Nine months earlier and a thousand miles to the east, another U.S. Navy sailor leaned on the rail of his ship, the USS *Congress*, which was anchored in the slack tide near the *Cumberland* off Newport News, Virginia. Quartermaster James A. Wicks watched as an oddly shaped ironclad ship slowly turned the point at the Crany Island lighthouse and headed for the small Union fleet anchored near the mouth of the Elizabeth and James Rivers. The ironclad was accompanied by three smaller escort ships, all bearing the Confederate naval jack at their staffs. With a quite unexpected naval engagement quickly brewing, the U.S. ships frantically beat to quarters. Wicks scrambled to his station as the newly completed Confederate ironclad *Virginia* (more frequently and incorrectly called the CSS *Merrimac*) and her escorts swung around a bend in the James and disappeared from view. Anxious moments turned into an agonizing wait, every gun crew at the ready for immediate action.

Finally, with Wicks and the rest of his crewmates sweating from both heat and fear, the *Virginia* rounded a bend and swung westward back into view, this time sailing straight for the *Congress*. The U.S. sail frigate opened with a thundering broadside, but her 32-pound shot just rattled like hail off the armored sides of the Confederate ship.

Wicks's gun crewmates kept up a steady, blistering, but ineffective fire on the Confederate ironclad and were soon joined by powerful gun-fire from the *Cumberland* and several shore batteries. All, however, proved equally ineffective against the thickly armored Confederate ship. The *Virginia*, moving at her top speed, was "like the roof of a very big barn belching forth smoke as from a chimney on fire," according to one witness. It rammed the luckless *Cumberland* while returning fire from her own guns, tearing open the Union ship below her waterline, but in the process, the *Virginia*'s own three-foot iron ram was broken off. Backing off, the *Virginia* answered, broadside for broadside, the intense fire coming from the *Congress*. Wicks and the other officers and masters crouched on the spar deck, feeling the huge cannon balls blasting through the ship beneath them, while their gun crews attempted to keep some sort of return to the raking fire from the *Virginia*. Lt. Joseph Smith, acting commander of the *Congress*, slipped his moorings and tried to back away from the action, while sounds of iron shot, thundering broadsides, splintering wood, and screaming men filled the air.

Then, Lt. Selfridge, commanding the forward division of five 9-inch guns that day on the doomed *Cumberland*, ordered his crews to continue firing on the fire-breathing ironclad, even as his ship began to sink. He barely escaped with his own life, leaping at the last moment through an open gun-hatch, leaving behind 121 of his men to go down with the ship, their colors still flying. One Confederate sailor aboard the *Virginia* remarked, "No ship was ever fought more gallantly."

Clear of the sinking *Cumberland*, the *Virginia* slowly turned toward the *Congress*, which had beached herself on a sand spit while scrambling frantically to get underway. Soon joined by two of her smaller escort vessels, *Virginia*'s gun crews kept up a merciless cannonade, raking the *Congress*'s decks and piercing her hull in many places as their heavy, slow ironclad came alongside. Incredibly, both ships' crews kept up a hot fire at point-blank range for nearly an hour, before the Union vessel signaled its surrender. Her decks were awash with heaps of dead and dying sailors among the blasted-open bulwarks and pierced decks. Lt. Smith lay dead as well, at the foot of the ladder to the after gun deck, shot down at his post by the murderous cannon fire. The *Virginia* moved off to deal with another helpless Union ship trying to unmoor, the 3,300-ton wooden screw steamer USS *Minnesota*, while the CSS *Beaufort* moved in closer to take off the *Congress*'s crew as prisoner. As the *Virginia* closed in, however, her men began to suffer casualties of their own from increasingly accurate fire pounding in from the shore batteries. Wounded in the exchange, *Virginia*'s commanding officer, Capt. Franklin Buchanan, angrily ordered *Congress* to be set afire with heated solid shot as soon as all the living and wounded crew were removed. *Congress* burned through the evening, finally exploding as the fire reached her powder magazines about 2:00 the next morning.

One of the men taken prisoner from the destroyed *Congress* was forty-three-year old Quartermaster Wicks, who declared that, as he was a loyal Southerner, a Virginian by birth, he was not in fact a prisoner of theirs, but had simply been freed from his U.S. Navy service. After the outbreak of war, Wicks, who had been with the U.S. Navy for ten years, had been barred from leaving the service and returning to his home state. One month later, possibly after a short visit home with his wife and four young girls in Fernandina Beach, Florida, Wicks walked into a Confederate navy enlistment office in Norfolk and volunteered for service. In short order he was assigned as a seaman to the CSS *Indian Chief*, a receiving ship in Charleston Harbor.

On board the *Indian Chief*, Wicks applied himself with equal, if not more, enthusiasm than he had in the prewar U.S. Navy, soon earning himself a promotion to Boatswain's Mate. On October 15, 1863, Wicks and the rest of the crew watched a strange, cigar-shaped, low-riding boat sail directly toward them and dive under their hull. It never resurfaced, and a few days later, Wicks also watched as naval engineers recovered the remains of the crew and craft. Three months later, CSA Lt. George Dixon came aboard, looking for volunteers to undertake a very hazardous naval mission. Wicks stepped forward, along with several other members of the crew, and Dixon selected Wicks, as well as four others. Dixon then explained that the men had just volunteered to serve on the third crew of a so-far luckless and highly experimental new war weapon, a submarine known as the *H. L. Hunley*—the very boat Wicks had observed taking its second crew to their deaths several weeks earlier.

Naval actions in the Civil War occurred under three major scenarios: First, and least frequently, were the "blue water" major ships of the line actions, ironically what one typically envisions when the word "naval" is invoked; secondly, the Union naval blockade of the Southern ports and coastline, and the Confederate responses to break it; and thirdly, the fights for the inland rivers, which featured perhaps the most innovative approaches to both the technological and tactical problems involved. Just as with the land forces, the war arrived before there was any real navy to fight in it.

The "blue water" actions of the Civil War, confined almost entirely to the period following the battles of Gettysburg and Vicksburg in 1863, were entirely concerned with Confederate attempts to bring the war against Union merchant ships, and the Union navy's attempts to eliminate the threat from these "commerce raiders." The Confederate navy never launched even a single ship of the line, the main battleship of the day, and confined their actions at sea not to confronting the vastly superior Union navy (which consisted only of such ships, and associated vessels, when the war began), but to seeking out the far-flung northern merchant and whaling vessels. This was an attempt to both bring economic crisis to the North, and help convince England and France that the South was a player on the world stage and a good partner to team with against their old, northern antagonists.

The U.S. Navy, prior to the outbreak of war, was nearly completely devoted to "blue water" naval vessels and tactics, those suitable to fighting on the open seas. Following the lead of Britain's Royal Navy, the rather smallish fleet was largely comprised of "ships of the line," which were massive, multi-decked battleships designed to fight in the 'even-by-then-archaic battle-line concept, using grouped, large, smoothbore cannons to wreck the rigging and pierce the hulls of enemy combatants. The U.S. Navy possessed ninety ships of all types when the war began, but only forty-two were listed "in-service" at spots around the globe, only eight were actually available for combat service in U.S. territorial waters, and not a single warship would suffice for fighting in shallow, debris-choked rivers. Although other navies had experimented with metal-clad, shallow-draft warships, and the French had used several to good success in the Crimean War, almost every U.S. ship was both of wooden construction and sail-powered.

On the other hand, the fledgling Confederate navy had not a single ship at the outbreak of hostilities, and they had a host of other problems to overcome. With the Union's tight blockade of the Southern coastline and ports, the Confederate navy would have to find some way to either break through portions of the blockade, to keep some trade flowing in and out, or at least prevent the Union navy from totally closing down the most critical ports. It was obvious that the Mississippi River was going to be a major area of conflict, and suitable ships for port defense were needed there as well. The greatest problem facing the newest navy was where these ships would come from, as nearly every major shipyard and heavy industrial facility was located in the North.

One of the major problems for both sides was designing a whole new class of fighting ship, along with developing a whole new doctrine of warfare, while the war these were going to be used in was already raging. While the naval authorities on both sides had a wealth of experience in fighting and sailing on the open oceans, they were going to have to adapt to fighting in shallow, narrow river channels, with little room to maneuver and always within easy range of shore batteries.

In one of the opening campaigns of the war, USA Brigadier General Grant and Flag-Officer Andrew Hull Foote (various sources list him as a Captain, Commodore, or Admiral at this point in time) were given the mission of opening up the great Southern rivers to Union control. Together, they decided to initially concentrate on taking control of the Tennessee and Cumberland Rivers in northern Tennessee. Early on, most of the available gunboats were simply modified civilian riverboats, with widely varying sizes and gun capacities. One carried only four 8-pounder guns, while others carried guns as heavy as 42-pounders and mounting as many as twelve guns. Foote himself commanded three unarmed boats and four ironclads in the opening battles of the Tennessee and Cumberland Rivers Campaigns, and his boats were manned by a rather motley assortment of 500 sailors who were formerly riverboat crewmen, Maine lumber-boat sailors, New England whalers, New York ferrymen, and several who were only described as "Philadelphia sea-lawyers."

Even before seeing how his new ideas worked out in these opening battles, Foote had supported the design and overseen the construction of a new class of navy craft specifically designed for such army-navy cooperative operations—heavily modified, ironclad riverboats initially nicknamed "Pook" boats, after the naval architect responsible for their basic design, Samuel Pook (an enigmatic figure about whom nearly nothing is documented). Built by the James B. Eads Company in Cairo, Illinois, these boats were relatively small (75 feet long and 50 feet wide on average), shallow-draft craft with protected mid-ship paddlewheels for propulsion. They were ironclad either entirely or at least protecting the gun decks, with rectangular casements covered by sloping iron armor and small hatches for cannons. Eads, a master riverman and engineer who had been called out of retirement for this specific purpose, produced his first "City" class ironclad, the *Carondelet*, in a mere forty-five days after initiating the design, and produced the other six boats of this class within another fifty-five days: the *Cincinnati*, *Louisville*, *Mound City*, *Cairo*, *Pittsburg*, *St. Louis*, and the much larger *Benton*. These relatively crude combatants were soon informally re-christened after what they most closely resembled, "Turtleboats."

Before the ill-fated Yazoo expedition, the *Cairo* had bloodied herself in two major actions at Plum Point and Memphis and had also taken part in the peaceful seizures of Clarksville and Nashville, Tennessee. Plum Point was anything but peaceful, however, as the entire Confederate River Defense Fleet savagely lashed into the larger Federal gunboat–led flotilla near then–Confederate held Fort Pillow, sinking the *Cincinnati* (which was later raised and put back into service) and badly damaging the *Mound City*, before breaking contact with heavy losses of both ships and men. The equally vicious brawl a month later at Memphis centered around both fleets' ironclad rams, which swirled about each other in the middle of the muddy river, while the *Cairo* and her sister gunboats poured shot and steel into anything that came into open range. Between the two disparate Union navy flotillas, the Confederate fleet was soon reduced to a single under-armed former towboat, the *General Earl Van Dorn*, which abandoned the city and fled south at full speed to the temporary safety of the Vicksburg defenses, while erratically firing its single 32-pounder at the pursuing Federals.

After entering the mouth of the Yazoo River, the *Cairo's* flotilla began encountering a series of the same isolated Confederate sniper posts that had challenged them upriver, and they answered with a near-continuous series of heavy broadside bombardments, while Confederate rifle shots pinged harmlessly off their heavily-armored sides. Warned previously of the new Confederate "torpedoes" that littered these waters, the flotilla moved cautiously deeper into enemy territory, frequently pausing to use hand-lines to snag the floating mines. The *Marmora* and *Signal* moved ahead of the *Cairo* and soon encountered more floating mines. *Marmora's* captain, George W. Getty, ordered his deck crews to shoot at them and explode them in the water. Just around a bend in the river, Selfridge, onboard the *Cairo*, heard the gunshots and explosions, assumed *Marmora* was under attack, and ordered his ship to steam full speed ahead to the rescue.

Very little is known about Seaman Burke, a twenty-six-year-old former blacksmith from New York, but as the *Cairo* was preparing for combat, he had to have been inside the ship's protective armored superstructure when Selfridge ordered the increase in speed. The noise inside was enough to cause the deaf to wince, as no soundproofing of any sort was between the engine machinery and the rest of the crew compartments. Outside was the cool, early December air, but inside was a combination of exposed steam boilers, hot cannons recoiling back inside the hull, sweating and shouting men feverishly reloading and running back out the guns on the tightly packed gundecks, firemen stoking both engines, and sailors struggling to keep the beast afloat and fighting. The interior became a fetid swamp of heat and humidity, enough to sap the strength of even the strongest man aboard.

Charging around the bend in the river, her twin smokestacks pumping out massive columns of black smoke, and her port and starboard batteries keeping up a blind cannonade into the woods on each side, *Cairo* rapidly swept up on the two smaller craft engaged in fishing the deadly torpedoes out of harm's way. Selfridge opened a hatch and hailed Getty, asking why his ship had stopped. "Here's where the torpedoes are," Getty tersely replied, turning back to his task. Selfridge, his habitual impatience showing, ordered the engines to idle and had a small boat prepared, presumably so he could go down and supervise the work first-hand. In the midst of this flurry of orders and scurrying sailors, the bow watch shouted a warning that the *Cairo*, still moving forward at a good clip due to its enormous bulk, was drifting dangerously toward shore. Selfridge then shouted out another set of orders, yelling for the engines to be reversed, and the crew to set lines for shore, to use in snagging the floating mines, and to anchor the gunboat in the slow current. Then, seeing that he was about to strike the other Union gunboat, he hailed Getty again and ordered him to move his ship out of the way.

Getty no doubt was wondering what to do, with the giant gunboat and its inept, but loud, captain bearing down on him rapidly, his own engines idle, and his men engaged in dealing with the deadly minefield. It was at this point that the Confederates decided to get in on the fun. Eight heavy guns atop Drumgould's Bluff, nearly 2 miles to the east, opened fire on the confused situation and were quickly answered by *Cairo*'s three forward 42-pounder, 7-inch rifled cannons. Most likely forgetting every order he had just issued, and no doubt the minefield that lay just off his bow as well, Selfridge ordered his ship to steam full speed ahead toward midstream. Just as his bow swung around and his paddles started churning the chocolaty water, two huge explosions literally lifted *Cairo*'s massive bow clean out of the water, breaking her keel in half at the same time.

The size of these two explosions can be measured by their effect, partially lifting a 512-ton craft straight up out of the water, lifting one 4-ton cannon clean off its mount, tossing the heavy iron anchor in the air like scrap paper, and bringing the entire operation to a screeching halt in the middle of the river. Inside was utter pandemonium, as Burke and his crewmates fought to get off the rapidly sinking ship. Water "rushed in like Niagara" from the massive holes in the bow and forward shell room, according to one crewman's account. In a desperate act, Selfridge ordered the turn continued and *Cairo* to be beached on the far shore of the river, while her single undamaged forward gun mount continued to fire at the distant Confederate battery Eventually, though, water sloshing around the gundeck made that task untenable. The *Queen of the West* came up alongside to help evacuate the crew, who pulled the *Cairo*'s jack staff colors as she slid down to the six-fathom-deep riverbed. From Selfridge's arrival on the scene until the moment he watched the *Cairo*'s pilothouse disappear underwater took less than twelve minutes.

Seaman Burke, along with the rest of the ill-fated *Cairo*'s crew, escaped with little more than their lives and the clothes they were wearing. They were taken back to the dockyards, along with Selfridge, who was doubtlessly nervously awaiting yet another formal hearing, or even a court-martial. Selfridge, a fighting officer during a time in the war when these were at a premium, however, not only escaped any official notice of his injudicious actions, he even managed to gain another command in short order. Burke disappeared into the mists of naval service; no further records of his service, discharge, or even survival of the war have been unearthed to date. An ordinary seaman in a most unordinary time, we are left with just the barest of facts about his physical appearance: he was dark-skinned with brown hair and grey eyes, and was a shade over five-feet-nine inches tall, by all standards quite ordinary for the time. In the USS *Cairo* Museum at Vicksburg National Military Park, where the recovered remains of that doomed ship are on display, there is quite a large collection of personal artifacts from the wreck. One can't help but wonder whether Burke ever replaced his eyeglasses or his favorite pipe, or whether he told his great-grandchildren many years later about his treasured *Bible* or nearly empty wallet, which went down that December day on the cold Yazoo River aboard the fighting *Cairo*.

Far to the east, another kind of naval war was being fought in Charleston, South Carolina. Once one of the crown jewels of Southern genteel society, the port had been reduced to hauling in only the barest trickle of European goods and luxuries that had once crowded her docks and warehouses—thanks entirely to an effective and ever-tightening blockade by the Union navy. The blockade ended up being so successful that it was rumored to have caused Charleston's commander, Confederate Maj. Gen. Beauregard's hair to turn gray nearly overnight during the worst of the import restrictions. Actually, he had been graying for some years, but vainly hid the fact by importing Egyptian henna to maintain his youthful, fiery appearance, before the Union navy cut this essential supply off.

Shortly after the evacuation of Fort Sumter, and the resulting land war brewing up across the nation, Union naval authorities decided to quickly implement part of Gen. Winfield Scott's previously derided plans for the war, and started setting up an armed blockade of the four major southern ports (Norfolk, Charleston, Pensacola, and Mobile). The intent was to deny access to as much of the 3,000-mile Southern coastline as was practicable. The first to arrive off Charleston was the USS *Niagara*, a 5,540-ton steam screw frigate built at the New York Navy Yard, and originally commissioned in April 1857. A few weeks after her arrival, her crew attacked and captured the Confederate blockade-runner *General Parkhill*, attempting to bring a load in from Liverpool, England.

By early 1863, the blockade was well in place and had changed from an offshore patrol by a few ships to a very large, static, anchored force that sat just outside shore battery range of every port of any significance. This blockade fleet stayed at anchor even during fierce storms, denying Confederate merchantmen a tactical advantage even during those high-risk times. However, although radically affected, the Southern ports continued to bring in supplies from the hundreds of blockade-runners helping to keep the South alive. Many of these runners were well-experienced British Royal Navy officers, "temporarily retired from service," along with regular Confederate navy officers and sailors, men drawn from the ranks of the various state naval forces, and not a few civilian "privateers" (quasi-legal pirates) out to make a buck or two. The best-known example of the latter, albeit a fictional one, is Rhett Butler, portrayed by Clark Gable in the 1939 movie, *Gone with the Wind*. By the spring of 1865, some 300-plus separate runners attempted the gauntlet of Union ships over 1,700 times, succeeding over 1,000 times. About 140 of these runners were captured and another 85 were destroyed by Union gunfire. The real testament to the runners is that they managed to bring in over 60 percent of the infantry weapons, mostly Enfield rifles, used by the Confederacy throughout the war.

Even with the help of these blockade-runners, the Confederacy faced a dire logistics crisis if the blockade was not broken in at least one major port. Both England and France had promised the fledgling Confederacy all the supplies it needed in exchange for the sought-after cotton crop, but neither was willing to do anything to risk another shooting war with the U.S., even the divided Union it had become. Confederate naval authorities in each port came up with a variety of locally produced craft designed to either directly confront the Union blockade fleet (mostly an assortment of ironclads and converted riverboat "tinclads") or to race past the relatively ponderous Union ships (shallow-draft, fast sloops). However, by late 1861, an unlikely pairing of an egomaniacal New Orleans businessman and a machine-shop owner originally from Cincinnati was working toward a solution that might not only open the Confederate supply lines, it would usher in another revolution in naval warfare.

To be perfectly blunt, Horace Hunley was Horace Hunley's number one fan. A very wealthy plantation owner from New Orleans, Hunley moved in the highest circles of society and politics, and was consumed with the idea of becoming a "great man," to be well noted by future historians. Similar to today's overextended Yuppies, Hunley kept a sort of nineteenth-century PDA, where he obsessively planned his appointments and tasks, scribbled inspirational quotes, noted his gambling winnings and losses, sketched plans of ever-more-elaborate business schemes, and ruminated about what was involved in "Great-Man-ness." However, when the war broke out, Hunley seemed to lose interest in nearly everything except a Confederate victory. The very model of a Southern patriot, Hunley set out to use his business talents and wealth to help the cause.

While not at all opposed to increasing his own wealth, New Orleans machine-shop owner James McClintock was more interested in working with his hands than increasing his society standing. Before the war, McClintock had worked as a Mississippi riverboat captain and had set up a small but profitable business producing steam gauges. Inspired by ideas and rumors floating around the Confederacy about underwater "fish-boats" that could simply sail underneath blockade ships, and buoyed by Hunley's financial backing, McClintock set out with a small group of other machinists and ship-fitters to develop a whole new genre of fighting warship.

The idea of submersible ships (deliberately submersible, rather than accidentally submersible) came about as early as 1580, with the unlikely plans of Englishman William Bourne, who proposed a system by which a ship could submerge and resurface by changing the size of the hull itself, and thereby changing the displacement of the ship. At least twelve other designs were proposed and some were even built, including the well-documented Revolutionary War *Turtle*, before Hunley and McClintock set up shop on the New Orleans docks.

Their first attempt, a 4-ton, 34-foot-long, 4-foot wide, doubled-pointed craft made from an old iron boiler, was designed to be crewed by only three men. Christened the *Pioneer*, it showed some promise in early testing on Lake Pontchartrain, and even earned the inventors one of the first privateering licenses from an excited Confederate government. Before McClintock would allow it to be released from testing and put to good use in the Gulf of Mexico, a combined Union army-navy offensive swept up the Mississippi River toward New Orleans in the spring of 1862, forcing him to scuttle the still-unfinished boat. Hunley moved his team to the safer environs of Mobile, where they set about creating a larger and more effective submersible.

The new boat, originally called *Pioneer II* and later the *American Diver*, was basically a larger, narrower version of McClintock's first craft. Made again of pieces from an old iron boiler, it featured a larger crew capacity and two conning towers instead of *Pioneer*'s single tower. McClintock, ever the tinkerer, didn't want to rely on hand-cranks to power the craft and delayed the launch of *American Diver* for months while he tried to produce an electric motor, an invention that would have been as advanced as a working submersible itself.

Mobile at the time was a well-guarded port town, full of soldiers and sailors on leave and recuperating from battle injuries. Since so much manpower was literally standing around, Hunley requested, and received, several unassigned soldiers to help out building the new boats. One of these men was a newly minted lieutenant, badly wounded in the Battle of Shiloh, George Dixon.

After McClintock reluctantly allowed the *American Diver* to be tested in the shallow waters of Mobile Bay, and after it was refitted with hand-cranks in place of the still-unfinished electric motor, George Dixon and four crewmen took it out for a series of tests, which showed the new boat had some promise. With the tests completed, and one unsuccessful mission just outside Fort Morgan (which guarded the entrance to Mobile

Bay), Dixon felt that he, McClintock, and his men had ironed out all the bugs. In late February 1863, Hunley joined Dixon and his crew on board a towboat hauling the *American Diver* 30 miles south to the entrance of the bay, with plans to launch her there against the Union blockade ships riding at anchor 4 miles out to sea. The day was a stormy one, with rough seas even in the shallow bay. The hatches of the *American Diver* were open to air the interior out, and when a rogue wave swept over the craft, enough water swept in the twin conning towers to sink her like a stone.

Hunley had just lost his second submersible boat, without even a single attack launched against the hated blockade. Undeterred, and still consumed with the desire to defeat the Union blockade (and with not a small amount of pressure from Confederate military sources), Hunley set out to try a third design.

The loss of the *American Diver* had nearly wiped Hunley out financially, and this time he allowed his business side to come forth by offering "investments" to interested commercial partners. Amazingly, considering his poor track record in building submersibles that also surfaced, several prominent Southern businessmen promptly bought in to the enterprise. Among the group of investors was Lavacans Edgar Collins Singer, a nephew of the future sewing machine inventor, and B. Gus Whitney, allegedly a cousin of the inventor of the cotton gin (which had indirectly led to the establishment of the Confederacy itself). With financial backing and the limited resources made available by the Mobile Confederate authorities, Hunley began construction of what for him was a somewhat more conventional design.

The submersible later christened the CSS *H. L. Hunley* was a bit larger than the *American Diver,* but was designed from the outset to be propelled by a hand-cranked prop shaft. Instead of using another cast-off boiler, he and his men built up the *Hunley* around a cast iron frame that was 42 inches in diameter and 40 feet long, with ⅜-inch iron plates flush-riveted to the frame to form a slick, low-drag hull. Hunley introduced several other innovations in his namesake's design, including thick glass skylights in two rows along the top of the hull, twin conning towers with glass view-ports all around each, and heavy keel ballasts that could be dropped from inside the hull, as a means of emergency surfacing. Concerned about the possibility of the propeller snagging on rope or some other obstacle, rending the small craft helpless in a combat situation, he designed a shroud around it, with the rudder mounted directly aft, which helped to both guide snags away from the prop and make steering possible even at very low speeds. A long wooden spar jutted from the top of the knife-like bow like a bowsprit, initially included as a sort of low-visibility collision sensor. The boat's commander would sit with his head jutting up into the forward conning tower, steering the craft with a complicated tiller-bar arrangement, and hand-pumping the forward ballast tank. Another crewman would sit at a hand-crank station below the aft conning tower and hand-pump the aft ballast tank as needed. In between would sit six more crewmen at their hand-crank stations.

With a now-experienced construction crew, assisted by assorted Confederate troops provided by the Mobile authorities, and with pressure from Hunley and his investors, the new submersible rolled down the ways into Mobile Bay in July 1863. It represented both the single most technologically advanced warship of its day and the best hope for the Confederacy to finally break the strangling blockade. This time naval authorities allowed only a short series of tests in Mobile Bay, which proved highly successful, before loading up the *Hunley* on a railcar and shipping it to Charleston under heavy guard.

McClintock, Whitney, and Singer accompanied their boat to Charleston, where its arrival was greeted with fanfare by the Confederate authorities. The builders were amazed to be immediately presented with the offer of $100,000 in gold ($1,759,934.14 in 2003 dollars!) to sink one of two specific Union blockade ships, the USS *New Ironsides* or the USS *Wabash*, along with equally generous offers to support their families should the effort prove fatal. However, McClintock, ever the soul of caution, insisted on another series of tests inside the safety of Charleston Harbor before he would allow it to go out on a combat patrol.

This "short series" of test runs turned into yet another series of twice-daily short trips that accomplished nothing (no modifications to the *Hunley* are noted during this time), but to infuriate the Confederate naval authorities. Finally, after Beauregard himself intervened to try to speed things up, he ordered the seizure of the vessel and ordered it to be manned with a combat crew. Navy Lt. John Payne was appointed its first commander and drew his first crew from a large number of volunteers eager to escape their otherwise stupefyingly boring duties. McClintock, angry that his boat had been taken away from him "before it was ready for such service," argued to no avail that it was much harder to operate than it appeared and that he was needed to properly train the crew. Ignored by all concerned, he soon left the city and returned to Mobile.

On August 29, Payne made ready for his first attempt at the blockade fleet. His crew that day consisted of Lt. Charles Hasker, Seamen Frank Doyle, John Kelly, Michael Caine (or possibly Cane), Nicholas Davis, Absolum Williams, and William Robinson. All were settling into their positions as Payne stepped gingerly off the dock and into the forward conning tower of the highly unstable craft. As he did so, a Confederate ironclad, moving slowly down the nearby channel, raised a low wake as it passed the *Hunley*. The *Hunley*, already riding dangerously low with a near-capacity load, still had its conning tower hatches open to let in fresh air. Before Payne could get into position, water raised by the ironclad's wake rolled over the open hatches and almost instantly filled the small crew space, taking all but Payne, Hasker, and Robinson to their deaths. Payne merely stepped back onto the dock, without even getting his uniform wet, while Hasker managed to free himself only after the boat hit the bottom of the harbor. He later claimed that Payne had caused the craft to sink by hitting the tiller as he dropped down and made a small fame for himself late in life as "the only man that went to the bottom with the 'Fish-Boat' (a popular nickname for the *Hunley*) and came up to tell the tale." Robinson probably escaped through the aft conning tower hatch, although there is some dispute whether he had even been on the boat that day. The dead were recovered some days later when the *Hunley* was raised by Confederate engineers. The crew's limbs had to be hacked off their bloated bodies to permit passage through the 15-inch hatches; the bodies were buried hastily and secretly in a nearby cemetery.

The *Hunley* was the central focus of a small, highly classified "special operations" mission. Almost everything surrounding the boat, its crews, and their missions were shrouded in several layers of secrecy. This was all done for a very good reason, for if the Union navy had uncovered any details about the submersible's capabilities, or lack thereof, it could have easily changed the deployment or composition of the blockade fleet, rendering the slow, barely seaworthy craft useless. Even in death, these naval commandos enjoyed no fame or renown. The location of their graves was kept so quiet that the Citadel later built a stadium atop them. When they were uncovered again in 1999, several were found to have been buried stacked one on top of another, obviously in the haste to have them interred and out of sight. Their coffins were easy to distinguish from other nearby graves of Confederate soldiers, as they were constructed quite a bit larger to accommodate the bloated bodies. Their hacked-off limbs were found dumped across their twisted trunks. None of the men proved to be older than twenty or so, while one body was of a teenage boy no more than thirteen years old.

None of the survivors would set foot in the raised boat again, and Horace Hunley wanted it back, thinking he could do a better job himself. The craft was already considered an "iron coffin," and Beauregard only briefly considered Hunley's request before granting it. Hunley immediately sent word to his workers in Mobile and began putting together a second crew.

On October 15, the boat had been scrubbed clean of the lingering effects of its first crew, and after a few test voyages proved the boat was at least passably workable, Hunley made ready for a final test of his main weapon, a towed mine. Hunley would command the mission personally. With crewmen Robert Brookbank, Joseph Patterson, Thomas Parks, Charles McHugh, Henry Beard, John Marshall, and Charles L. Sprague, he planned to head directly for a nearby Confederate receiving ship, the *Indian Chief*, which was anchored in the harbor. The *Hunley* would dive under her as they approached, and demonstrate that the dummy mine they were towing on a rope 100 feet aft could strike the ship's hull as they safely passed underneath.

Leaning against the *Indian Chief*'s rail that rainy, dreary afternoon was Boatswain's Mate James A. Wicks, possibly smoking his ever-present pipe, and watching as the strange, low-riding craft slid under his own ship's keel. It did not surface on the other side.

Some days later Confederate divers found the *Hunley* and helped raise it a second time. Horace Hunley and his men were buried with full military honors, under Beauregard's orders, in nearby Magnolia Cemetery. When cleaned of the crew's remains and silt, engineers discovered the reason it had sunk—Hunley had forgotten to close the valve to the forward ballast tank, allowing water to rapidly fill the hull. Beauregard ordered the submersible to be abandoned, citing that it "was more dangerous to those who use it than the enemy."

On hearing of this second tragedy, George Dixon and William Alexander immediately traveled to Charleston, both to honor Hunley at his burial and to see what they could do to help get their boat back in service. Asking for and gaining an audience with Beauregard, they pitched their case for another try. The fiery Confederate commander was at first adamantly against putting the "iron coffin" back to sea again, but was soon swayed by the heroic young lieutenant. After the war he remarked:

> After this tragedy I refused to permit the boat to be used again; but Lieutenant Dixon, a brave and determined man, having returned to Charleston, applied to me for authority to use it against the Federal steam sloop-of-war Housatonic, a powerful new vessel, carrying eleven guns of the largest calibre, which lay at the time in the north channel opposite Beach Inlet, materially obstructing the passage of our blockade-runners in and out.

Dixon finally had command of the *Hunley*, and immediately set about building a third crew. Along with Seaman Wicks, the *Indian Chief* provided most of the *Hunley's* final crew, including Arnold Becker, Fred Collins, Joseph Ridgeway, and possibly the mysterious crewman known only as "C. Simkins" or "C. F. Simpkins." They immediately set about refitting and making small changes to the *Hunley's* design, with Dixon driving hard to set out on combat patrols as soon as humanly possible. The major design change was to abandon the idea of towing a mine into place, as the danger of pulling it into the *Hunley's* own hull was too great. Instead, at the suggestion of one of Beauregard's staff officers, the explosives were moved to the end of the wooden bow spar. Three months later, all was ready.

Twilight on February 17, 1864, was a clear, bitterly cold beginning to the night, as Dixon led his crew down the wooden dock on the east side of Sullivan's island, next to the fourteen-gun Battery Marshall. Like Hunley and McClintock, he had attempted to cram in as much training and testing as he could, without incurring too much wrath from the local Confederate command. By this time Charleston, the one-time "Jewel of the Confederacy" was for the most part a burnt-out collection of shell-blasted buildings, occupied almost exclusively by troops, sailors, blockade-runners, and what few civilians dared the constant Union bombardment. Dixon knew he had to make the Hunley earn its keep, and soon, or his small command would be broken up and returned to front-line service. Doubtlessly his crew knew this as well, as they carefully eased through the twin tiny hatches and squirmed into their assigned positions, with Wicks at his post at the sixth hand-crank station.

Before he climbed into his own station, Dixon spoke briefly with Lt. Col. O. M. Dantzler, Battery Marshall's commanding officer, and reminded him of the signals they had previously agreed on; when his mission was complete, Dixon would shine a small, blue phosphorus lamp at the post, and Dantzler would order a large bonfire to be lit on the beach, to help guide the *Hunley* safely home. Dixon then climbed into his boat, clamping the hatch down immediately.

Although the men were dressed for the cold winter weather outside, they could not have escaped the cold, damp chill that permeated *Hunley*'s hull. The few candles they kept lit would have only highlighted the claustrophobic darkness inside. As they pulled slowly away from the dock and swung into the main shipping channel, the effort needed to hand-crank the large iron propeller would have resulted in little conversation, only grunts and gasps for more of the soon-fetid air inside. Dixon turned the tiller to starboard and headed for their target, one of the hated Union blockade ships riding at anchor, just outside the mouth of Charleston Harbor.

The USS *Housatonic*, a 1,900-ton, 207-foot-long "Ossipee" class steam screw sloop, was built in 1862 at the Boston Navy Yard and had arrived off Charleston, South Carolina, that August to join the United States Navy South Atlantic Blockade Fleet. That cold night was no different from so many others, incredibly boring for the 160 officers and crew, maintaining the regular watches as the vessel bobbed slowly in the calm waters. One difference that particular night was that there had been vague warnings that the Confederates were up to something and might try to attack the fleet some night soon, possibly with a new type of torpedo-boat they were known to have been developing. The *Housatonic* had seen little action in the year and a half she had rode at anchor off Charleston. One of the handful of times she had fired her nine heavy guns was the previous January, when she had unfortunately fired at one of her sister blockade ships in the confusion of an attack by Confederate ironclads.

The night had stayed clear, and to Dixon's dismay, a full moon shone on the calm waters. It did help outline his target, but it also made it far easier for Union sailors to spot his boat on the approach. It was just after 8:30 when he whispered back to his crew that they were about to make contact with the enemy vessel.

Wicks probably received the news without a word either way. He had been in the navy, both navies, long enough to not anticipate much of anything. His world that night consisted of a hard wooden bench in a dank, dark, sweltering iron box, a crank to pull, and the aches and pains that accompany hard manual labor in such a tight, sweaty place.

On the *Housatonic,* reveille had sounded at 8:00, and the first evening watch had settled into their duty stations. Six lookouts and a handful of officers kept a close eye on the harbor for any sign of another Confederate foray. At just about 8:40, the starboard bow watch shouted that he saw something. It looked like a log, about a football field's length away, but it didn't float like a log. It was moving against the tide, straight at them. Master John Crosby, the Officer of the Deck during that watch, moved across the quarterdeck to get a better look. By the time he realized he was in fact not looking at a log or a porpoise (his own first thought), the *Hunley* was less than 100 yards away and bearing down fast. Crosby immediately turned, sounded general quarters, and ordered the anchor line slipped and the engines immediately set into reverse.

As the *Hunley* bore in the last few yards, Dixon noticed that sailors were starting to fire at him with rifles, but their shots pinged harmlessly off his boat's iron hull. He was relieved to have gotten in so close before being noticed, as the *Housatonic's* main batteries could not depress enough to hit him. At 8:45, his explosives-tipped spar rammed into and through *Housatonic's* wooden hull. He immediately ordered his crew to reverse and get away quickly. As he backed away, a line attached to the 135 pounds of explosives now inside the Union ship's hull tightened, then detonated the mine.

The resulting explosion rocked the big ship onto its port beam, blasting a huge hole in the wooden hull, and knocking dozens of sailors off the decks and out of their bunks, many of them splashing down into the cold Atlantic water. Amazingly, only five sailors were killed. As the remaining crew scrambled up the rigging, the *Housatonic* soon settled on the bottom in twenty-five feet of water. At least one lookout, still watching the strange boat that had attacked them, claimed he saw a blue light shining out from it.

Back at Battery Marshall, 4 miles from the scene of action, Dantzler neither heard nor saw the explosion, but at about 9:00, he did see the blue light signal he had been anticipating. He ordered the bonfire lit, and then went off to bed, knowing it would be hours before the submersible made it back to her mooring.

But the *Hunley* never returned to port.

Many theories about what happened to the *Hunley* and her third crew came and went over the next century, and several searches for her wreckage bore no fruit. Her remains were finally located in 1995, 131 years after her disappearance, east of the *Housatonic*'s position and further out toward open sea—the last place, literally, anyone had thought to search. After five more years of careful underwater archeological exploration and preparation, the *Hunley* broke surface again at 8:30 A.M. on August 8, 2000. At this writing, her remains are in a Charleston naval laboratory, undergoing a lengthy conservation process.

When archeologists carefully opened and dug into *Hunley*'s silted-up hull, they found the crew mostly at their duty stations, where they had been seated for 136 years. Some early reports indicate that the crew did not drown, but for some reason sat calmly while their air supply ran out. Normally, a crew that died from oxygen starvation would be found heaped up next to any available exit, but the tiny hull size, the experience of the crew, and the knowledge that they literally had no chance to escape their tomb probably led them to this sad acceptance. No damage to her hull or windows was found, and as of this writing, no one is really sure why she went down.

Most of the crew has been tentatively identified through forensic analysis, including James Wicks. From family accounts we know a bit more about him than any of the other enlisted crew, and far more than we know about William Burke of the *Cairo*. Wicks was born in North Carolina sometime around 1819, making him one of only three of the final Hunley crew that was actually from the South. He was a stout man, well accustomed to the harsh life of a sailor and was particularly fond of pipe tobacco. He had light brown hair, blue eyes, and a ruddy, florid complexion. The night of his last voyage, he wore his old navy wool peacoat, part of which was later found in the muck. "Goodyear" and "U.S. Navy" were still visibly imprinted on his large, black rubber buttons. He married an Englishwoman, Catherine Kelley, in 1850, and she eventually bore him four daughters. Not much is known about his family after his disappearance, but Catherine is believed to have remarried and moved away from their home in Fernandina Beach, Florida.

James Wicks and the rest of his crewmates were buried with full Confederate military honors in a grand spectacle, befitting their landmark service, on April 17, 2004. There are no known records as to where William Burke's remains are interred. Both the *Cairo* and the *Hunley* represented the very cutting edge of naval architectural breakthroughs of the day, but tragically neither would survive to demonstrate their real abilities. And just like Burke and Wicks, both lay buried in the earth, forgotten by all but a handful who had known and loved them, long after the war itself had nearly been forgotten.

The 1st Georgia State line Regiment Capturing the DeGress battery at Atlanta, June 22, 1864.
ENGRAVING BY ALFRED R. WALTER, COURTESY ATLANTA HISTORY CENTER

Union Pvt. D. W. C. Arnold. NATIONAL ARCHIVES

A group from the Irish Brigade at Harrison's Landing, Virginia, July 1862. LIBRARY OF CONGRESS

Fredericksburg, February 1863, from the Federal positions across the Rappahannock River.

Interior of Fort Fisher, North Carolina, 1865. LIBRARY OF CONGRESS

The "Pulpit" inside Fort Fisher, North Carolina, 1865. NATIONAL ARCHIVES

Union Private Emory E. Kingin, 4th Michigan Infantry.
NATIONAL ARCHIVES

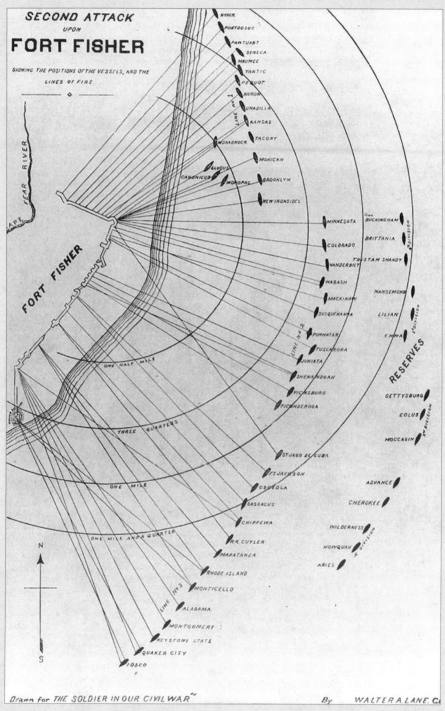

SECOND ATTACK
UPON
FORT FISHER

SHOWING THE POSITIONS OF THE VESSELS, AND THE
LINES OF FIRE

Map of fleet actions on Fort Fisher, North Carolina, January 15, 1865.

U.S. NAVAL HISTORICAL CENTER

...bruary 1863, from the Federal positions across the Rappahannock River.

...itzer on deck of USS Pawnee. U.S. NAVAL HISTORICAL CENTER

Artillery position in Fort Fisher, North Carolina. LIBRARY OF CONGRESS

Ambulance Drill at Headquarters, Army of the Potomac, near Brandy Station, March 1864. As bandsmen served as hospital corpsmen, these Zouaves may have been members of Frank Rauscher's cornet band, attached to the 114th Pennsylvania Volunteer Infantry. LIBRARY OF CONGRESS

1st Tennessee Colored Battery at Johnsonville. LIBRARY OF CONGRESS

Church service on deck of the USS Passaic. U.S.

Fredericksburg, F
NATIONAL ARCHIVE

"Army" howitzer gun crew exercise on board USS Le

An 8-inch Hou

Artillery position in Fort Fisher, North Carolina. LIBRARY OF CONGRESS

Ambulance Drill at Headquarters, Army of the Potomac, near Brandy Station, March 1864. As bandsmen served as hospital corpsmen, these Zouaves may have been members of Frank Rauscher's cornet band, attached to the 114th Pennsylvania Volunteer Infantry. LIBRARY OF CONGRESS

1st Tennessee Colored Battery at Johnsonville. LIBRARY OF CONGRESS

Church service on deck of the USS Passaic. U.S. NAVAL HISTORICAL CENTER

"Army" howitzer gun crew exercise on board USS Lehigh. U.S. NAVAL HISTORICAL CENTER

Fredericksburg, February 1863, from the Federal positions across the Rappahannock River.

An 8-inch Howitzer on deck of USS Pawnee.

The bombardment of Fort Fisher, North Carolina, January 15, 1865.
U.S. NAVAL HISTORICAL CENTER

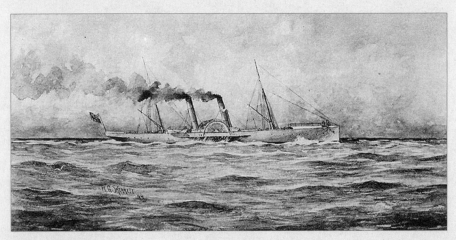

Union fleet in a storm off Fort Fisher, North Carolina, December 21, 1864.
U.S. NAVAL HISTORICAL CENTER

Blockade Runner Banshee. U.S. NAVAL HISTORICAL CENTER

Private Henry Taylor McKay, Company H, 26th Alabama Infantry, with wife Vinnie, around 1900. AUTHOR'S PERSONAL COLLECTION

Inaccurate wartime sketch of the CSS H. L. Hunley. U.S. NAVAL HISTORICAL CENTER

Deck of USS Lehigh. U.S. NAVAL HISTORICAL CENTER

Postwar photo of gun crew cleaning the 10-inch Dahlgren cannons, on board the USS Nahunt.
U.S. NAVAL HISTORICAL CENTER

Deck scene on board the USS Catskill, 1865. U.S. NAVAL HISTORICAL CENTER

Gun deck of the USS Pawnee, 1865. U.S. NAVAL HISTORICAL CENTER

Lieutenant Joseph B. Smith, USN, 1861. U.S. NAVAL HISTORICAL CENTER

Colonel Daniel N. McIntosh, commanding 1st Creek Regiment. LIBRARY OF CONGRESS

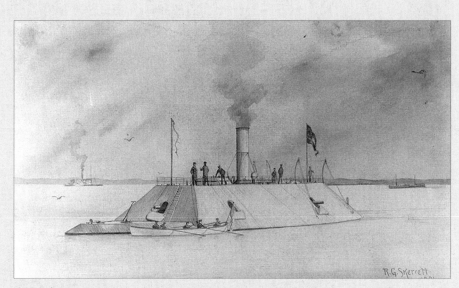

CSS Palmetto State. U.S. NAVAL HISTORICAL CENTER

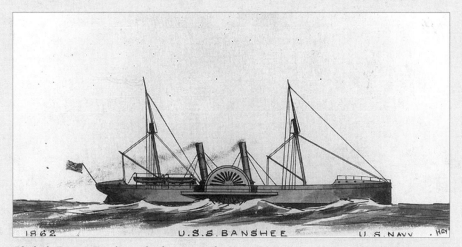

1862   U.S.S. BANSHEE   U.S. NAVY

Blockade Runner Banshee, *after her capture by Union Navy.* U.S. NAVAL HISTORICAL CENTER

US Sergeant Major Christian A. Fleetwood, 4th United States Colored Troops.
LIBRARY OF CONGRESS

26th United States Colored Troops in camp. NATIONAL ARCHIVES

Ambulances from the 57th New York Infantry. NATIONAL ARCHIVES

Unknown Union cavalry troop on a pontoon bridge over the Rappahannock River at Fredericksburg, 1863. NATIONAL ARCHIVES

Union hospital at Chancellorsville, 1863. NATIONAL ARCHIVES

Brigadier General Stand Watie, commanding Indian Cavalry Brigade. NATIONAL ARCHIVES

"Old Salt" on gun deck of USS Pawnee, next to her 100-Pounder Parrott Rifle.
U.S. NAVAL HISTORICAL CENTER

Captain William Jasper Worley, commanding Company D, the "Blue Ridge Rangers," 1st Georgia State Line Regiment. AUTHOR'S PERSONAL COLLECTION

5

SUTURES AND SAWS: BATTLEFIELD MEDICAL CARE

Dr. Thomas Smith Waring, Surgeon, 17th South Carolina Volunteers

Scorched by the cannon's molten breath,
They'd climbed the trembling walls of death
And set their standards tattered --
Had charged at the bugle's stirring blare
Through bolted gloom and godless glare
From the dead's reddened gulches, where
The searching shrapnel shattered.

—"THE LAST CHARGE AT APPOMATTOX," BY HENRY JEROME STOCKARD

THE SHRIEKS OF THE WOUNDED AND DELIRIOUS ECHOED OFF THE wooded hillsides as Dr. Thomas Smith Waring briefly rested between surgeries. Since leaving South Carolina with his regiment two months before, he had been in near continuous movement, but had witnessed very little combat action. That traveling holiday came to an abrupt halt on this, the sunny afternoon of August 30, 1862, in the north Virginia countryside, near the small town of Manassas Junction.

Waring and the 17th South Carolina had arrived the day before, just in time for the second battle for Manassas Junction. There, the Carolinians fought a long day's battle nearly in the center of the line, suffering 188 dead, wounded, and missing. A couple of weeks later, after moving north with Lee's great gamble to invade the north, the 17th collided with several Pennsylvania regiments atop Crampton's Gap on South Mountain. The losses in that short fight were staggering, but the few South Carolinians still able to fight would see even worse three days later, at Sharpsburg, near the meandering Antietam Creek. The 17th had left Charleston with 304 men barely a month before. After these three pitched battles, only nineteen unwounded still stood beside the flag.

Now nearly every building in Shepherdstown had been converted into a clinic, morgue, surgery suite, or sickroom, turning the northern Virginia town into one vast hospital. Waring, wounded during an artillery barrage on the hospital tents while treating the wounded after 2nd Manassas, was about to crack under the strain of so many wounded. He wrote to his wife:

> *You have no idea of the work I have to do. Our corps is woefully deficient in number & quality and my name is being called from morning to night by the poor fellows who want attention & almost all in the camp prefer me. I am almost worked down and have not changed my clothes—or washed my face decently—in two days.*

Dr. Waring of Charleston, South Carolina, was a prewar doctor and plantation owner. He had graduated from the College of Charleston in 1851 and the Medical College of the State of South Carolina in 1853. He was considered to be an exceptionally well-educated doctor, one of several prominent Charleston doctors in his family, and he was already quite well known in medical circles as the war began, having published several papers on surgery and infectious diseases. Specialization was an unknown premise at the time, and Dr. Waring also published at least one research paper on difficulties in labor.

Waring offered his services to the State of South Carolina even before Fort Sumter was fired upon, and was assigned to Morris Island the day before the war began. His initial assignments had little to do with his profession; instead, he was placed in charge of moving ordnance from inland locations into Charleston's various batteries. Camp sicknesses soon made him return to his physician roots, however, and he was promoted to Assistant Surgeon at the rank of Captain, and reassigned to a garrison on Johns Island. The records are not very clear, but it is presumed that at this point he was assigned to the 17th South Carolina.

CIVIL WAR MEDICINE

The care of the sick and wounded during the Civil War is simultaneously one of the most notorious and one of the least understood stories of the war. Family stories and Hollywood movies have tended to emphasize how great the sufferings of the men were, but oddly enough, have also tended to draw up short of just how intense this suffering was. These same stories and movies have also referenced how prevalent sickness was in camp and on the battlefield, but again oddly enough, both drew up short of the actual extent. Both also have featured lurid stories about untreated wounds and amputations without anesthesia; these, again oddly enough, are the few areas of the story were things are grossly over-claimed.

Battlefield medical care in the Civil War was, as one Northern surgeon commented, "at the end of the medical medieval era." Theories of sepsis were just then under study, mostly by the great Dr. Joseph Lister, but conditions in the field hospitals would cause anyone to recoil in utter horror. Surgeons worked without any sort of gloves and without washing their hands before they, quite literally, plunged into the next patient. They wore aprons splattered with blood and pus, and used instruments that were, at best, quickly washed off in cold water and put right back into service. Instruments and dressings that were dropped on the floor would be put back into service with, at most, a quick wipe with an equally filthy towel, while many "quick cutting" surgeons habitually held their scalpel in their teeth as they positioned the patient on the operating table. Wounds were expected to become infected, producing "suppuration," also known as "laudable pus." This rampant infection was so common that surgeons regarded the onset as a positive sign that "proper healing" was underway.

Training and experience for the nearly 11,000 Union and 3,000 Confederate surgeons was, at best, inadequate. Of all the Northern surgeons, only about 500 had actually performed any surgical procedure at all before the war, while only 27 Southern surgeons had done so. Medical school in those days consisted of a mere two years of training, with the second year being just a blow-by-blow repeat of the first. There were no licensing boards or national standards to be met, and anyone who wanted to work as a "doctor" only had to hang out a shingle, advertising as much. Most of these new Army combat surgeons would have to learn their grisly task completely on the basis of on-the-job training.

Not only were the doctors under-trained for their job, they were usually under-equipped as well. In complete contrast to today's myriad of available tools and materials, the "one-size-fits-all" Civil War surgeon had a minimal number of tools to work with. Most surgeons brought along their own "surgeon's kits," or were given them. These were usually kept in small, finely made, wooden chests, with lots of attention paid to the visual aesthetics and not one whit to the cleanliness of the instruments inside. According to Dr. Stephen Smith's Handbook of Surgical Operations, published in 1863, a well-equipped kit would contain:

> One long amputation knife; one amputating knife; one catling; two small amputating knives; one metacarpal saw; one bone forceps; one tenaculum; one short bistoury, sharp; one pair slide artery forceps; one pair bull-dog artery forceps; one pair large scissors; one pair small scissors; one pair dressing forceps; one long silver bullet probe; one whalebone bullet probe; one small silver probe; two dozen serrefines; two dozen needles; one tourniquet, screw; one tourniquet, field; one director; one conical trephine; one elevator; one Hay's saw; one brush; three bullet forceps; two retractors; one needle forceps; one plain aneurysm needle; one set Dr. Mott's needles; silk and silver wire.

EFFECT OF CIVIL WAR BATTLE TACTICS

The surgeons' bill was based on the fact that, as so often happens in warfare, technology had far outstripped the ability of the general staff to understand what profound changes to the battlefield had been introduced. Most of those in high command at the beginning of the war had come up through a system that was well versed in Napoleonic theory, and emphasized drill and precision maneuvers over weaponry considerations; for the most part, they ignored the groundbreaking work in infantry longarms (or shoulder-arms) developed in the previous twenty years.

Infantry weapons of the Napoleonic age were based around very large caliber, smoothbore muskets, which had the advantage of rapid reload capabilities and produced a great shock effect on whoever it hit. The disadvantages were that they didn't have an effective range any longer than ancient archery (100–125 yards, maximum), and so even a seasoned marksman had a very hard time hitting a target more than 200 feet away. As a result, a battle-tactics theory developed that was based on massed firepower mixed with the more familiar blade and sword charges. Armies stood in long lines because the prevailing military thought was that warfare was "linear"—that is, the object of battle was to confront the opposing army in the field and force it to give ground.

By far, the most influential military strategist during the Civil War period was a Frenchman, Baron Antoine-Henri de Jomini. Although his early nineteenth-century theories were criticized even by his own contemporaries (Napoleon himself dismissed his writings out of hand, while the Duke of Wellington thought him a "pompous charlatan"), Lee, Johnston, Longstreet, McDowell, and Grant were all familiar with his work, and their initial (and sometimes late) battlefield strategies reflected this.

In short, Jomini held that: offensive warfare was by far superior to defensive warfare; the establishment and maintenance of "interior lines" was of great importance; the key to winning a battle was to discover the "decisive point" (he always held that there was only one in a given battlefield), and to place superior power there; war was a stage for heroes, a "great drama," and that this spirit had to be developed within the armies themselves (called the "spirit of the bayonet" at the time).

This last point may well be the crucial element of determining why the war developed as it did. One of the most influential American military tacticians prior to the war was William J. Hardee, who later rose to the rank of Major General in the Confederate army. His primary work, *Hardee's Rifle and Light Infantry Tactics,* is a "nuts and bolts" version of Jomini's theories, giving practical steps to commanders on how to train and lead their troops into battle. It is worth noting that both the Union and Confederate armies officially used *Hardee's* as their leading tactical manual in the early parts of the war, and that the Union army never officially dropped its use, despite the fact that its author was eventually in command of a Confederate corps.

Hardee's most lasting influence on the war was its heavy emphasis on "stand up and face the enemy like a man" use of close-order drill and employment of the bayonet. Lines of infantry were to use their firepower to blow holes in an opposing enemy's line of battle, then "give 'em the cold steel" to force them off the field. To be a man among men, you had to stand up and face the enemy; hiding in holes or behind big rocks was for shirkers and cowards. Most ordinary soldiers were a step or two (or ten) ahead of their commanders as to the real tactical situation on the battlefield, and they turned to digging in whenever possible. Most commanders of that era had little clue on how to handle attacks on entrenched, fortified positions, and few were inclined to begin engaging in such seemingly unmanly practices. Confederate Capt. John Ellis wrote of such in 1862 to his father, "We want Stonewall Jackson fighting that hurls masses against the enemy's army. The policy of entrenching will ruin our cause if adopted here. The truth is it never paid anywhere."

NEW WEAPONS

As mentioned in earlier chapters, the primary new technology introduced on the Civil War stage was the rifled musket, a far more accurate and powerful weapon than the earlier smoothbore muskets. A series of lands and grooves cut in a spiral fashion down the inside of the barrel "grabbed" the bullet as it was fired and gave it a spinning motion that helped stabilize its flight, much like a football quarterback giving a spin to the ball as he releases it. This simple change not only helped stabilize the round, increasing its accuracy, but dramatically increased its effective range (again using the football analogy, imagine throwing a football by grabbing one end of pushing it forward—which will most likely result in the ball tumbling wildly and not going very far—just like a ball leaving a smoothbore weapon).

The Union adopted the 1861 Springfield rifled musket, .58 caliber, weighing a bit over nine pounds, with a 39-inch long barrel, about 56 inches in length overall, and capable of hitting targets well over 500 yards distant. The Confederacy used a wide variety of weapons and calibers throughout the war, but the most prevalent was the imported British 1853 model Enfield three-band rifled musket, .577 caliber, weighing about nine and a half pounds, 55 inches long with a 38-inch barrel, and even more accurate than the Springfield in the right hands. The paper cartridge ammunition used in both weapons was interchangeable, making resupply from captured enemy ammo chests easier.

Much has been made of the incredibly high casualty rate during the war—more were killed in the single-day battle of Sharpsburg (Antietam) on September 17 than in all previous American wars combined (26,134 dead, wounded, and missing, total) — and the main reason was due to the new class of infantry weapon, the rifled-barrel muzzleloader, combined with another ground-breaking technology, a new bullet designed in the 1840s by French Army Captain Claude Minié, that was elongated, with a hollow base, and slightly smaller than the rifle's bore diameter. This meant the bullet could be rammed down the barrel much faster, and the gases from discharge would expand the base, engaging the rifling and giving the bullet a very stable flight. The soft lead bullet (called a minié "ball," in the parlance of the day), weighing 500 grains (about the same as 11 modern copper pennies), tended to "mushroom" when it struck anything solid, depleting the entire kinetic energy of the shot onto the target. For example, this meant that if an infantryman was struck in the shoulder, his arm would most likely be ripped off, or a hit in the leg would shatter the bone into so many irreparable fragments that amputation was the only option. This radical treatment would still be indicated today, in fact, as medical technology has never developed any other method to deal with massively splintered and shattered bones.

Through the first months and years of the war, as a result of these pre-war theories, nicely dressed massed lines of battle were drawn up fifty to seventy-five yards from the enemy, as the earlier smoothbore weapons had a limited effective range, and massed firepower was the only reliable way to break up an enemy's line. Using this same formation with the more modern weapons—with their effective range of six times that of smooth-bores, an ability to fire about three times as fast, and the incredible dam-age the minié ball could inflict on the human body—made any wound life-threatening at best, and almost always rendered the victim combat-ineffective. It took far too many casualties before the powers-that-be woke up and realized a new day had dawned in combat technology. Battlefield surgery had also not caught up with the new technologies, dooming many a fine infantryman hit in the wrong place at the wrong time.

Battlefield casualties during the war were impressive, even at extreme ranges. Common infantrymen were able to pick off individual targets at ranges of 500 to 600 yards, using just their ordinary issued weapons. Special "sniper" rifles were acquired in both armies, and issued either to special riflemen units, mostly in the Union army, or to one or two of the best shots in a regiment, as was the fashion in the Confederate army. The most common of these special weapons, the British-made Whitworth, had a heavy barrel and a full-length scope, weighed about thirty-five pounds, and in the hands of a trained sharpshooter could pick off moving targets at ranges over 1,000 yards. One of the better-known examples of long-range sniping occurred at Spotsylvania. Union Maj. Gen. John Sedgwick was walking the ramparts of his redoubts, fully exposed, looking over at the Confederate lines, which were a good 800 yards away, nearly one-half mile. When his men pleaded for their beloved "Uncle John" to get under cover, after Confederate sharpshoot-ers had sent several rounds their way, he merely laughed at them, "What? Men dodging this way for single bullets? What will you do when they open fire along the whole line? I am ashamed of you. They couldn't hit an elephant at this distance." About two minutes later came the crack of a Whitworth rifle fired by CSA Sergeant Grace of the 4th Georgia, from the distant Confederate trench line. Sedgwick stiffened, then fell dead, a neat hole about one-half inch under his left eye.

In addition to the fearsome wounds suffered from rifle-fired minié balls, wounds sustained from the preferred pre-war weapon, bayonets, took their toll as well, albeit at a much lower rate than previously thought.

As mentioned in an earlier chapter, both Union and Confederate rifles could fit an "angular" bayonet, triangular in cross-section and 18 inches long, at the muzzle end—a fearsome weapon indeed. However, it took a high degree of expertise and discipline to properly use a bayonet in combat. Imagine trying to hold a poorly balanced, eleven-pound, 6-foot-long stick with an off-center pointed end (the bayonet attached to the muzzle end off the weapon and was offset from the center of mass about 2 inches, so the weapon could be fired with it attached), and try to stick it in a moving, similarly equipped and very highly motivated (to move out of the way) target, while your hands are slick with sweat and shaking with fear and adrenaline. This is also the reason why less than 2 percent of all battlefield casualties were attributed to edged or pointy weapons, including the hallowed bayonet.

The huge disparity in the instruments of battlefield injury can be seen in the Union Army of the Potomac medical reports, where 108,000 wounds from minié balls were recorded throughout the war, versus only 16,000 from round shot fired by smoothbore muskets (the resulting injuries were quite different and easy to distinguish). Those same records indicate that there were only twelve artillery-related injuries and six saber or bayonet wounds, out of the 7,302 casualties treated at the battles of the Wilderness in 1864—despite the heavy use of artillery by both sides and frequent hand-to-hand combat during the week-long set of battles.

EFFECT OF NEW WEAPONS

These weapons, seemingly so primitive by today's standards, were far advanced for the day, to the point that not only had tactics suffered along, trying to catch up, but battlefield medical care had lagged even further behind. Records indicate that over 70 percent of wounds suffered were to the extremities, but this is a very misleading statistic. For a variety of reasons, wounds to the head, chest, or abdomen were usually so immediately or decisively fatal that few men presenting these injuries showed up in field hospitals.

Unlike the earlier, relatively low-velocity round balls used in Revolutionary-war era smooth-bore muskets, which tended to push smooth tissues out of the way, rifled minié balls tended to tear and smash their way through internal organs, making any chest or abdominal wound a near-certain fatal event. This idea was well known by the combat troops, and the relatively few photographs showing the dead on battlefields illustrate this. The overwhelming hydrostatic shock from a minié ball hit was such that the soldier would not know immediately where he had been struck. If knocked to the ground by the force of the hit, the immediate reaction for most soldiers was to tear their coat open and jerk their shirt up. If the hit were a chest or abdominal wound, most would simply lie down, make their peace with God, and quietly remain there until they died, usually within minutes from the severe hemorrhage. This is the reason so many of these photographs show the soldier's clothing in disarray, not because of rigor mortis or posthumous bloating.

Head wounds most often resulted in instantaneous death. Hard blows to the head from hand-to-hand combat or glancing hits from musket fire usually resulted in depressed skull fractures—where part of the skull is driven into or near the brain itself, resulting in massive swelling and a rapid death if not treated. The only treatment in such cases was called trephining, a technique first known to be used by the ancient Egyptians. It was effective only if done within a few minutes or hours of the injury, and was performed by cutting a hole in the skull and allowing excess fluid to flow out and reduce the pressure on the brain. The technique, a variation of which is still used today in such cases, was usually successful, but well over 90 percent of the patients died anyhow, usually from infections caused by surgeons putting their filthy hands into the brain material and scooping out skull fragments.

The wounded men who did make it to field hospitals, as mentioned earlier, were overwhelmingly suffering from leg or arm injuries, and a large number of those injuries were treated with little more than a hasty amputation of the limb. The field hospital, by the second year of the war, was pretty close to being an assembly line, with junior and less experienced medical officers checking the wounded in, shuttling the lightly injured off to a clinic (usually outdoors), and steering those with head, chest, and abdominal wounds off to a quiet corner to spend their last minutes.

Those needing surgical intervention were rapidly moved to the operating theater, where the more experienced surgeons would rapidly prep and position them on wooden tables and quickly apply anesthetics before wiping their oft-reused, seldom cleaned amputation knife once or twice across their apron and diving into their grisly work. The lurid stories of amputations performed without anesthesia, along with equally lurid stories of "bite bullets" used by the patient, are for the most part baseless legends. Even at the lowest point of supplies deprivation in the Confederacy, surgeons reported they had "adequate" supplies on hand, most of the time. The familiar stories of men shrieking and screaming in pain, for the most part, were the results of being roughly handled inside the surgical suites, along with trauma-induced delirium, and the terrifying sight of bloody amputations performed in the open, in plain sight of the next ones in line.

Since the widespread use of anesthetics had only recently come into play, antebellum surgeons were noted for their speed more than their skill, and they retained their quest for speed through the war years. Once the patient was sufficiently sedated, the surgeon would make two quick incisions through the skin and muscle tissue above the injury location, leaving one side longer than the other. Tossing the amputation knife aside (or sticking it between his teeth, à la Errol Flynn), he would snatch up his steel amputation saw, and with a few strokes, cleave straight through the bone. Then, discarding the severed limb (there was usually a gory basket nearby), he would rapidly tie off the arteries with a piece of silk or softened horsehair suture, pull the longer flap of skin over the bone end, and suture the wound shut, leaving a small hole at the end for the inevitable putrid drainage. The whole procedure usually took less than ten minutes.

This is where the differences between Northern and Southern hospitals came into play. The industrial-rich North had a surplus of both fabrics to make bandages and otherwise idle women to roll them up, and their hospitals were well equipped with stacks and stacks of clean bandages. Following an amputation, a Union soldier was typically swaddled in a massive dressing, which was intended to absorb the drainage, to keep the putrid smell down, and to make it more comfortable for him to rest the raw end of his amputated limb. The South, bereft of most industry even before the war began, had a severe shortage of textiles and an even shorter supply of non-working women to roll bandages (scenes from Gone with the Wind notwithstanding). The Confederate soldier was lucky to get a thin piece of used cotton rag to absorb the worst of the drainage, leaving his stump to fester in the open air.

These disparate situations had a most unusual and unexpected result; far more Union soldiers died of septic shock from gangrenous wounds than did their Confederate counterparts with similar injuries. It seems that the generous bandages afforded to Union troops had the effect of cutting off any open-air exposure to the wound, setting up a perfect situation for the growth and spread of oxygen-hating bacteria that cause gangrene. The Confederate soldier, on the other hand, whose bare bandaging did not keep out air and flies, usually developed maggot-infested wounds after just a few days. This admittedly gross situation was actually the best possible under the circumstances, as the maggots would eat away necrotic tissues, allowing the wound the best chance to properly heal.

One of the facts of all wars is that the most rapid advances in medical sciences and technology usually arise from them. This was true even in this medically primitive age, with some surgeons, toward the end of the war, experimenting with "resections" of shattered arms rather than simply amputating them. This involved a more tedious and time-consuming process of removing the shattered bone fragments, grinding down the remaining open bone ends so they would not cause further soft-tissue damage, then cutting away torn skin over the wound and sewing it all back together again. The wounded soldier would have to keep that limb strapped to a brace or splint for the rest of his life, as there was now no underlying skeletal structure to give it support, but he would still have the use of that hand.

RECOVERY

Recovering in hospitals, as is the custom today, was a foreign concept during the Civil War. Even the best and cleanest Northern hospitals were little more than massive, open rooms, where legions of wounded and sick soldiers were crowded together, spreading disease and infection. Some of the Southern "hospitals" during the last two years of the war were no more than a designated spot in a field, hopefully shaded by trees, where the men lay on the open ground, sometimes, but not always, covered by a rough blanket. These arrangements, again running against common sense, sometimes provided much better opportunities for the men to recover with fewer complications and a lower mortality rate than their Northern counterparts. As stated before, the concept of cleanliness to avoid sepsis was unknown during the war, and a pus-filled, swollen incision site was seen as a positive thing, the "very beginning of the healing process," as one medical journal of the day claimed. The most dangerous infection, known as "hospital gangrene," could be treated only by doing a further amputation of the affected limb and had an extremely high mortality rate.

Other diseases frequently seen postoperatively were pyemia, erysipelas, and osteomyelitis—infections of the blood, tissue, and bone, respectively. These infections had combined mortality rates approaching 90 percent of their victims. Other problems arose as a result of hasty field amputations performed under less-than-ideal conditions: bone protrusions, stumps that refused to heal, serious nerve damage, and a whole host of secondary infections. One Union surgeon even claimed that "exhaustion" was a leading cause of the deaths of his patients.

With all of this, it is easy to understand the high mortality rates following surgery. The U.S. Army Medical Department reported after the war that the various Union armies reported death rates of 3–6 percent for finger or toe amputations, 14–24 percent for arm, 38 percent for lower leg, 45 percent for shoulder, 54 percent for above-the knee, and 88 percent for hip joint amputations.

DISEASE

Even with all the problems and mortality rates from combat injuries, the real killer during the Civil War was disease. Nearly 60 percent of all Union casualties and nearly 70 percent of all Confederate casualties were a result of the myriad "camp sicknesses," aggravated by exposure, fatigue, malnutrition, and close proximity of groups of men that by and large had come from relatively isolated farming communities. The problems started at the recruiting depots, where by the third year of the war, all pretense of any medical examination was abandoned, allowing the chronically ill and acutely sick to join and spread their infections across the tightly packed camps.

The younger men in the camps were exposed to a host of diseases that today we consider relatively innocuous childhood illnesses: chicken pox, mumps, measles, and whooping cough. Few had gained any natural immunity from these problems, and this resulted in a high mortality rate, mostly in the initial camps. Close confines in camp led to outbreaks of tuberculosis, and simple colds frequently turned into lethal pneumonias. Even more lethal were the intestinal disorders that resulted from the usual unsanitary conditions in camp and on the march: cholera, typhoid fever, and dysentery. The last was considered to be the single largest killer of soldiers during the war, far outstripping every other cause of death. One Union postwar report claimed that well over 95 percent of all soldiers had contracted this disease in some form during the war years.

To treat all of these diseases and injuries, the surgeons on both sides had a list of supplies and treatments that was just as concise as the number of surgical instruments they had available. This is a list of an unusually complete pharmacopoeia chest that accompanied one Union corps:

1. CERATUM CANTHARIDIS. (Spanish flies) Three ounces

2. ARGENTI NITRAS. (silver nitrate) One ounce

3. ARGENTI NITRAS FUSUS. (crystalline silver nitrate) One ounce

4. IODINIUM. (iodine) One ounce

5. ANTIMONII ET POTASSAE TARTRAS. (tartar emetic) One ounce

6. HYDRARGYRI CHLORIDUM MITE. (mild chloride of mercury; calomel) One ounce

7. EXTRACT OF BEEF. One pound

8. EXTRACT OF COFFEE. One pound

9. CONDENSED MILK. One pound

10. BLACK TEA. Four ounces

11. SPIRITUS FRUMENTI. (spirits of nitric ether) Twenty-four fluid ounces

12. SPIRITUS AETHERIS NITRICI. (sweet spirit of nitre) Eight fluid ounces

13. ALCOHOL FORTIUS. (strong alcohol) Twelve fluid ounces

14. COUGH MIXTURE. Twelve fluid ounces

15. WHITE SUGAR. Ten ounces

16. CHLOROFORMUM PURIFICATUM. (chloroform) Twelve fluid ounces

17. LINIMENT. Twelve fluid ounces

18. SYRUPUS SCILLAE. (syrup of squill) Eight fluid ounces

19. AQUA AMMONIAE. (ammonia water) Eight fluid ounces

20. SPIRITUS AETHERIS COMPOSITUS. (compound spirits of ether) Four fluid ounces

21. TINCTURA OPII. (tincture of opium; laudanum) Six fluid ounces

22. EXTRACTUM CINCHONAE FLUIDUM. (fluid extract of cinchona; Peruvian bark) With aromatics, four fluid ounces

23. EXTRACTUM VALERIANAE FLUIDUM. (fluid extract of valerian) Six fluid ounces

24. EXTRACTUM ZINGIBERIS FLUIDUM. (fluid extract of ginger) Six fluid ounces

25. OLEUM OLIVAE. (olive oil) Six fluid ounces

26. OLEUM TEREBINTHINAE. (oil of turpentine) Six fluid ounces

27. GLYCERINA. (glycerine) Six fluid ounces

28. TINCTURA OPII CAMPHORATA. (camphorated tincture of opium) Six fluid ounces

29. LIQUOR FERRI PERSULPHATUS. (liquid iron persulphate) Four fluid ounces

30. SPIRITUS AMMONIAE AROMATICUS. (aromatic spirits of ammonia) Four fluid ounces

31. PILULAE CATHARTICAE COMPOSITAE. (compound cathartic pills) Fifty dozen

32. PILLS OF COLCYNTII AND IPECAC. (colocynth and ipecac) Fifty dozen

33. PULVIS IPECAC: ET OPII. (powder of ipecac and opium) In five gram pills, thirty dozen

34. PILULAE QUINIAE SULPHATIS. (quinine sulphate pills) Three grams, forty dozen

35. POTASSAE CHLORAS. (potassium chlorate) Four ounces

36. POTASSAE BICARBONAS. (bicarbonate of potassium) Four ounces

37. POTASSII IODIDUM. (iodide of potassium) Four ounces

38. SODAE ET POTASSEA TARTRAS. (tartrate of potassium and soda; Rochelle salt) Four ounces

39. LIQUOR MORPHIAE SULPHATIS. (morphine sulphate solution) Sixteen grains to the fluid ounce, four fluid ounces

40. PILLS OF CAMPHOR AND OPIUM. Twenty dozen

41. PILULAE HYDRARGYRI. (mercury pills; blue pills) Forty dozen

42. PILULAE OPII. (opium pills) Sixty dozen

43. ACIDUM TANNICUM. (tannic acid) Half an ounce

44. ALUMEN. (alum) Three ounces

45. COLLODIUM. (etheral solution of gun cotton) Three fluid ounces

46. CREASOTUM. (creosote) Two fluid ounces

47. EXTRACTUM ACONITI RADICIS FLUIDUM. (fluid extract of aconite root) Three fluid ounces

48. EXTRACTUM COLCHICI SEMINIS FLUIDUM. (fluid extract of colchicum seed) Three fluid ounces

49. EXTRACTUM IPECACUANHAE FLUIDUM. (fluid extract of ipecac) Three fluid ounces

50. TINCTURA FERRI CHLORIDI. (ferric chloride; tincture of muriate of iron) Two fluid ounces

51. PLUMBI ACETAS. (acetate of lead) Three ounces

52. ZINCI SULPHAS. (zinc sulphate; white vitriol) Three ounces

—FROM AN EXHIBIT BROADSHEET, COURTESY OF THE NATIONAL MUSEUM OF CIVIL WAR MEDICINE IN FREDERICK, MARYLAND. A NEARLY IDENTICAL LIST WAS PROVIDED BY THE NOW-DEFUNCT CIVIL WAR SOLDIER'S MUSEUM IN PENSACOLA, FLORIDA.

It is hard to overstate just how awful the hospitals truly were, filled to the brim with the sick and dying, the air poisoned with the stench of putrefying wounds, the shrieks and cries of the delirious and mentally insane cackling off the walls, and with little to no human comforts, save the momentary ministrations of an overworked nurse. Most soldiers considered them to be a place to go to die and avoided them like the plague. Even the surgeons themselves thought likewise; one of Waring's compatriots, Surgeon William L. Daniel of the 8th South Carolina Volunteers, said in a letter, "The most disgusting and repulsive sights I ever saw in my life have been in Hospitals and on the Battle Field." This letter, however, was written to his sister on August 5, 1862, well before things took a distinct turn for the worse.

As more and more stories describing the ghastly conditions in field hospitals took hold in the newspapers, demands from citizens that "something be done" were either met with indifference or with hotly worded letters defending the "advanced medicine" being practiced there. When the Union War Department expressed some growing unease over reports about the treatment of the wounded at Sharpsburg (Antietam), Lt. Col. Jonathan Letterman, Medical Director of the Army of the Potomac, fired back angrily:

> The surgery of these battle-fields has been pronounced butchery. Gross misrepresentations of the conduct of medical officers have been made and scattered broadcast over the country, causing deep and heart-rending anxiety to those who had friends or relatives in the army, who might at any moment require the services of a surgeon.
>
> If any objection could be urged against the surgery of those fields, it would be the efforts on the part of surgeons to practice "conservative surgery" to too great an extent.
>
> I had better opportunities, perhaps, than any one else to form an opinion, and from my observations I am convinced that if any fault was committed it was that the knife was not used enough.

DR. WARING OF THE 17TH SOUTH CAROLINA

Most of the known facts about Dr. Waring's service come from a collection of his letters to his wife, which may have been partially lost. Aside from some early comments about his military, versus medical, adventures, Waring confines the majority of his letter-writing to mundane household considerations, and not a few comments about his growing homesickness. Also missing is much in the way of commentary about his medical duties. For example, he mentions to his wife that there had been a hard fight on June 19, 1862, referring to the Battle of Secessionville, on James Island near Charleston, but says almost nothing about the casualties he undoubtedly treated (more than 200 Confederate and 600 Union, left behind by retreating Union forces), even though his own regiment was not engaged.

Waring and the 17th South Carolina left for points north not long afterward, entering their first major battle at Rappahannock Station on August 23. Although his brigade was caught in the middle of a heavy artillery duel and ninety men were killed or wounded, Waring didn't even mention it in a subsequent letter, instead complaining of the food situation, the expense of his officer's mess (officers had to pay for their own food supply, usually doing it in small groups called "messes"), and the difficulty he has had finding proper (possibly meaning finer quality) clothing to wear. A week later the 17th was heavily invested in the second battle at Manassas, centered in the middle of the swirling fight at the Chinn House and suffered the loss of its commanding officer, Colonel John Hugh Means, as well as 187 other officers and men. Means was the former governor of South Carolina and was also a friend and evening walking companion of Waring's. Waring himself was slightly wounded during the battle, which prompted a more somber, direct, and longer letter to his wife immediately afterward:

> How shall I describe to you my Dear wife the horrors that have come under my observation the last four days . . . I was struck by a piece of schrapnel shot while following one of the fiercest charges and hottest fires (I am told) of the war. Gen'l Jenkins was shot there also 8 out of our 10 captains in Means reg't and the Col. mortally wounded. Cote & Paul Seabrook both killed and the ground for half a mile square literally strewed with the dead–dying. I received my wound thus. I was told by a soldier that Col. Means was shot and the adjunct looking for me. I immediately started from left to right of the reg't to find him and so ran the gamut of the entire line, when about midway a shell exploded so near me that I was knocked down stupefied and

thrown about 10 feet. After recovering myself I got up and moved on when about 20 steps further the shot that struck me exploded struck me slightly [and] killed one man on my left & wounded one on my right. The Blood & hair of the poor fellow killed was thrown all over me–My wound thank God was so slight that I have not a moment had to give up my duties and although it compels me to go with my shoe down at the heel gives but little pain and will very soon be quite well . . . Give love to all–Kiss Mother & the girls. Let not little Blue eyes cease to know & love poppa who thought of and saw her sweet little face amid the din and Carnage of battle.

Waring was clearly rattled over his near-death experience, but had little time to recover. The remains of the 17th moved out almost immediately, entering battle again on September 14 at Crampton's Gap on South Mountain, where they suffered sixty-one casualties. Three days later, they endured the hell-fire of Sharpsburg (Antietam), and suffered an additional nineteen casualties. There, the 17th almost ceased to exist as a fighting unit, having only forty officers and men left to follow their colors south with Lee, back into Virginia. Waring stayed behind in the Confederate hospital complex at Shepherdstown, where he treated the massive numbers of wounded, until ordered to rejoin his regiment at Winchester, Virginia, in mid-October. His letters home during this period carried the same somber, reflective tone as the one following 2nd Manassas, with vivid descriptions of the wounds and privations he had witnessed, along with not a few comments concerning his sought-after promotion and transfer back to Charleston.

After his return south to Virginia, Waring was clearly not in the mood to continue in his position. He asked for, and was denied, a transfer to Beauregard's command, headquartered in Charleston, citing rather vague "health reasons." He then asked for, and was denied again, a leave of absence "for the purpose of restoring [his] health." His good friend Col. Fitz William McMaster, who was in command of the 17th following the death of Colonel Means, advised him to simply get a certificate of medical disability, resign his commission, and go home. On December 25, 1862, he finally received an order signed by his brigade commander, Brig. Gen. Nathan George "Shanks" Evans, accepting his claim of disability and his resignation. Waring's brief military career was over.

The 17th South Carolina went on to fight in the Western Theater, attempting to break through the Union siege at Vicksburg, and defending Jackson, Mississippi, before returning east to Charleston and the Bermuda Hundred fight at Clay's Farm, the nine-month siege of Petersburg, and the final big battle at Sayler's Creek, Virginia. Colonel McMaster surrendered three days after that last fight, at Appomattox Courthouse, along with what was left of the 17th: eight other officers and 110 men.

Of all the Union surgeons who served during the Civil War, thirty-two were killed in action, nine died in accidents of various sorts, eighty-three were wounded in action—ten of these mortally—four died in prisoner of war camps, and 281 died of diseases contracted during the war. There are no complete records for Confederate surgeons, but it is safe to assume they suffered casualties in like numbers.

Both sides seemed struck deeply by what they had endured, and even more so by what their patients had endured during the long war. Countless medical journal articles, reminiscences, and books by former surgeons spoke of the bravery of the men they treated, perhaps none more eloquently than that by Dr. Francis Peyre Porcher, former Surgeon of the Holcombe Legion, which served alongside Waring's own regiment in Evan's Brigade. In an 1889 speech to an association of former South Carolina Confederate surgeons, he said:

> *There was no one so uncomplaining as the Confederate soldier. Every surgeon who has seen active service will confirm the truth and accuracy of a picture drawn without exaggeration. In your daily rounds to offer him relief he gazes upon you, but does not complain that you pass him by, asks for nothing, does not bemoan his fate, nor murmur at the insufficiency of either food or attendance. He may lay sick under a broiling sun, in a heated tent; or wounded, he may languish in the hospital amid the dying and the dead, surrounded by everything to appal even well men* crudelis, Ubique luctus, ubique payor, Et plurima mortis imago; *yet the mere stripling possessed his soul unterrified, and uttered neither cry nor groan. There was always a courage and a resolution mingled with his apparent indifference, which has extorted our admiration and has compelled us involuntarily to recall the noble description of the invincible Cato: "The whole world was subdued, save the intrepid soul of Cato."* Omne terrarum subacta, Preter atroeem anitaurn Catohis.

Waring himself survived the war without further injury, though leading a much quieter postwar life. The "little Blue eyes" his letters frequently referred to was his daughter, Sarah, the only child to survive to adulthood of eight children born to his first wife, Josephine Gabriella (Ella) Seabrook, whom he had married in 1853. It is not recorded when she died, but he married again in 1895, when he was sixty-three years old, this time to Mary Virginia Chaplin, who bore him three additional children—all of whom survived to adulthood. He died in 1901 on Yonges Island, South Carolina and is buried there in his family's small plantation cemetery.

6

HELL ON EARTH:
PRISONERS OF WAR

William J. Crouse, Co. G, 7th Pennsylvania Reserves

IN THE EARLY SPRING OF 1864, SHORTLY AFTER BEING PROMOTED AND given overall command of all Union armies, Lt. Gen. Ulysses S. Grant planned out a strong, three-part offensive against Confederate Gen. Robert E. Lee's forces in northern Virginia, intending to end the war in the Eastern Theater with one big push. Grant coordinated this strategy with his friend and subordinate in the West, Maj. Gen. William T. Sherman, who was ramping up to start his own spring offensive, aimed at taking the critical rail juncture and manufacturing center of Atlanta. The hoped-for, near-simultaneous fall of both Richmond and Atlanta would have ended the war, for all practical purposes.

Grant sent Maj. Gen. Benjamin "Spoons" Butler's Army of the James to an amphibious landing at the Bermuda Hundred, with orders to march westward toward Petersburg and Richmond, destroying any portion of Lee's army that stood in their way. Maj. Gen. Franz Sigel was ordered to take a small, 10,000-man force from his Department of West Virginia, march south through the Shenandoah Valley to Staunton and Lynchburg, destroying supplies and railroads along the way, and then threaten the rear of Lee's lines. Finally, Maj. Gen. George Meade's Army of the Potomac was ordered out of camp due south toward Richmond, taking the same roads used in the previous year's Chancellorsville Campaign, with Grant himself along to observe firsthand the centerpiece of his campaign. Grant told Meade that his primary objective was the destruction of Lee's Army of Northern Virginia, who had danced back and forth in front of innumerable Union armies for three years at that point, protecting the Confederate capital with great success. Meade would take his 118,000 men and 274 field guns against Lee's 62,000 men and 224 guns, with Butler and Sigel sapping off an unknown number of Lee's forces to boot. Defeat for the Union forces seemed impossible, at least on paper.

Amid Meade's vast army that started out on the muddy Virginia roads at midnight on May 3, was a private in Maj. Gen. Gouverneur K. Warren's V Corps, William J. Crouse, of Company G, 7th Pennsylvania Reserves Regiment. Like so many other private soldiers of the war, he arrived on the scene anonymously, appeared without comment on the unit muster rolls, fought without recorded distinction or documented merit, and seemed destined to either die equally anonymously in the ranks, or at best, quietly go back home to pick up his life again. Crouse, however, was to have a central role in one of the war's most controversial events.

Later in the morning of May 3, their movements screened by Brig. Gen. James Wilson's Cavalry Corps, Crouse and the rest of Warren's V Corps crossed prepared bridges over the Rapidan River at the small settlement of Germanna Ford. From there, they proceeded without resistance to march down the Germanna Plank Road to Wilderness Tavern. In the middle of a large, tangled, thick woods, pierced only by four crude roads, Meade thought it relatively safe to collect up his scattered corps and prepare for sustained battle—even though this was the very site where Confederate Maj. Gen. "Stonewall" Jackson had so thoroughly routed then-Army of the Potomac commander Maj. Gen. Joseph Hooker exactly a year before. Wilderness Tavern, in fact, was the very building where Jackson subsequently had his arm amputated, after being accidentally shot by his own troops. Despite the connection, neither Meade nor Grant expected any immediate action.

Lee, however, had correctly predicted several days beforehand exactly where Grant would deploy his forces, down to naming the fords where they crossed the Rapidan, and had positioned his much-smaller Army of Northern Virginia amid the thick woods of the Wilderness, waiting for the opportunity that Meade had now handed him. Meade was further delayed by the difficulty in transporting his supply wagons over the various river crossings; the 65-mile-long supply train took until late on the afternoon of May 4 to arrive. Crouse and his fellow soldiers of the 7th, assigned to the all-Pennsylvania 1st Brigade commanded by Colonel William McCandless (part of Brig. Gen. Samuel W. Crawford's 3rd Division, V Corps), were camped in an open field in the center of the

5-mile-long Union line, just southwest of the tavern, astride the Orange Turnpike, and facing west.

Early in the morning of May 5, Lt. Gen. Richard Ewell's Corps moved out, heading east on the Orange Turnpike, and aiming to destroy Warren's V Corps. They were supported on their right flank by Lt. Gen. James Longstreet's Corps and Lt. Gen. A.P Hill's Corps to his right. Grant had gotten wind that Lee's forces were moving in the area, and at 7:15 A.M., he ordered Warren to move west on the Orange Turnpike until he made contact. By 8:00 A.M., that contact was made.

With the sound of skirmishers firing to his front, McCandless deployed his brigade in a semi-circle astride the road, with the 7th Pennsylvania to the far right of the line in another small clearing. He then sent a hasty message back to Crawford that he had just encountered enemy skirmishers. When the firing died down a few minutes later, McCandless ordered his men out and advancing again. Ewell had not retreated, as McCandless had presumed, but was well deployed on a small ridge, waiting for his Union opponents to approach. With the 2nd Pennsylvania Reserves in front, redeployed as skirmishers, the 7th, supported by the 11th Pennsylvania Reserves, advanced westward again. Within minutes they encountered Ewell's main line, which retreated under the pressure. Closely pursuing, Crouse and the 7th Pennsylvania plunged through the thick, unbroken woods, trying to turn the Confederate's flank. Instead, they became lost, with the sounds of heavy combat in all directions.

Turning to their left, without orders, the men of the 7th Pennsylvania tried to push through a seemingly thin line of Confederates, only to be thrown back with losses. Turning then to the right, again without orders, and entering another woody thicket, they initially thought they had escaped the Confederate noose. The renewed sounds of fighting to their front and musketry to their rear showed they had entered a trap. With Confederates rapidly closing in on three sides, the commanding officer of the 7th, Col. Henry C. Bolinger, had no choice other than to surrender or watch his dwindling force be chopped to pieces (some records indicate Maj. LeGrand B. Speece was actually in command at the scene). Bolinger signaled his regiment's surrender, and 272 officers and soldiers dropped their weapons and ended their war. None of them suspected the real fight for their lives was just beginning.

One of Crouse's companions, Pvt. Samuel Elliot of Company A, kept a diary during the long months of confinement. His first entry expressed well the dread the Pennsylvania men felt as soon as they arrived in their Southern prison camp:

> *Sunday, May 22: The camp contains about fifteen thousand Union men, most of-whom have been prisoners from eight to ten months, and were once strong, able bodied men, but are now nothing more than walking skeletons, covered with filth and vermin, and can hardly be recognized as white men. The horrible sights are almost enough to make us give up in despair—the ground is covered with filth, and, vermin can be seen crawling in the sand. In the centre of the camp is a stream of dirty water so warm and greasy we can scarcely drink it. The sights I saw on this, my first day . . . so filled me with horror that I can give but a poor idea of this prison den.*

OVERVIEW OF THE PRISONER OF WAR SYSTEM

No one had ever expected to have to house and feed prisoners, at least for any serious length of time. Until well into the second year of the war, the old European tradition of exchanging and "paroling" prisoners prevailed. After a given battle, equal numbers of prisoners from both sides were released, and those who remained were sent home, after first signing an oath that promised they would not take up arms again. In theory this system worked rather well for the holding side; by allowing the prisoner to go home, you no longer had to feed, house, or guard him, and by virtue of his oath, he had become a non-combatant. The downfall, of course, was that it relied on the fallen natures of quite fallible men.

This system required the mutual cooperation and honesty of each side, which did exist, for the most part, in the early part of the war. Prisoners, particularly officers, were usually treated quite well during the brief period they spent in captivity. It was routine for relations on opposite sides to "look each other up" if in the same area. Tobacco, whiskey, and rations were often exchanged between inmates and guards, and even newspapers, debating societies, dances, and other parties were organized at some prisons. Local communities, both in the North and South, did make at least superficial efforts to assist the imprisoned foes, to the point where several romances flourished between captives and local ladies bringing refreshments into the camps.

In contrast, both sides were so unprepared to deal with any substantial number of prisoners in the beginning that some were held in local jails, along with murderers, thieves, and other riff-raff. In fairness, this was consistent with the situation across the board, as both sides expected a "ninety-day war," tops, and went so far as to turn away "excess" recruits and limit the purchase of military supplies. To hold the rapidly increasing numbers of prisoners, the North began using old coastal fortifications, and the South began using old factory buildings. Even with exchanges and paroles, administrative bottlenecks soon caused overcrowding in prisons on both sides.

The situation finally became critical after July 1863, when the exchange system collapsed. What had once been a system of honor and efficiency had become simply a farce, with most Northern paroled prisoners making good their promise, and heading home right after their release. Most Southern paroled prisoners, on the other hand, usually either went back as quickly as possible to their old unit, or found another regiment to join. Grant finished off the practice once and for all, putting a swift end to the exchange and parole system as soon as he was promoted to supreme commander. In fairness, as the North had several times the number of military-aged men in its population, it could afford to honor the system, while the South desperately needed every single fighting man it could scrap up.

The numbers of Prisoners Of War (POWs) taken by both sides rapidly climbed, helped in no small part by the increasing number and severity of battles taking place in late 1863 and early 1864. The North attempted to control the problem by appointing a central authority over all the prison camps, Col. William H. Hoffman. A POW himself at the beginning of the war, Hoffman set up a vast bureaucratic network of regulations, inspections, and standards for his camps. The South followed suit by appointing Brig. Gen. John H. Winder to a similar position, in charge of all the Richmond POW camps, where nearly all the Union prisoners were being held at first.

LIFE IN THE PRISON CAMPS

Again in theory, the two formalized and organized POW systems should have worked to treat prisoners in a relatively humane manner, but unfortunately neither lived up to its charge. Both sides' camps became crowded very rapidly, and space to house prisoners and build more camps became harder to find. By early 1864 both sides resorted to building simple wooden enclosures with no interior housing to "corral" the prisoners, in short, building something actually less humane than the WWII Nazi concentration camps.

By the spring of 1864, the South was barely able to feed its own army and citizens, and despite the efforts of camp commandants, most Union prisoners barely subsisted on diets of rough corn bread, occasionally supplemented by half-rotted and spoiled meat. To be perfectly honest, this was frequently what the camp guards and staff were eating as well. Rail routes were being decimated by Union attacks, and what little food was being produced often rotted in warehouses for lack of available transportation. The situation became so desperate by the summer of 1864 that overtures were made to Grant to either renew the parole system, this time with a strict promise of honesty on the part of the parolees, or even to simply hand over to him all the Union prisoners, as the South had no real capability for taking care of them properly. Grant consistently refused, recognizing that even as his own men under captivity were suffering and dying from lack of food and medical care, it was burdening the already strained Southern logistics system nearly to the breaking point just to give the prisoners those meager supplies. Grant's hope was that the sacrifice of the Union prisoners would help bring a swifter conclusion to the war.

News leaking out of the South about prison conditions was amplified by the Northern press, which was, unbelievably enough, even less "fair and balanced" than today's media. Indignant articles and gruesome stories about rumored deliberate, savage, and widespread Southern "abuses" of POWs enraged the public, who demanded that "justice be done" and that their own Confederate prisoners be treated the same. Some Union officers were more than happy to satisfy this lust for misplaced vengeance; at war's end, Hoffman returned $1.8 million to the Federal Treasury (roughly equivalent to $38 million in today's dollars), bragging that this was money he had saved by cutting prisoner rations. Responding to public polls is not a modern phenomenon, as this well illustrates.

Over 150 prison camps were built on both sides during the war. Within weeks after opening, almost all were filthy, disease-ridden hellholes. None of them required any routine cleaning or maintenance, other than whatever the local commander deemed absolutely necessary, this being the "end-Medieval" era of prisons as well as medical care. Many prisoners vomited uncontrollably on entering the gates of Andersonville or its Northern counterpart Elmira, where the overpowering stench of open sewers, dead bodies, and rotting flesh hung like a cloud over the wide-open, shadeless fields. At most prisons, "fresh fish" (new prisoners) had to be shoved through the doorway, where they would stand for hours at first trying not to touch or sit on anything. The walls and floors of prison buildings were normally covered with thick layers of greasy slime, dirt, mold, dead lice, and other vermin. The ground in "open air" camps like Elmira and Andersonville became covered over time with a thick layer of mud, slime, human waste, and vermin as well.

The prisoners themselves were nearly universally filthy, infested with lice and fleas, and covered with open sores and rashes. Many became despondent after endless weeks in the camps, no longer caring what happened to them or others; they quit bothering to use the slit latrines to relieve themselves, or even to cover up the mess afterward. Diarrhea, dysentery, and typhoid fever ran rampant, killing far more prisoners than starvation or failed escape attempts.

Boredom was an equally lethal killer. By the height of the war, many camps were so crowded that it could take literally hours to walk from one side to another, and most activities were forbidden for security reasons. Sitting in the same spot in encrusted, filthy clothes day after day, too hungry to sleep and too tired to talk, with the noise from dying and delirious fellow prisoners ringing in their ears day and night, and with no hope for release or exchange, some prisoners finally chose suicide as a means of escape. Andersonville became notorious during the war for newspaper stories about its "deadline," a small wooden fence twenty feet inside the main stockade wall, where guards could and usually did shoot anyone who ventured inside (actually, most open prisons on both sides had this feature). Some prisoners "went over" just to end their suffering.

On both sides, the filth that these prisoners endured cannot possibly be overstated. Several prisoners wrote in their journals about how their skin actually changed color from the layers of grime, and a Northern surgeon testified that it took months of bathing to completely remove the encrusted dirt. Most prisoners were not allowed to bathe for most or all of their incarceration; many reported that if they were allowed a bath, it would be six months or longer before another.

COMPARATIVE RATIOS OF PRISONER DEATHS

By the third year of the war, vast numbers of prisoners were falling into Southern hands, times were tough for everyone as a result of the Union naval blockade and the cutting of railroads throughout the Confederacy, and few were in the mood to deal kindly with the "Northern invaders." However, although this chapter deals specifically with the most notorious prison of all, it is important to note that the North did not treat their prisoners much better.

Roughly 29 percent of Andersonville's 45,000 prisoners died in captivity, where conditions were wretched for all concerned; by way of comparison, 24 percent of the 12,123 Confederates held at Elmira, New York, died in captivity. Elmira suffered from many of the same supply and environmental problems faced by Andersonville, but there is a great deal of evidence that at least part of their prisoners' suffering was deliberately induced. The evidence is much stronger for this deliberate retaliation at other notorious Union prisons, including Camp Douglas and Rock Island, Illinois, and Camp Morton, Indiana—all of which had relatively high prisoner mortality rates.

CAMP SUMTER, ANDERSONVILLE, GEORGIA

As the war intensified in late 1863, Confederate officials searching for a place to hold thousands of Union prisoners found what they thought was a perfect place. It was located at Station Number 8 on the Georgia Southwestern Railroad track, a place that locals in the adjacent tiny village called Andersonville. Confederate Capt. William Sidney Winder, the officer in charge of the search, apparently had no intention of creating a hellhole when he chose this location. On the contrary, in his official report he mentioned the "plentiful food" and water available, with transportation easily accessible and far from the battle lines.

Construction of the new camp, soon named Camp Sumter, was delayed for a few months by both local opposition to the project, which was mostly due to a fear of vindictive escaped prisoners and a general shortage of labor. By the time work crews started on the new facility, in early January 1864, shortages of money and rapidly increasing numbers of Union prisoners caused the Confederate government to order that just a strong fence be built, without any interior buildings to house the POWs. Under pressure to have the facility ready as soon as possible, the workmen simply stripped the entire area of all but two trees, using the felled pines to build a 15-foot-high double wall of roughly shaved logs butted closely together. Guard towers, known as "pigeon roosts," were built against the outside of the interior wall, spaced every thirty feet.

A star-shaped fort on the southwest corner and six other earthwork emplacements guarded against any Union cavalry attempts to free the prisoners, and inward-facing cannons guarded against prisoner uprisings. Artillery crews manned the cannons, which fired blank charges on a regular basis, as part of "quick-action drills" for the garrison. On at least one other occasion, they fired live shot over the camp as another sort of demonstration. Private Elliot commented on this shot in his diary:

> Thursday 28 (July 1864). The rebels fired a solid shot over the camp for the purpose, I suppose, of showing us they had ammunition on hand. They are very much afraid of us making a break when the gates are opened to pass prisoners through. When the shot was fired a loud cheer was given, and cries of "lay down," "stand to your guns," &c., could be heard in all parts of the camp.

A smaller enclosure called Castle Reed, located one-half mile west, housed the only officer prisoners sent to this area, until all were transferred to Macon's Camp Oglethorpe in May 1864. Afterward, only enlisted prisoners languished in Andersonville's stockades.

The first prisoners moved in on February 25, 1864, even before the stockade walls were completed. Within a week the first escape attempt was mounted, when prisoners climbed the stockade wall using a homemade rope of torn shirts and blankets. All were caught within a day or two, but their attempt inspired the construction of the ill-famed "deadline." Lacking even the crudest structure to protect themselves from the elements, the first arrivals were able to use leftover scraps of wood to build huts. Later prisoners built "shebangs" by digging shallow pits in the red clay ground and covering them with some sort of tarp, or else they simply sat out in the open, totally exposed to the sun, wind, and rain.

HENRY WIRZ

The commandant of the camp then and through most of the early buildup was Col. Alexander W. Persons, commanding officer of the 55th Georgia Infantry. He was replaced by Gen. John Henry Winder (Captain Winder's father) on June 17. By that date the prison already held more than twice the number it was designed for. Many of the arriving prisoners had been held at other Confederate POW camps, and arrived already filthy, weak, sick, and diseased. The stage was set for a real disaster to take place, the responsibility for which would be placed on the next arrival, Winder's subordinate, Capt. Henry Wirz.

Wirz was not a Southerner. In fact, he was not even an American citizen. A native of Switzerland, he had immigrated and was living in Louisiana when the war broke out. Wounded during the Battle of Seven Pines in the spring of 1862, he was promoted and assigned as Adjutant General to General Winder in Richmond. Given various tasks after that, including a mysterious "secret mission" to carry documents to Confederate agents in Europe, he was eventually assigned as keeper of the inner stockade of Camp Sumter in March 1864.

Wirz had a disagreeable personality and no real flair for command. Some of his more outrageous orders and comments were later used as "evidence" against him in his war crimes trial. Many escape attempts were made by prisoners tunneling under the walls, digging in the open under the pretense of excavating wells for water (there were also some legitimate wells dug by the prisoners). Wirz decided at one point that the Union prisoners were literally "covering up" their digging with their shebangs, so he ordered that no prisoner build or inhabit any sort of overhead shelter. This insane command was soon overturned.

There were also quite a few reports that Wirz habitually walked around the stockade with his pistol in hand, and that he personally shot several prisoners, although this last allegation is the object of heated debate. Camp Sumter's best-known inmate, Pvt. John Ransom, the author of *Andersonville Diary*, certainly was no great fan of Wirz:

> *May 10. Capt. Wirtz [sic] very domineering and abusive. Is afraid to come into camp anymore. There are a thousand men in here who would willingly die if they could kill him first. Certainly the worst man I ever saw.*

THE DECLINE AND FALL OF ANDERSONVILLE

By the end of the summer of 1864, Camp Sumter's population reached 33,000, making it the fifth largest city in the entire Confederacy. Thirteen hundred prisoners occupied each acre of land within the compound, and things went from bad to worse. Atlanta was under siege and Sherman's cavalry were ranging all through the northern half of Georgia and Alabama, laying waste to railroads and warehouses. Rations started to run out, then nearly disappeared. Salt was the first to go, followed by fresh vegetables, and then meat. Most prisoners started to subsist on rough cornmeal delivered only four days a week, and turned to eating rats and even birds that some of the stronger men were able to catch.

Some of the less enlightened guards started amusing themselves by dropping bits of food over the wall into the mass of prisoners, just to laugh at the riot that would ensue. A few of the nastier ones dropped food within the dead line, just for the opportunity to kill a prisoner.

A very small stream ran through the stockade site close by. When the camp opened this was the only source of drinking, bathing, and toilet water in the entire facility. Needless to say, it became overwhelmed and contaminated in short order, and no other source of decent water was to be had. In August 1864, when a violent thunderstorm reopened an old spring that had been covered with construction debris, the prisoners insisted that God himself had opened the spring with a lightning bolt; they named the spot Providence Spring in gratitude.

The number of prisoners dying from diarrhea and dysentery skyrocketed, claiming over 4,500 in just a five-month period. Deaths were so common that some prisoners managed to escape by pretending they were dead, and then waiting until after they were carried outside the walls to the rude "death house." Elliot talked about this charnel house in his diary:

> *Thursday 25 (August 1864). Charles Jarimer, a recruit of our Company, and a bunk-mate of mine, died to-day, after a long and painful illness; helped to carry his body to the "dead house"—a house built in the rear of the hospital, outside the stockade. There were about twenty-five other bodies, most of which had been stripped of all their clothing, and were so black and swollen they could not be recognized. While I was there I saw them piling the bodies one on top of the other, into the wagon, to be hauled to their graves or ditches. I passed through the hospital on my way back, and the sights I saw there were enough to make one sick: the tents were filled with what could once have been called men, but were now nothing but mere skeletons. The short time I was there I saw several die. A man is never admitted to the hospital until there is no hope of his recovery, and when once there it is seldom, if ever, he returns.*

By the end of the war, exactly 12,919 had died and another 329 had escaped. Largely through the work of a single prisoner, Union Pvt. Dorence Atwater of the 2nd New York Cavalry, only 460 of the graves are marked as "unknown." Atwater had been assigned by Wirz the responsibility of recording the names of all who died at the camp. Fearing the loss of this record in the Confederate archives, Atwater painstakingly handwrote another copy, which he kept in hopes of notifying the families of the deceased.

Prisoners were also stalked by some of their own number. A group of thugs known as the "Mosby Raiders" beat, robbed, terrorized, and even murdered their fellow prisoners quite openly for many months. Led by a particularly unpleasant character, Pvt. William "Mosby" Collins of Company D, 88th Pennsylvania Infantry, they were finally brought down by another group of prisoners. With Wirz's approval and cooperation, the Raiders were subjected to a trial by the prisoners themselves, and six of them were hung. Three others were later beaten to death by their former victims. The six who were hung were buried in a special part of the cemetery, away from any other prisoner's grave by their request.

After the fall of Atlanta in September 1864, many prisoners were quickly relocated to other camps, farther away from the action. Only the sickest 8,000 remained by the end of September, and all but about 1,300 of that number died by the end of November. The camp stayed open with a much-reduced number of prisoners, operating mainly for the sick and dying, until the end of the war. Some of the prisoners evacuated from Andersonville were sent to a newly built, and short-lived, camp near Millen, Georgia, then south to a swampy hellhole near Blackshear, as Sherman's troops rampaged across central Georgia. Others were sent to Savannah and Columbia, South Carolina.

Crouse and the surviving members of the 7th Pennsylvania were loaded up on boxcars, after a long wait in the open woods on the night of September 12, and sent via Macon and Charleston to Florence, South Carolina. Of all the Confederate prison camps, indeed of all prison camps of all wars of all times, Andersonville has the reputation of being at the bottom of the list. However, the new camp at Florence actually exceeded the wretched excesses of the Georgia camp, as Elliot noted:

> Monday 31 (September 1864). While at Andersonville I did not suppose the rebels had a worse prison in the South, but I have now found out that they have. This den is ten times worse than that at Andersonville. Our rations are smaller and of poorer quality, wood more scarce, lice plentier, shelters worn out, and cold weather coming on. I have stood my prison life wonderfully, but now I am commencing to feel it more sensibly,

*and am getting too weak to move about. To add to my misery I
have the scurvy in the gums.*

The war was already winding down by this time. Atlanta had fallen,
Grant was pressing Lee hard at Petersburg, and Sherman was preparing
to march on Savannah. Food rations dwindled to the non-existent point
at Florence, and after two more months of hard living, Confederate
authorities in Charleston finally arranged for a special parole and
exchange of the sick and wounded. Crouse, Elliot, and most of the dwindling band of 7th Pennsylvania survivors were picked to end their confinement:

*Wednesday 7 (December 1864). Cold, rainy, windy morning;
called out before day-light with the glorious news to fall into line
to be examined for parole. Can it be possible that the day of
deliverance has at last arrived? While our hundred were marching inside the dead line I trembled with fear lest I should not be
taken, but my fears were allayed when the surgeon pressed upon
my arm and told me to go. I cannot say how I felt when he told
me this; I trembled, not with fear, but joy. Eleven hundred and
eighty of us were marched outside the stockade, where we signed
the parole papers, and stood around small smoky fires until late
in the afternoon.*

*Sunday 11. Rained nearly all night; could not sleep on account
of the cold and lice. It seems as if for every one we burned two
came in its place. Still raining this morning. Fell into line at one
o'clock and were again marched to the rebel truce boat and
steamed into the harbor. Passed Fort Sumpter (now nothing but
a mass of ruins) and Moultrie, when we met our boats. It would
be impossible to describe the feelings of the men when our dear
old flag came into view; tears of joy filled many eyes, and cheer
after cheer rent the air. After we were marched on our boats we
each had a pound of boiled pork, nine hard tack and a quart of
coffee issued to us. It was an amusing sight to see us devour
these rations—any person would have thought we had not had a
bite of anything to eat for a week.*

AFTER THE WAR

Crouse's war was not yet over. Although the Andersonville and Florence prison camps ceased to exist by late April 1865, when the last of the dead had been buried and the dying relocated to proper hospitals, Northern politicians and civilians, enraged by lurid stories in the press, compounded by red-hot outrage over the assassination of President Lincoln, demanded a blood sacrifice. The imperfect sacrificial lamb selected was Henry Wirz. Too many half-fictional newspaper stories had been printed that too many well-sheltered Northerners had read and believed, and there were innumerable magazine articles and books written by former prisoners, most of them based on rumors and half-truths that had spread like wildfire through the overcrowded camp of terminally bored men.

Wirz had remained at Camp Sumter until his arrest on May 7, 1865, by Union Capt. H. E. Noyes, of Brig. Gen. James H. Wilson's staff. Wilson had just completed a lengthy raid through Alabama and Georgia and had divided his forces into smaller raiding parties, looking for Confederate President Jefferson Davis (then known to be on the run through Georgia and heading for Mexico), and other "persons of interest," as his orders straight from Washington read. Wirz was placed under guard and transported to Washington to await trial.

Davis was captured at Irwinville, Georgia, on May 10, 1865, and confined to Fortress Monroe, Virginia, as a war criminal. At first he, along with Lee, Confederate Vice-President Alexander Stephens, and most of Davis's cabinet and military high command, was accused of participating in the conspiracy to assassinate Lincoln. After no evidence linking anyone outside the known conspiracy group surfaced, Davis was charged as a co-conspirator to "impair and injure the health and to destroy the lives of large numbers of Federal prisoners at Andersonville," along with Wirz, both Winders, Lee, Howell Cobb, and a lengthy list of pretty much every ranking Confederate officer who had ever possibly heard of the place. From this group, Lee's name was soon removed, John Winder was already dead, and Howell Cobb received a presidential pardon from Andrew Johnson. Of the remaining men, only Wirz was ever tried on the charge. Davis was released without trial and all charges against him were dropped in May 1867, and the rest of the affair quietly forgotten, probably as prominent newspapers had turned their limited attention span to the alleged scandals and excesses of the Johnson administration.

Beginning on August 23, 1865, Wirz was placed on trial before a military tribunal, based on this initial charge, and an added thirteen counts of murder or deadly assault on prisoners, in violation of the Articles of War. Specifically, Wirz was accused of murdering helpless Union prisoners with his own hands, or ordering his guards to do it in his stead. Interestingly, not one of the thirteen allegedly murdered prisoners was mentioned by name in the indictment; they were all referred to as a "United States soldier whose name is not known." This anonymity occurred despite the work of Private Atwater, whose meticulously maintained log of the dead was ordered by none other than Wirz himself.

Wirz had as counsel five military lawyers, who put up a spirited effort at pre-trial motions. They raised the issue that Johnston's and Lee's surrenders put a blanket pardon on all Confederate soldiers, but the court ruled that this pardon "did not extend to war-criminals." They next argued that the military tribunal itself was not a proper venue, as Wirz was now a civilian who had never served in the U.S. military. However, the court ruled that the South was still "a rebellious, armed camp," and that combat might break out again at any second, making a military rule and tribunal necessary and proper. Finally, his defense team argued that the charges were unconstitutionally vague and lacking in the specifics required by the Sixth Amendment. The court denied the petition without comment. With this, three of Wirz's five lawyers quit the case, and the trial began.

William Crouse was one of 160 witnesses called to testify for the prosecution, most of whom were former prisoners in Camp Sumter. Like 145 other former soldiers, Crouse testified to his intense sufferings, there and later at Florence, but could only say that he "had heard about some rumors" that Wirz had personally shot prisoners. Of the entire group of witnesses, only two men could give compelling eyewitness testimony, and another ten gave "friend of a friend" hearsay testimony. One man testified that he alone, of approximately 30,000 prisoners in the camp that day, saw Wirz enter the gate, randomly select a prisoner, and fatally shoot him in the head, as one of the indictments claimed. The only problem was that the date given on the indictment was different than the date the former prisoner insisted on. The indictment was then (illegally) changed, so the transcript would be consistent.

The other eyewitness was one Felix de la Baume, a good-looking, well groomed man who testified that he witnessed Wirz personally shoot several prisoners, amazingly each one in exact accordance to the charge in several indictments. De la Baume was an amazing witness, truly gifted in his near-photographic memory of exact dates and times that Wirz had committed these foul deeds, and he added a laundry list of lurid details to each story that the newspaper reporters eagerly passed on to their readers. One witness at the trial stated, "His omnipresence while at Andersonville seemed something bordering on the supernatural. Nothing escaped him. Witness de la Baume held the surging crowd like an inspiration." He was remarkable, also, for his seemingly outstanding state of health after such an extended period of horrid imprisonment. Immediately after his testimony, de la Baume was given a commendation by the officers of the military tribunal itself, citing his "zealous testimony," which he immediately used to gain a position in the Department of the Interior.

Shortly after the trial, de la Baume was exposed as a deserter from the 7th New York Infantry. His real name was Felix Oeser. In short order Oeser was ousted from his government job, and he admitted he had perjured his entire testimony at the Wirz trial. Nothing, however, was changed about Wirz's situation.

One prosecution witness, who ultimately was not allowed to testify, was Union Lt. James Madison Page. Page had been held at Andersonville for seven months. He had been prepared to testify that the murder and assault charges against Wirz could not possibly be true, as he had heard not one word about any of them until the trial process began. He explained later, in his 1908 book, *The True Story of Andersonville Prison*, that the intense boredom and lack of anything to do but talk and gossip would have ensured that any such tales, true or not, would spread like wildfire through the camp. Since he had never heard any of the stories, the only possible logical conclusion was that they had simply not happened. After the prosecuting team interviewed him, he was released from the witness list.

Page was not allowed to testify for the defense, because, in a special rule for this trial alone, all defense witnesses had to be interviewed and approved beforehand by the prosecutors. The defense did manage to bring to the stand sixty-eight of its own witnesses, who consistently testified that Wirz was an irritable, cross, and frequently angry man, who was personally unpleasant, but who did try with all his might to bring relief to the men in his camp. They introduced documents showing Wirz had sent four men under a special parole to Washington, to plead with the Lincoln administration to restart the parole process; the court ruled that as irrelevant testimony. Wirz had released several hundred prisoners in late 1864, and sent them on their own to the Union authorities in Jacksonville, as he was completely unable to properly house them. The Jacksonville commandant had refused to let them in and forced them to return to Andersonville. The court ruled this, too, as irrelevant. The only documents actually accepted by the court, ironically, were Confederate records introduced by the prosecution as a part of the conspiracy charge, showing that Wirz had frequently begged and pleaded with the Confederate authorities for more supplies, food, and medical care for his camp. These, too, were ruled irrelevant to the defense's case.

In late October, both sides rested, and Wirz's remaining defense team asked for a brief recess to prepare their closing statement. When the court denied this routine motion, both remaining lawyers quit in disgust; it was abundantly clear to all that this was a show trial at best. Instead, on October 23, 1865, Col. N. P. Chipman, the lead prosecutor, gave both the prosecution's and the defense's closing statements. The next day the tribunal announced a guilty verdict. Wirz was sentenced to be hanged.

No appeal was permitted. Instead, the U.S. Army's Bureau of Military Justice "reviewed" the case, assigning the task to Brig. Gen. Joseph Holt, the Judge Advocate General who had been part of the team preparing the prosecution of Wirz. In confirming the sentence, Holt charged that Wirz was a "demon," whose sadistic treatment of Union prisoners gave him "savage orgies of enjoyment." Needless to say, Holt confirmed the utter and complete fairness of the trial and sentence.

On November 10, 1865, in Old Capital Prison, Wirz was brought before a howling mob of soldiers and civilians, all screaming, "Andersonville! Andersonville!" He ascended the stairs to the gallows, where he was read the charges and the sentence, and a noose was placed and tightened around his neck. When the trap was sprung, the hanging failed to break his neck, and Wirz was left to slowly strangle to death, while hearing the ringing derision of the jeering crowd.

7TH PENNSYLVANIA RESERVES

William Crouse shows up as a private on some of the earliest muster rolls for the 7th Pennsylvania Reserves, also known as the 36th Pennsylvania Volunteer Infantry Regiment. This regiment drew its members from the far western part of the state, and first encamped together in March 1861, originally for three months of service. Amazingly, they were not accepted for service, because the Army believed they had too many regiments already. However, at the request of the governor and the urging of their officers, they maintained their own barracks and uniforms at their own expense, and taught themselves drill and rifle maneuvers. In early June, they were finally accepted for state service, mustering in on June 26, and re-equipped with proper military uniforms and equipment. Following the Union's defeat at Manassas (Bull Run), they were called up for Federal service around Washington. On August 2, they were assigned to Brig. Gen. George G. Meade's 2nd Brigade, Army of the Potomac.

Although the 7th was assigned to a central line corps during McClellan's unsuccessful Peninsular Campaign, they were initially kept far from any action, first inside one of Washington's defense fortifications, then later marching from camp to camp, all without hearing a single shot fired. Their first action occurred during the Seven Days Battle, on June 26, 1862, at Beaver Dam Creek, where half their number was deployed as skirmishers, and the other half anchored the left side of the line. The next day, at Gaines Mill, they were, literally, in the very center of the action. On June 30, they were on the right of the line, astride the Richmond Road, and while routed in the effort, they helped fight off a savage, two-corps Confederate attack, which broke the lines at several points and even managed to capture their divisional commander, Brig. Gen. George Archibald McCall. Badly beaten up in a several-hour hand-to-hand fight protecting the Union supply trains near Willis Church Road, the 7th sat out the final battle of the Seven Days, at Malvern Hill, on July 1. It marched with the rest of McClellan's defeated army back to Harrison's Landing, where they were redeployed as pickets. The short campaign had cost the 7th an amazing 301 casualties; they had less than 200 men still standing and fit to fight.

Less than two months later, with the Army of the Potomac reconstituted under its new commanding officer, Maj. Gen. John Pope, the 7th marched out on the Northern Virginia Campaign, seeing heavy action at 2nd Manassas and Upton's Hill. Pope faired no better than his predecessor in reaching Richmond or defeating Lee in open battle, and soon retired back to Washington.

Pope's men had little time to rest. Lee was seizing the opportunity to raid the North, intending to roam through Pennsylvania while whittling to size every Union army sent his way. With no other general officer available that had even close to what was needed to take on the task, Lincoln reluctantly fired Pope and replaced McClellan as commander of all the Eastern Theater forces. As previously discussed, McClellan got an incredible break when he was handed a copy of Lee's deployment order, found wrapped around a bundle of cigars in an old campsite by one of his sergeants. Knowing where and when he needed to strike the seemingly invincible Lee gave even a battlefield-incompetent like McClellan an almost certain route to victory. Lee was concentrating his forces around Sharpsburg, Maryland, west of the South Mountain range, and McClellan ordered his three armies to move rapidly to strike him there.

Moving in the northernmost column, the 7th's first engagement was on September 14 at Crampton's Gap, atop the steep eastern slope of South Mountain. There, along with two other Pennsylvania reserve regiments, they pushed a single Alabama unit (26th "O'Neal's" Infantry) off the mountain, with heavy casualties (including the author's great-grandfather). Colonel Bolinger was seriously injured in the fight, but remained in the line. The next day, they followed hard on the heels of the retreating Confederates, through Boonesboro and Keedysville, where they moved over to the right of the Union line at Antietam Creek.

At dawn on September 16, the 7th charged through the cornfield at Sharpsburg, in the midst of a thunderous artillery duel, and encountered heavy Confederate resistance. They fell back, only to repeat the charge and retreat several times throughout the morning. Ordered forward one last time, the 7th and supporting regiments managed to advance to the Confederate line of battle, at the rail fence on the other side of the cornfield, primarily with the help of single and double loads of canister from supporting artillery. Soon, however, they found the position untenable. Their shattered ranks fell back, escaping annihilation solely due to the murderous fire of Union artillery batteries.

Badly beaten up yet again, the 7th was pulled completely off the Antietam line of battle. They were briefly reassigned as gravediggers, and rested a bit more before rejoining the Army. McClellan, who never missed an opportunity to miss an opportunity, decided not to pursue Lee's army, retreating back into Virginia instead, and taking the Army of the Potomac back to Washington for a parade and grand review—presumably in celebration of his resounding victory at Sharpsburg. Lincoln sacked him, again, shortly afterward.

On November 14, newly installed Army of the Potomac commander Maj. Gen. Ambrose Burnside sent one of his corps to the high ground across the Rappahannock River from Fredericksburg, threatening the entire Falmouth area. Lee, alerted that Burnside intended to move the rest of his army forward to seize the city, moved his entire Army of Northern Virginia to a high ridgeline commanding the other side of the city, and dug in securely behind a well-constructed stone wall. The 7th was placed on the right of the line again, charging through the woods and surprising part of Longstreet's Corps, who promptly retreated to their pre-arranged fighting positions atop Maury's Heights. The 7th managed to grab about one hundred prisoners, and more significantly, they captured the battle flag of the 19th Georgia. This ended up being the single battle trophy obtained during the terrible Union defeat. The 7th limped back across the Rappahannock three days later, with one hundred casualties missing from its ranks.

The 7th had been much reduced by hard fighting through the summer and fall, and were reassigned to a garrison command in the Washington fortifications, where they remained for nearly a year, slowly rebuilding their shattered ranks. In late April 1864, they, along with the other Pennsylvania Reserves regiments, were brought back into the line for the Wilderness Campaign, and attached to the 1st Brigade of the 5th Corps.

When mustered in at Philadelphia a short three years earlier, Company G of the 7th Pennsylvania Reserves boasted 103 officers and men. In its final battle, every last surviving man, a total of thirty, was captured. Eight long months later, William Crouse and twenty other gaunt, starving Company G survivors walked onto a Union receiving ship in Charleston Harbor. They left behind the graves of nine of their friends and what remained of the flower of their own youth.

7

WEEKEND WARRIORS: THE MILITIA

Capt. William Jasper Worley, Company D, "Blue Ridge Rangers," 1st Regiment, Georgia State Line

L ATE IN THE AFTERNOON OF JULY 22, 1864, LYING IN THE SCRUB BRUSH woods east of Atlanta and enduring blistering heat and hours of pounding artillery fire from a four-gun Union battery, the men of the Blue Ridge Rangers, Company D of the Georgia State Line's 1st Regiment, heard the sounds of battle increasing around them. A courier suddenly came crashing through the brush, and hastily relayed orders to their recently appointed captain, William Jasper Worley. With cannon fire bursting around him, Worley ordered his men up and headed southeast along with the rest of Confederate Col. Abda Johnson's (Stovall's) Brigade, across the Georgia Railroad tracks, then eastward, directly into battle. Calling for his men to follow him and raising a hair-raising yell, Worley burst out of the tree line and headed straight into the storm of Yankee shell and shot.

Following right on his heels, Worley's fast-moving Rangers slammed into the entrenched remnants of Union Brig. Gen. Joseph Lightburn's Division. Worley's color sergeant was killed as he exited the tree line, the colors dropping from his hand before being quickly snatched up by the following corporal. As the Rangers gained the Union emplacements, this color-bearer, too, fell from a mortal wound. Worley stopped, reached down, snatched the colors from the ground, and personally charged with them to the top of the Union breastworks, where he planted them for all to see. After a few minutes of heavy hand-to-hand fighting, the Union troops broke and ran north, away from the Georgia men, while Worley led his men into the abandoned Union trench lines just south of the railroad. He quickly realized that he had charged far ahead of the general

Confederate line, and that he and his men now stood alone amid the center of the whole Union line. As Worley hastily organized his men into a defensive position for the expected counter-attack, twenty-four guns of combined Union artillery, personally directed by Sherman himself, began a heavy and accurate barrage. Minutes later, just as a supporting brigade led by Confederate Col. Bushrod Jones finally arrived and began digging in to their left, the reorganized Union infantry charged in.

Worley's Rangers, assailed by increasingly accurate cannon fire and facing assault by three Union infantry brigades moving into position to their east, held fast to their entrenched line and even sent word back that they could hold indefinitely if further reinforced. Instead, the regiments and brigades to either side of them began to break under the Union assault and were quickly ordered to retreat. The Rangers held on for another forty minutes of galling fire from two sides, ignoring orders to retreat, before Worley reluctantly ordered them out and back to their original positions. Behind, they left two of their number dead and carried away four others who had been seriously wounded.

Captain Worley commanded a company that had marched out of Dahlonega with 103 officers and men just eighteen months before, and had enlisted a total of 139 volunteers while on "safe" railroad guarding duties in various parts of the state. But now, after only a month of nearly continuous combat, his unit had been reduced to less than fifty effective combatants. Even this casualty rate was not enough to keep the hardy mountaineers out of the fight, as they would later prove at Griswoldville and Savannah. For all this sacrifice and courage in the trenches, the surprising fact is that Worley commanded a unit that was "only" an ill-trained and ill-equipped variation of a state militia, saddled with the sardonic epithet of "Joe Brown's Pets."

William Worley was born in the small mountain town of Dahlonega, Georgia, on May 29, 1837, the son of the first justice of the peace and later sheriff of the rough mining community, James H. Worley, who had commanded a company of infantry during the Florida Seminole War. Unusual for the day and the area, William Worley had received an "academic" education, as opposed to an industrial or agricultural one, before turning to farming shortly before the outbreak of war.

There is very little known about Worley before the war, but judging from his postwar reputation, and the fact that he did not volunteer to join the first companies raised in Dahlonega, it is safe to assume that he did not relish the idea of going off to war. Worley was among the first volunteers, however, later in the war, for Georgia Governor Joseph Brown's third attempt at creating his own, personal state military force, the Georgia State Line. While not exactly meeting the classic definition of a militia and understood description of a local part-time military unit, the State Line was one of the countless irregular and militia forces formed for home defense both before and during the war.

Civil War militias are not exactly replicated by anything in today's society, and they took on different forms as the war progressed. Prewar militias were in fact the real fighting force of the nation (the "well-regulated militias" referenced in the Second Amendment to the U.S. Constitution); the "regular" U.S. Army was merely a small corps of officers and cadre, organized and maintained primarily to coordinate the use of these local units. Initially raised in the very earliest days of the colonies to protect against Indian attacks and to provide some semblance of an armed community policing force, militias first saw battlefield military action as a distinctly American fighting force in the early days of the Revolution (the oft-mentioned "Minute Men"). After Independence and the War of 1812, most local militias gradually fell apart from misuse or outright apathy, especially in the Northern states.

A violent slave uprising in 1831, led by an enslaved preacher named Nat Turner, resulted in the deaths of fifty-seven whites and the immediate rebirth of the militia system in the South. Turner and all of his sixty to seventy followers were later executed, as were an unknown number of innocent slaves (sources claim anywhere from thirty to over 1,000). In addition to Nat Turner's Rebellion, at least fifty other slave insurrections of lesser success occurred in the subsequent decade. The fear spread in the white population by these rebellions, fanned into a near-panic by the press, led the newly revised militias to dedicate themselves to a serious study of the military arts, most especially those theories espoused by various Napoleonic and anti-Napoleonic generals and scholars.

Among these, as previously discussed, the theories of Baron Antoine-Henri de Jomini, a former general in Napoleon's army, proved to have the largest impact and the greatest effect on the American wars of the nineteenth century. Jomini maintained two significant points: first, that an army represented the might and prestige of the state itself and needed to therefore uniform and comport themselves as such; and secondly, that war was a "grand stage for heroes," where men of honor were to fight righteously and upright on the battlefield, facing their opponents standing up and looking them in the eyes.

By the late 1850s, slave revolts had been largely eliminated, and many of the militias had evolved into fancy marching and drilling companies, manned by social elites, who adopted grand uniforms in the spirit of Jomini's theories. Spurred on by tours of European elite fighting units, who displayed magnificent command of precise marching and bayonet drills, many American militias adopted similar gaudy uniforms—most notably, the wildly dressed Zouave units found in both Northern and Southern militias. With the outbreak of war in 1861, these local militias were largely absorbed into the growing national armies, and eventually lost both their distinctive uniforms and their socially prominent membership.

The small mountain town of Dahlonega, in northeastern Georgia, is perhaps best known for its central role in the first major gold rush, thirty-three years before the war. Despite the area's widespread Unionist bent, and even stronger isolationist character, this small community put nine companies with well over 500 soldiers in the war on the Confederate side, including its prewar militias. As a fitting tribute to the area's obtrusiveness, a bit later in the war, another unit formed in the surrounding hills, the 1st Georgia State Troops (Volunteer), a Union guerilla force made up partly of men who had deserted these nine companies. Worley was a native of these rough parts, and his father and grandfather had both settled in and tried to bring some semblance of law and order to the newly opened mountain territories.

After nearly two years of war, and with the first Dahlonega volunteer troops already returning home, some for just a brief rest before joining new units, the call went out for men to join yet another local infantry company, the Blue Ridge Rangers of the new Georgia State Line. Neither a regular army force nor a true militia, nor the typical late-war rabble of untrained "old men and boys," the Georgia State Line (or GSL) was a unique private "state army," formed by the governor and totally at his disposal. In theory it was formed strictly for defense within the state borders. Brown, an ardent states' rights advocate, refused to submit to what he termed a "tyranny of Richmond," although faced with a serious quandary about the military defense of Georgia. Obviously, a purely state army would have no chance against the combined forces of the Union, yet Brown believed that to submit all able-bodied combat troops to the service of the Confederate government would undermine his grounds for secession from the Union itself.

Early in the war, Brown tried on two separate occasions to create his model of a "state army." The first time, he raised and equipped a brigade that was shortly thereafter offered voluntarily for Confederate service. The second time, a three-brigade "1st Division, Georgia Volunteers" was broken up immediately after their six-month enlistment by the Confederate Conscription Act. Neither unit was involved in combat, but both gave Brown the opportunity to appoint many influential officer posts, which may have been part of his political aim all along. A consummate politician, many of Brown's speeches and acts during the war seemed to be aimed not at winning the war but at collecting votes.

On April 12, 1862, a group of northern guerillas led by James J. Andrews stole a train in Big Shanty, just north of Atlanta, and sped northward, planning on destroying the tracks and infrastructure of the Western and Atlantic Railroad as they went along. Chased down and caught in what became known as the "Great Locomotive Chase," the raiders failed to do any actual damage to this vital link, but the incident badly shook Governor Brown. Fascinated by railroads and their profit potential, he had been dependent on this specific rail link for trade and transport in his early political days. As governor, the Western and Atlantic had been his pet project as a source of patronage and pride since it began turning a profit during his first term. Politics aside, the raid pointed out the vulnerability of this essential military supply and transport link. Combining the need to protect this link with his desire for a state military force, Brown conceived and raised a company called the "Railroad Bridge Guard," intended and destined to become the nucleus of a grander state force.

Brown placed command of the Bridge Guard on one of his hometown political connections, Capt. Edward Machen Galt, and placed his own brother, John M. Brown, as unit Quartermaster. One hundred and fifty men filled the ranks, and a second company of equal strength was soon raised. No uniforms were issued, and, as very few state weapons were available, the state gave a $50 annual compensation for the men to provide their own. For just under a year, until February 1863, these two companies guarded over 100 miles of railroad and bridges, from near Chattanooga to just above Atlanta. The men saw no recorded combat along their posts. The only action seen as a unit was during a short-lived raid into the Dahlonega area in early 1863, ostensibly to confront a reported Union force heading that way, but the men ended up searching for deserters and rounding up "Tories."

Governor Brown kept the pressure on to expand these Bridge Guard companies into his vision of a 10,000-man "state army." After intense political wrangling during the fall of 1862, the Georgia Legislature, who did not share Governors Brown's isolationist views, reluctantly gave him permission to raise two regiments of state troops, limited to no more than 2,000 men, "for protection of her people against invading forces of the enemy, and for internal police duty." Recruitment began almost immediately, and one company was manned to near full strength within one week. Seventeen other companies were raised in a little over one month. In a letter, Brown remarked that surprisingly many had been turned away. "I could have formed five regiments almost as easily as two," he wrote. Obviously the lure of seemingly easy duty meant available manpower would be the least of his problems.

In the custom of the day, elections were held on February 20 to choose officers. Colonel Galt of the old Bridge Guard was chosen as 1st Regiment commander, and Richard Storey, a farmer from Wilkinson County, was elected 2nd Regiment commander. Two of the governor's own brothers were appointed to posts in the 1st Regiment: Maj. John M. Brown again, this time as Commissary, and Maj. Aaron P. Brown as Surgeon.

Special attention was given to the troublesome northern mountain counties, where three companies were specified by General Order to be raised. In Dahlonega, even with over 300 local men already in the field, little time was required to fill the ranks. Early in January 1863, officers were elected by ballot, and the troop formally mustered in on January 24 as Company D, 1st Regiment, the "Blue Ridge Rangers," Georgia State Line, with 105 men officially enrolled and eighty-nine showing up for the muster ceremony. Initially commanded by Capt. Robert A. Graham of Auraria, and with William Worley showing up as a "Private" on the very first muster roll (he joined a few days after the death of his eldest son, Thomas Jefferson Worley), the troop immediately set out combing the northern Georgia mountains for deserters and Union loyalists.

The Rangers were anything but an archetypical, hodge-podge militia. Every single man had formal military training in the regularly established prewar state militia, and fifteen had been militia officers. Two of the enlisted men were Mexican War veterans. While most were small-lot farmers, two owned gold mines, one was an inferior court judge, one was a lawyer, and one was a county official. Worley listed his occupation as "Artist," and stated that he was married to one Georgia Victoria Goodrum Worley, but with no children or slaves to claim. All told, the 105 men owned twenty-six slaves among them, but not one man owned more than five. The physical fighting ability of these men was never checked, no formal medical screening took place, and at least one man died before he could even report for duty. Two more died, of pre-existing conditions, within three months.

Although they were not immediately sent into battle, the Rangers' early service was anything but happy. Typical of wartime militias, or other irregular units, the Rangers received a hodge-podge of smoothbore muskets, and initially only seventy-five were made available for the 105 men and officers. Within a few months, the situation was rectified, and the Rangers alone of the entire GSL were issued the most desired of Confederate rifles, .58 caliber, English-made Enfields. Also typical of militias, no uniforms or shoes of any sort were issued, and the men were expected to make do with what they had, or what they could get the home folks to send. Food and clean water were constant problems, as Confederate commissaries were reluctant to supply the "foreign" fighting force, and Brown was more concerned with lofty concepts of sovereign state government than the boring details of army life.

The first duty assignment outside the Rangers' home territory was in Savannah, as part of the general buildup to guard against an expected Union invasion. Three months later, without seeing any action, they were ordered back to north Georgia to guard the Western and Atlantic Railroad bridges at the Etowah River near Cartersville. They remained on the rail line in relative comfort without seeing action for nearly a year, until Sherman's invasion in May 1864. While there, Worley was elected to take over as captain, after Graham was forced to resign due to illness. At the time, manpower was critically short in General Johnston's Army of Tennessee, and it was not long before the Rangers were ordered into the fight.

With Johnston's army falling back rapidly before the Union assault, it took little time to lose Confederate control of the area surrounding the State Line posts at Cartersville. By this time the 1st Regiment, GSL, was down to only 550 men; disease, desertions, and other commands had stripped the ranks. Hastily called up, the Rangers marched for three days before arriving in line of battle on May 29, 1864. They were assigned with the rest of the 1st Regiment, GSL, as part of Brig. Gen. Marcellus A. Stovall's Georgia Brigade (Stewart's Division, Hood's Corps), in the midst of the ongoing fight in the rough, tangled woods and scrub near New Hope Church and Pickett's Mill, part of the Dallas Line campaign. This battle had started the day the Rangers moved out to the line, as Sherman tried to force through what he thought was (ironically) only some "local militia," and attack Marietta from the west. Instead, he ran into the bulk of Johnston's Army of Tennessee, which was well entrenched, with plenty of well-placed artillery, and well aware of Sherman's intentions. The resulting combat was so devastating to Sherman's commands that he later "forgot" to mention the week-long fight in both his official dispatches and his memoirs.

Worley's Rangers started their combat service with fifty-eight of the original 103 available for duty. Assigned as pickets with other State Line companies off one wing of the brigade, they engaged in active combat for the first time on June 2, suffering three wounded, one of whom later died of his wounds. Alternating as pickets, skirmishers, and reserves, the Rangers moved out two days later with the rest of Johnston's army to Lost Mountain and Big Shanty, before deploying near Kennesaw Mountain on June 18. Despite officially being in reserve status, the Rangers and other companies of the GSL came under heavy fire for several hours during the move.

That afternoon, Worley was sitting on a log, waiting for the order to bring his men into the line of battle, when a Union artillery shell struck directly behind him, passed under the log, and burst in front of him blowing up a great mound of dirt and trees and flinging Worley several yards back. He was quickly recovered by his men and was standing up again when Major Brown rushed up and asked, "Captain, are you hurt?" Worley replied, "No, I think not," to which Brown exclaimed, "Thank the Lord! Here, sit down on this log." "No thank you," Worley replied pleasantly, "I prefer standing. I was sitting on that log when that ugly shell came hunting for me!"

The Union fire on the reserve lines that afternoon continued to be accurate and hot. Sixteen more State Line troopers were wounded, including Major Brown.

Johnston expected Sherman to send his forces flanking the south of Kennesaw Mountain in an attempt to seize Marietta and sent Hood's Corps out to block them. Meeting at Kolb's Farm on June 22, Hood rashly charged the entrenched Federal line with two divisions, achieving almost nothing at the cost of 1,085 casualties, including eighty GSL men of the 2nd Regiment. Held in reserve during the initial combat, Worley's Rangers were ordered up afterward to help hold the line until all forces could be withdrawn back to what had become known as the "Kennesaw Line." Five days after Kolb's Farm, the Rangers were on the far left of the line of battle when Sherman's combined forces stormed Kennesaw Mountain, skirmishing but missing once again the brunt of fighting.

Less than a week after the Union defeat at Kennesaw Mountain, the Rangers had their first major fight directly on their hands, at a heavily entrenched post above the Chattahoochee River, called Nickajack Creek. On July 2, after realizing he could not extend his lines far enough to prevent Sherman from flanking his position, Johnston began withdrawing from his mountaintop stronghold. Failing to hold the line during a running battle at nearby Smyrna, Johnston was desperate to get his forces intact across the Chattahoochee, into the northern fringes of Atlanta, and escape the overpowering Union frontal assault. Governor Brown offered the services of the just-reformed, 3,000-man-strong Georgia Militia under Maj. Gen. Gustavus Woodson Smith, who, along with an "appropriated" four-gun battery of 12-pounder Napoleon cannons, proceeded to stage a delaying action on a small hilltop along Turner's Ferry Road, 3 miles north of the river.

These militiamen only managed to delay the Union advance a few hours, and they were quickly withdrawn to man an interlocking series of hastily but exceptionally well-constructed trench lines just south of Smyrna, near the north bank of the Chattahoochee, along a steep ridge-line above Nickajack Creek. This near suicidal and expendable position again directly confronted the full corps strength vanguard of Sherman's army, but this time the line of battle lacked any clear and protected lines of retreat. With the Federal forces bearing down, Worley and his Rangers were sent in with the rest of the 1st Regiment to reinforce the line on July 4. Relieving the Militia at the forward primary fighting positions, the Rangers had barely gotten into place before forward elements of Union Maj. Gen. John M. Palmer's XIV Army Corps began their assault.

Palmer soon reported fierce resistance in this line, but Sherman accurately believed that it represented a token rear-guard action while Johnston retreated his main force across the river. Believing the line could be easily brushed aside, he ordered Palmer to "fiercely assault" the line with everything he had, nearly 20,000 men at that point. The total combat-effective manpower available to the State Line by this time was about 300 men, with the 3,000 mostly ill-equipped and barely tested Georgia Militia serving as emergency reserves, and their "appropriated" four-gun battery of artillery as the only heavy fire support. Palmer's men assaulted and skirmished with the State Line all through July 5 without result, until Sherman personally came up to reconnoiter. Upon seeing the strength of the State Line's redoubts, he called off the attack, stating later that it represented "the best line of field entrenchments I have ever seen." Impressed with the fighting resistance of the State Line, and worried that to continue the frontal attack would result in another disaster like Kennesaw Mountain despite his overwhelmingly superior numbers, Sherman instead sent part of his army far to the left, to locate a place to cross the wide river at some unguarded site.

The Rangers stayed in their trenches on the steep ridge until the afternoon of July 9, then gradually pulled back toward Atlanta, skirmishing with Union scouts and pickets, until digging in near Peachtree Creek on July 18. Although not directly involved in the major battle there two days later, the Rangers skirmished with the rest of the 1st Regiment in the thick woods to the battle line's right. Colonel Galt was seriously wounded in the exchange, leaving the previously wounded Lt. Col. John Brown to take over. That same night, the Rangers marched with the remnants of Hood's army rapidly through the center and around the southern part of Atlanta—inadvertently panicking the citizens, who thought the army was deserting their city—before taking up positions on either side of the railroad line to Decatur by the morning of July 22.

After the previously described Battle of Atlanta, the Rangers pulled back to within the strong wall of fortifications surrounding the besieged city. Newly appointed 1st Regiment commander John Brown, never fully recovered from his wounds at Kennesaw Mountain, was wounded again, this time in the thigh, a mortal injury. Capt. Albert Howell, the highest ranking remaining officer in the 1st Regiment, took over command in the midst of battle. Brown was transported quickly to join his brother at the Governor's Mansion in Milledgeville, where he died on July 25.

On July 27, Worley and his Rangers moved around the western side of Atlanta and once again entered combat. Sherman had grown more and more frustrated with his inability to pound or starve Hood's troops out of the city and ordered yet another attack on the remaining railroad tracks to try and force the Confederates out in the open, where they could be destroyed once and for all. On August 4, Schofield's XXIII and

Palmer's XIV Army Corps swung around to the southwest and after many delays, headed toward the two remaining railroad tracks near East Point.

Hood got word of the slow Union movement on August 5, and ordered a new line of emplacements built along Utoy Creek at the Sandtown Road (now called Cascade Road). These were soon manned by Bate's Division of Hardee's Corps and reinforced by a two-gun artillery battery, the Georgia State Line, a brigade of the Georgia Militia and CSA Brig. Gen. Lawrence S. Ross's Texas Cavalry Brigade. At dawn on August 6, USA Brig. Gen. Jacob D. Cox's 3rd Division (Schofield's XXIII Army Corps) advanced with a 2,500-man front against the now heavily entrenched Confederate left. This attack came within thirty yards of the Confederate line before being broken up with severe losses and thrown back. Several other multi-brigade assaults were attempted with the same result, and in the end, there were nearly 600 casualties. Total Confederate losses for the day also totaled about 200, included those captured in their forward skirmish positions in the early part of the battle. Sherman tersely described the action later as "a noisy but not bloody battle."

The two regiments of the State Line stayed in reserve during the Utoy Creek battle, but immediately after, they went into the main battle area as pickets and skirmishers, as the rest of Hood's army invested the Atlanta trench lines. Sixty-one State Line troopers were killed or wounded in this brief duty, while the Rangers spent the entire month of August continuously scouting and skirmishing with the Union troops in the western Atlanta defense lines, suffering four casualties as a result.

Frustrated with his inability to cut the rail lines, Sherman pondered his next move. A direct assault on the Atlanta fortifications was completely out of the question. Two, and in some places three, interlocking rings of artillery batteries and infantry parapets surrounded the city a little over a mile out from its center. It was reinforced by as many as four rows of abatis and long lines of chevaux-de-frise (both were types of wooden stakes used like barbed-wire fences of today), and manned with the tired, hungry, and undersupplied, but highly experienced, Confederate Army of Tennessee. Planned and constructed by Georgia's chief military engineer, CSA Capt. Lemuel P. Grant, and using slave labor from nearby plantations, the fortress city was "too strong to assault and too extensive to invest," according to Sherman's own Chief of Engineers, Capt. Orlando M. Poe. Sherman decided instead to bombard the city into submission.

On August 1, Sherman ordered Schofield's artillery to increase their rate of fire, and after the disaster at Utoy Creek, he sent for large artillery guns and plenty of ammunition. Two 30-pounder Parrott rifles were brought in from Chattanooga, and eight huge 4.5-inch siege guns were brought in and mounted by August 8. On August 9, Sherman ordered every battery within range to open fire, "and make the inside of Atlanta too hot to be endured." That day alone, over 5,000 shells slammed into the city's heart.

Along with the rest of the 1st and 2nd Regiments of the State Line, Worley's Rangers endured weeks of heavy shelling from rapidly increasing numbers of Union artillery pieces. Pvt. A. J. Jackson, of Company G of the 2nd GSL Regiment, later recalled the experience:

> I have watched the burning fuses of shells as they passed over our heads for many nights, and while we were doing picket duty between our lines and the enemy, the shot and shell were continually passing over our heads, crashing into houses and mowing down trees and playing havoc with everything they came in contact with.

Sherman kept up the intense bombardment for over two weeks, gradually wearing away the strength and endurance of the hollow-eyed soldiers within the city fortifications. Then, suddenly, on August 25 all the guns fell silent. The ragged Confederates in the Atlanta lines hoped for a moment that Sherman had given up and was withdrawing, but hopes were dashed when word came of yet another Union flanking attempt. Thomas's entire Army of the Cumberland and Howard's Army of the Tennessee had moved around the right of Atlanta, and were sweeping down again on the Atlanta and West Point Railroad, 9 miles southwest of East Point. Hood could not hope to muster any force to stop them, but pulled nearly his entire army out of Atlanta to try and protect the last remaining railway, leaving Stewart's Corps and Smith's Georgia Militia alone to hold the city lines. The remains of both State Line regiments moved out to Jonesboro along with Hood's army.

After dark on August 30, realizing that Sherman intended to strike at Jonesboro and cut the railway, Hood ordered Hardee's and Lee's Corps to move hastily to defend the small town. Encountering Union pickets about 3:00 A.M. and not wanting to risk a night battle, the two Confederate corps moved slightly to the east, not arriving in line at

Jonesboro until just after noon on the August 31. Hood was almost frantic to defend his railroad, sending Hardee message after message to attack "as soon as you can get your troops up."

At 3:00 on the afternoon of August 31, the order came: fix bayonets, up and at 'em, and drive the Yankees from their trenches. Attached to Stovall's Georgia Brigade (Lee's Corps), Worley and his Rangers prepared for a desperate battle, joining the line near the center, in the second wave of infantry. The two-corps-wide Confederate assault, advancing through open fields and concentrated artillery canister fire towards the well-fortified Union-positions, never made it closer than sixty yards away at any point along the line before withdrawing. Losses were staggeringly one-sided: at least 1,700 Confederate casualties versus a mere 179 Union. By incredible fortune, the Rangers only suffered a single casualty during the vicious brawl: Pvt. William Wade was wounded in the shoulder.

At the same time, Schofield's Army of the Ohio, reinforced by Maj. Gen. David S. Stanley's IV Army Corps, moved around the southern Atlanta defenses and struck the Macon and Western Railroad near Rough and Ready, which is now called Mountain View. Quickly overwhelming the small, dismounted Confederate cavalry unit stationed there, the Union troops quickly ripped up the tracks and moved north toward East Point.

At 6:00 that evening, the battle for Jonesboro winding to a close, Hood ordered Lee's Corps back north to help defend Atlanta against the new attack, leaving Hardee's battered corps to retreat alone back inside the Jonesboro city limits, where they would face three full Union corps regrouping for the final kill. At midnight, Hardee sent a message by courier to Hood (the telegraph wire had been cut about 2:00 P.M.), advising that the attack had failed and that Atlanta should be abandoned. Through the rest of the long, hot night, Hardee's forces shifted around to cover the gaps left by Lee's departure, and dug in as best they could. All knew their real job was to hold the main Union armies at bay long enough for Hood to get the rest of his army out of Atlanta.

The last Union attack began at 4:00 P.M. on September 1, led by two brigades of Brig. Gen. William P. Carlin's 1st Division (Brvt. Maj. Gen. Jefferson C. Davis' XIV Army Corps) and quickly followed by brigade after brigade, division after division, until all three Union corps were engaged in the assault. Amazingly, although one side of his line caved in, and 865 soldiers and two full batteries of artillery were captured, Hardee's single decimated corps managed to hold the main line of battle until the

Union attacks ended after nightfall. About midnight, he withdrew his three remaining divisions south to Lovejoy's Station, leaving behind about 1,400 dead and wounded. The Union force fared little better, losing a total of 1,272, but at last taking and cutting the last railway they had sought for so long.

The State Line regiments suffered heavily in the desperate fighting for Jonesboro. Howell's 1st Regiment, attached to Stovall's Georgia Brigade, suffered sixteen killed in action, while Wilson's 2nd Regiment was for all practical purposes destroyed. Out of the approximately 200 men Wilson had led into battle, 105 were killed or wounded, and a number of others were captured or ran away, all in the space of just four hours.

On the morning of September 1, having received Hardee's dreadful message about the first day of battle at Jonesboro, Hood at long last ordered the evacuation of the doomed city. With the railway cut, it would be impossible to take much in the way of supplies with them, so warehouses were ordered opened up for the civilians. With the last Union attack underway south at Jonesboro, Stewart's Corps and Smith's Militia began marching out around 5:00 P.M., with Maj. Gen. Samuel Gibb French's (Polk's) Corps providing rear guard divisional pickets, and the bare remnants of the State Line, the last combat troops in Atlanta, withdrawing about 11:00 P.M. Sappers (specialists who constructed fortifications) and other combat engineers hastily prepared the abandoned military supplies for destruction. Around midnight a thunderous roar announced the end of a large ammunition train Hood had been unable to withdraw. Sherman heard the blast 15 miles away in his headquarters at Jonesboro and knew he had the city. Hood continued his retreat well south of Jonesboro, finally turning and building defenses for an expected fight near Lovejoy Station.

Rather than face the small but combat-hardened veterans of Hood's army at their new defense lines near Lovejoy Station, Sherman elected to simply march his army into the city himself and take over the strong belt of fortification. Hood, faced with the prospect of bleeding his army dry against the very fortifications they had built, decided instead to take his army north, cut the Union supply line, and try to starve Sherman out. The Rangers and the rest of the State Line initially tagged along, following Hood north as he tagged and sparred with various Union outposts along the Western & Atlantic Railroad line. Finally, as Hood prepared to leave Georgia, intending to capture Nashville and then "march on

Cleveland," the State Line troopers turned back, heading south to regroup for the inevitable fight with Sherman in southern Georgia.

As Sherman evacuated Atlanta of its civilian population, and prepared it for destruction, Worley and his Rangers moved with the rest of the State Line west to Anniston, Alabama, then took a long, circuitous route south into Macon. There, they rested and refitted for the first time since entering combat nearly five months before.

On November 16, after thinning his army down to a hard core, and thoroughly destroying the heart of Atlanta, Sherman mounted his horse, Sam, and slowly led his men out of the ruined city, bound for Savannah and the Atlantic Ocean. The 60,598 Union soldiers were deployed in two huge columns, sometimes called "wings."

On the morning of November 15, even before the incineration of Atlanta had begun, USA Brig. Gen. Alpheus Williams's XX Corps headed off to the due east toward Augusta, and USA Gen. Peter Osterhaus's XV Corps joined with USA Gen. Frank Blair's XVII Corps to form the right column, under overall command of Maj. Gen. Oliver O. Howard, and moved south toward Macon. Early on the morning of November 16, accompanied by Sherman himself, USA Maj. Gen. Jefferson C. Davis's XIV Corps moved out behind Williams's Corps. The two-pronged attack was designed to fool Confederate defenders into thinking that Augusta and Macon were the targets of the separate wings, and force them to divide their already inadequate forces, whereupon the two columns would then swing south and east and converge on the Georgia capital of Milledgeville.

Opposing the Union juggernaut was a pitiful handful of mostly irregular troops: CSA Maj. Gen. Gustavus W. Smith's Combined Georgia Militia; the battered remnants of the State Line, who were freshly arrived after leaving the march north with Hood's army; a few "home guard" and hastily organized local militia groups; and the remnants of CSA Maj. Gen. Joseph Wheeler's Cavalry Corps. All told, less than 8,000 men were available to try and stop Sherman. Most of them had never fired a rifle in combat before.

Both columns moved separately out of Atlanta, proceeding initially east and south, with almost no opposition. Following Sherman's orders to the letter and spirit, nearly everything of any value was confiscated or burned, and assigned work gangs destroyed most of the railroad tracks. The rails were lifted and the crossties were pulled out from under them, piled high, and set afire. Next, the rails were held over the burning ties until they were glowing red hot, and they were then twisted and bent into unusable pretzel shapes called "Sherman's bow-ties."

Almost without opposition, the two huge columns moved through central Georgia, their flankers, skirmishers, and foraging parties creating a nearly 60-mile-wide path of destruction as they went. Slocum's left wing moved like a blue buzz saw through Stone Mountain, Lithonia, Conyers, Social Circle, and Madison, before encountering any real resistance. At Buckhead (a small town, not the Atlanta suburb), Confederate sharpshooters caused a relative handful of casualties before being driven off; Sherman ordered the town totally burned to the ground in reprisal.

Howard's right wing had moved more in a southeasterly direction, hoping to give the impression that Macon was their destination. Moving through McDonough and Locust Grove, Howard ordered a turn more to the east at Indian Springs, to close in tighter with the left wing and head more directly to Milledgeville. By November 20, the closest flanks of both wings were within 10 miles of each other, and were just a day's march from the Georgia capital.

From the start of the march, USA Brig. Gen. Judson Kilpatrick's 3rd Cavalry Division had ridden to the far right of Howard's massed columns, ordered to travel south as close to Macon as he dared, tearing up the railroad tracks as he went, and then to close up again near Milledgeville. On November 20, he had a brief skirmish with Wheeler's cavalry just east of Macon and quickly drove the Confederates back into the line of entrenchments surrounding the city.

The next day, a single regiment, USA Capt. Frederick S. Ladd's 9th Michigan, was sent to assault the small industrial town of Griswoldville, 10 miles east of Macon. Moving in without resistance, the cavalrymen soon destroyed most of the buildings in town, including the railroad station, a pistol factory, and a candle and soap factory. As they mopped up, USA Col. Eli H. Murray's 1st Brigade settled in for the night about 2 miles to the east.

At dawn on November 22, Wheeler's cavalry suddenly struck Murray's encampment. A short but furious fight ensued, ending when reinforcements from USA Col, Charles C. Walcutt's 2nd Brigade rushed to Murray's aid. Together they pushed the Confederate cavalrymen back through the burned-out town of Griswoldville, before breaking contact and returning to their original positions, where they heavily entrenched atop a small, wooded ridge.

The previous day Hardee, commander of the Confederate forces facing Sherman, had become aware that the Union forces were bypassing his location at Macon and made the assumption that they were heading toward the critical supply and manufacturing depot at Augusta. A hastily assembled force was pieced together around CSA Major General Smith's four regiments of the Combined Georgia Militia and ordered to move out post-haste to protect the river city.

Besides the four brigades of Georgia Militia, the small task force contained CSA Maj. Ferdinand W. C. Cook's Athens and Augusta Local Defense Battalions, CSA Capt. Ruel W. Anderson's four-gun Light Artillery Battery, and the decimated ranks of the combined two regiments of the Georgia State Line under CSA Lt. Col. Beverly D. Evans. With the exception of the State Line, which had been in nearly-continuous combat since May 29, the overwhelming majority of the command were the archetypal "old men and boys"; this force represented the literal bottom of the barrel for reinforcements.

By Hardee's direction, Col. James N. Willis's 1st Brigade of the Georgia Militia, along with Cook's command, left early on the morning of November 22, bound for Augusta via the road to Griswoldville. They were to be followed later that same day by the remaining commands. Hardee left at the same time for Savannah to help prepare its defenses, and Smith elected to remain in Macon to handle administrative chores, leaving command of the task force to the senior officer present, Brig. Gen. Pleasant J. Philips. As they left Macon, quite a few in the ranks remarked how much Philips had been seen drinking that morning.

As Philips's command moved out, Howard's entire right wing was also on the move, swinging a little more to the south and heading straight toward Griswoldville. Philips left Macon with the main part of his command and marched steadily on, arriving outside Griswoldville just after noon. There he found Cook's defense battalions drawn up into a defensive perimeter, having spotted the well entrenched Union lines just up the road.

Despite his explicit orders from both Hardee and Smith not to do so, Philips ordered preparations for an attack. Arranging his men perpendicular to the railroad tracks on the east side of town, Brig. Gen. Charles D. Anderson's 3rd Brigade, Georgia Militia, was placed on the left, just north of the tracks; Brig. Gen. Henry K. McKay's 4th Brigade was placed on Anderson's right, just south of the tracks; and Philips's own 2nd Brigade (now commanded by Col. James N. Mann) moved in reserve to the rear of McKay. Worley's Rangers and the rest of the State Line troopers moved forward in the very center as skirmishers, and Cook's small battalions took the extreme right of the line. Captain Anderson's battery set up just north of the tracks near the center of the line.

Facing Philips's small command was Walcutt's strong 2nd Brigade, 1st Division, XV Corps, which consisted of no less than seven reduced-strength Infantry regiments (the 12th, 97th and 100th Indiana, 40th and 103rd Illinois, 6th Iowa and 46th Ohio), two cavalry regiments (5th Kentucky and 9th Pennsylvania), and Capt. Albert Arndt's Battery B, 1st Michigan Artillery. In all, about 4,000 poorly trained and poorly equipped Georgia troops faced about 3,000 well-armed, well-entrenched, and combat-hardened veteran Union troops.

About 2:30 P.M., Philips ordered an all-out assault, and the ragged force began moving across the open field toward the Union entrenchments. USA Maj. Asias Willison of the 103rd Illinois wrote in his after-action report what happened next:

> As soon as they came within range of our muskets, a most terrific fire was poured into their ranks, doing fearful execution . . . still they moved forward, and came within 45 yards of our works. Here they attempted to reform their line, but so destructive was the fire that they were compelled to retire.

While most of Philips's militiamen were being blown apart behind them, the State Line charged up the slope toward the Union position, only to be thrown back to the wooded base. The State Line charged several more times, meeting the same result, until Evans was seriously wounded and all retired from the field.

Most of the militiamen never came closer than within fifty yards of the Union position, but bravely held their ground and returned fire until dusk. Philips ordered a retreat off the field then, and the shattered ranks limped slowly back into Macon. Left behind were fifty-one killed, 422 wounded, and nine missing. The Union lines were never in any real danger of being breached, but losses amounted to thirteen killed, seventy-nine wounded, and two missing in the brief fight. Walcutt himself was among the wounded, and had to be carried off the field during the engagement, replaced by Col. Robert F. Catterson. Incredibly, although the Rangers were in the very thick of this pitched battle, they only suffered a single casualty, Pvt. J.W. Eberhart, who received an injury to his right arm.

From there, the Rangers and the rest of the State Line were engaged in combat or on the move until the last few men were captured on May 12, 1865, with the exception of three short rest breaks. Worley, however, was absent for all of this. His beloved wife Georgia had fallen seriously ill as he was fighting near Atlanta, and with the blessing of the Adjutant General, he was allowed to return home to be by her side. She eventually recovered, but Worley himself fell seriously ill in the meantime, resulting in his reluctant resignation from the Rangers. He remained at home for the rest of the war.

With Worley gone, command fell to the only other remaining officer, 1st Lt. Robert C. Burns. During this time the Rangers moved from Macon to Jonesboro below Atlanta back up into northwest Georgia, into Alabama, across middle Georgia again, then to Savannah and into South Carolina briefly before returning to Savannah. The company engaged in combat nearly continuously during August and fought in nine more battles and major skirmishes before the end of the war. By mid-November both regiments of the entire State Line numbered less than 400. Only about twenty-five officers and fighting men of the Rangers were present and accounted for, although they were scattered in small, unorganized groups across the state from Augusta to Columbus.

During their brief, violent life, Worley's Rangers fought in nearly every major engagement in the Atlanta and Georgia campaigns after New Hope Church, fighting in no less than eighteen major actions. Of the 139 men enrolled at one time or another before they entered battle, five were killed in action, nine were wounded in action, six were captured by Union troops, sixteen were discharged for wounds or illness, forty-six deserted, and nine died of diseases. No original officer and only one original non-commissioned officer were present at the end. Despite being treated with general disdain by the rest of the Confederate Army, who called them "Joe Brown's Pets," and despite being refused uniforms and proper supplies because they were "only militia," the Rangers fought with uncommon courage and ability. Even though they were substantially outnumbered, the Rangers charged the field at Atlanta, Griswoldville, and Columbus, and held their line nearly without support at Nickajack Creek. Although nearly forgotten immediately after the war, their valor moved even Sherman to mention them in his reports and memoirs. Governor Brown may not have successfully made his point about "state armies," but his Rangers performed at least as well as the best Confederate army units.

William Worley recovered from his illness as the war ended, moved into a new home in Dahlonega and quickly became one of the pillars of that small community. He helped establish North Georgia College, now the senior military institute of Georgia, and served for many years as the clerk of the Lumpkin County Superior Court. He was a Dahlonega City Councilman for three consecutive terms, and at the time of his death, was serving as the United States Commissioner for the region. He remained loyal and beloved to the men of his old command, who frequently asked him to confirm their service and sacrifices to the pension committees. Worley, although a sober and upstanding Christian (one source noted that he "never drank intoxicating liquors and never played cards"), had no qualms in "bending" the truth, if necessary, to help out his destitute former comrades in arms. In support of one former soldier's pension application (one who had actually been admitted to the hospital with a "cutaneous eruption" just before the Rangers entered combat), Worley wrote:

> So sorry to hear that you was broken down in health and also finantially [sic]. It's bad for an old true and tried soldier to be in such circumstances, but I reckon it's the good Lords Will or it would not be so'. . . . a braver soldier never shouldered a gun, in my opinion, than you.

Often bed-ridden and ill in the last years of his life, Worley remained a beloved figure around Dahlonega, as noted in a February 10, 1898, *Dahlonega Nugget* newspaper article:

> Capt. W.J. Worley has had the grip too which robbed him of nearly all his beauty like it did us while we had it. The Captain is a great mineral man who talks about our rich country from morning until night except while in the garden alone, but while the grip had him he was never heard to utter a word about either gold or mica. Capt. Worley is a good clever man and we like him—he neither harms man nor makes love to the women. Often when we take the blues we go and sit down and talk with the Captain who soon gives us a dose of conversation—telling what a big boom we are just on the eve of having—which drives them entirely out of our system and we go away feeling like a new man.

While working on his barn in 1907, Worley suffered an injury that left him nearly blind for the rest of his life. He died in his own bed at home in Dahlonega, on Friday, November 21, 1913, and was laid to rest two days later with full military honors, accompanied by the full cadet corps of his beloved North Georgia College.

8

PIRATES AND PRIVATEERS: BLOCKADE RUNNERS

Tom Taylor (Civilian)

IT IS A LITTLE-REMEMBERED FACT THAT THE UNITED STATES GOVERNMENT is expressly authorized, by the Constitution no less, to hire pirates for the purpose of national defense. In Article I, Section 8, Clause 11, Congress is granted the authority both to declare war and to "grant Letters of Marque and Reprisal," which authorize private citizens, or even non-citizens, working on behalf of the U.S. government, the right to conduct military-style raids for plunder or take any other action they so desire, without a formal declaration of war being issued. Such "private citizens" doing this type of work on the high seas would normally be called "pirates," but since they operate under the dignity and protection of the U.S. government, they instead are known by a much sweeter name, "privateers."

The original intent of this clause was to give the fledgling nation some stab at naval power, recalling that it had just gained a tenacious independence from the world's most overwhelming superpower, Great Britain, who had both a massive navy and a roaring inferiority complex that frequently required its use against all who dared stand in its path.

A quite similar situation presented itself to the Confederacy in 1861. It was an infant nation, with no navy and only the barest hint of a national army, and they were facing an overwhelmingly powerful foe with an effective heavy industrial base and, at least in relative terms, a powerful navy. Taking a cue from the founding fathers, the Confederacy decided to enter the "letters of marque" business itself. They did not tarry long in consideration of this, either. Four days after the surrender of Fort Sumter, on April 17, 1861, Jefferson Davis issued the brand-new government's first proclamation, asking for the service of privateers to the Confederacy:

Now, therefore, I, Jefferson Davis, President of the Confederate States of America, do issue this, my proclamation, inviting all those who may desire, by service in private armed vessels on the high seas, to aid this government in resisting so wanton and wicked an aggression, to make application for commissions or letters of marque and reprisal...

Davis obviously had in mind the use of privateers in conducting combat operations. But the brand-new Confederacy was bereft of anything resembling a proper merchant marine, and the use of such mercenaries was quickly reconsidered for an even more important task—obtaining critically needed supplies from friendly foreign nations.

As mentioned in previous chapters, after Lincoln's election and the ensuing parade of Southern states seceding from the Union, it was not initially thought that any grand strategy for defeating the strong Confederate armies would have to be devised. Aged USA Gen. Winfield Scott, Commander-in-Chief of all Union armies, suggested early on a plan that would cut off trade and supply to the South, effectively starving it into submission. This so-called "Anaconda Plan" was initially rejected by Northern politicians. In the manner of politicians everywhere and throughout history, they demanded a "quick 'n' easy" solution to a complex and deadly problem. Their idea, which was happily carried out by the army, was to simply march out, "show the grand old flag," and watch as the Southerners ran screaming from the field.

Southerners, however, proved a bit more intractable than the Northern politicians had predicted. With the Union disaster at 1st Manassas (1st Bull Run to the Yankees), realization set in that this was not going to be a "ninety-day war," and that a real, workable strategy would have to be adopted. Based on Scott's original plan, a three-part strategy was approved, which involved: first, a tight naval blockade of the entire Southern Atlantic and Gulf coasts, to cut off supplies and trade with foreign nations; second, an invasion of Virginia as soon as possible with the goal of capturing the Confederate capital of Richmond; and third, the capture and control of the Mississippi, Cumberland, and Tennessee Rivers, which comprised the major river systems in the heartland of the Confederacy.

By July 1861, the naval blockade was put into place on over 3,500 miles of Southern coastline, or rather some small stretches of that vast coastline. USA Maj. Gen. George Brinton McClellan's feeble attempts to take Richmond, however, proved much less successful. The third part of the strategy, wresting control of the river systems, would take another two years and multiple campaigns to accomplish.

The Union's blockade of the Southern coastline harbors was one of the very few early success stories for the hapless Union military machine and had the effect of legally prohibiting those waters to neutral shipping. Unbelievably enough, much time was spent discussing the legalities of a blockade during the first months of the war. In observation of several hundred years of admiralty court decisions, the Union Navy was able to impose a shutdown of most Southern ports simply by declaring them blockaded, even if there were no Union ships outside most of these ports. In response, foreign-flagged ships would avoid sailing into these ports, rather than risk armed confrontation, or worse, having their insurance rating lowered by Lloyd's of London.

The Union's blockade declaration was very much a bluff. At the beginning of the war, they only had eight ships suitable for battle in port, and the relative handful of other, newer ships were on far-flung overseas stations from Japan to the Mediterranean. To enforce a blockade the Union brought its industrial capacity to bear and commenced a massive shipbuilding program that was supported by the conversion of suitable merchant ships to warships. Although ships were built in record time (one class was known as "ninety-day gunboats," referring to the duration of their construction), the blockade took a while to become effective. However, the Confederacy never really took advantage of this delay to declare the blockade broken and open the ports to neutral ships, who carried the war supplies they so desperately needed.

The Confederacy never had the naval capacity to break the blockade, although they came close to it once. In early 1863, two small ironclad rams, the CSS *Chicora* and CSS *Palmetto State*, sortied out of Charleston Harbor. The Union blockading squadron had no armored ships and was completely outclassed by the smaller and cruder Confederate crafts. In just a few minutes of furious battle, the *Palmetto State* rammed the USS *Mercedita*, which surrendered before sinking, and the *Chicora* temporarily disabled the USS *Keystone State*, which also surrendered. Two other Union ships struck their colors (a signal of surrender) in fear of being sunk in turn. Officially the blockade had been broken, putting an emphasis to the lie the Union's proclamation to the world made a few months earlier, if only for a very short time. Unfortunately, since the Confederate gunboats were unable to put prize crews on the surrendered Northern ships, the surviving vessels simply raised their colors again, un-surrendered themselves (releasing themselves on their own recognizance, so to speak), and sailed off, leaving the slower ironclads in their wake.

The Union navy reinforced Charleston with powerfully armed and armored ironclads that put a stop to any further sorties by *Chicora* and her fellow ironclads. Two months after the Confederate sortie, in an attempt to stop the Rebel naval actions once and for all, the Union navy gathered the largest ironclad fleet ever assembled to that time, with the intent of blasting past Fort Sumter and taking Charleston Harbor by direct naval assault. Centered around the 4,120-ton broadside armored frigate USS *New Ironsides*, the fleet included the odd-looking 677-ton, twin-turreted, composite-ironclad USS *Keokuk*, and the more familiar looking, "cheese-box on a raft" style, 1,335-ton, ironclad, single-turreted monitors USS *Passaic, Patapsco, Nahant, Montauk, Weehawken, Nantucket,* and *Catskill,* all commanded by Rear Admiral Samuel F. DuPont. On April 7, DuPont ordered the fleet to attack.

Within minutes of approaching firing range, the ironclad fleet showed that it was not nearly as effective against land fortifications as it was against warships (or unarmed blockade-runners). Fort Sumter's gunners raked the column with a hot, accurate, and heavy fire, sinking the *Keokuk* and damaging most of the monitors. The *New Ironsides* never got into the fight, but wallowed around just out of range with steering problems. DuPont ordered his fleet to break off after several hours of exchanging fire, to no avail on his part. Confederate authorities in Charleston jubilantly wired their superiors in Richmond, claiming a decisive victory and affirming that, with the withdrawal of the Union fleet, the blockade had been "legally" broken, and foreign emissaries should be thus notified. Davis's administration in Richmond was divided, as usual, over what to make of this report, and, again as usual, ended up doing nothing.

Several months later the ironclads returned to Charleston Harbor with a new commander, USA Rear Adm. John A. Dahlgren, and a new mission: to support the Union army in a series of amphibious assaults around the Charleston area—including Morris Island and its main fortification, Battery Wagner. Dahlgren's fleet was the same one used by DuPont, with the USS *Lehigh* replacing the sunken *Keokuk*. His ironclad gunboat fleet continued to operate in Charleston-area waters for the rest of the war.

With the failure of the attempt to blast open the blockade around Charleston, and with other, equally critical ports already closed off or nearly so, the Confederate government turned to the only real option available—the use of "privateers" to bring in essential supplies from friendly foreign nations . . . for a handy net profit, of course. As these "privateers" would sneak through the Union blockade fleet, the ships and the captains who commanded them were soon dubbed "blockade-runners." There were a number of ports available all along the Southern coastline, and blockade-runners operated out of Norfolk, Beaufort, New Bern, Charleston, Savannah, Pensacola, New Orleans, and Mobile until they either fell or to the end of the war. The two "hotspots" for blockade-runners, however, were Galveston, Texas, and Wilmington, North Carolina. Both ports were well protected by Confederate fortifications, and were difficult to completely "seal off" by the blockade fleets.

The most successful of all blockade-runners was an Englishman named Thomas E. Taylor, who was an employee in the Liverpool merchant firm of Edward Laurence & Company when the war broke out. While he had formerly been in charge of the firm's trade with the United States and India, his firm saw no real profit in supporting one side or the other in the war and did not seriously intend to challenge the Union-proclaimed blockade until the *Trent* incident occurred.

In October 1861, Confederate President Jefferson Davis appointed John Slidell of Louisiana and James M. Mason of Virginia as diplomats to France and Great Britain, respectively, charging them to obtain both economic and military support for the Confederacy from the European powers. The two traveled through the Union blockade safely aboard the *Theodora*, to Cuba, where they were greeted by the British consul and escorted aboard the Royal Mail steamer, *Trent*. The U.S. government uncovered the moves of the Confederate diplomats and ordered Captain Charles Wilkes of the USS *San Jacinto* to hunt them down. Wilkes went about his duty with great enthusiasm and ran down the *Trent* 300 miles east of Havana on November 8. Firing a shot across her bow to order a halt, Wilkes personally boarded the British steamer with a company of Marines and forcibly removed the Confederate diplomats before allowing the civilian vessel to continue on to England. Although Wilkes became an overnight celebrity and national hero upon delivering his prisoners to Boston (receiving the thanks of Congress, a high honor back in those days), his rash actions had provoked an international incident. The British government soon fired off an angry note of protest to the Lincoln administration, threatening to attack from Canada in support of the Confederacy over this outright act of war. Within a few days, reports leaked out that 80,000 British troops were being loaded aboard troopships to reinforce the Canadian garrison, along with a serious amount of war supplies. After much heated debate with his cabinet, most of whom were of the "let them hang" variety of statesmen, Lincoln reluctantly let the diplomats go free, allowing a British-flagged ship into Boston Harbor to pick them up, stating that it was prudent to fight "only one war at a time."

The *Trent* affair was very big news in England, where the U.S. seizure was seen as yet another action of the immature, overly powerful nation. Taylor himself felt a personal anger over the incident, writing a friend in South Carolina, "There is no doubt that we are prepared to make any sacrifice to resent this outrage. Feeling runs very deep here and we await for the answer to our demands for redress. The federal government is apparently the spoiled child of democracy." He didn't have long to wait to contribute a personal effort to the cause. Taylor's bosses, recognizing a lucrative opportunity, called him into their offices early in 1862, offering him the chance to supercargo (the officer aboard a merchant vessel charged with the purchase and sale of its cargo) a blockade-running vessel they were planning to underwrite. Although Taylor mentioned in his 1896 memoirs, *Running the Blockade*, that he had developed a very strong pro-Confederate attitude, which motivated his enthusiastic acceptance of the offer, the opportunity to become quite wealthy in short order possibly had some effect on his swift decision, as well.

The twenty-one-year-old Taylor turned out to be exactly the right man for the job. He sailed across the Atlantic aboard the first vessel commissioned by his firm, the *Dispatch*, loaded down with military supplies and coal until her decks were nearly awash, and was bound for Nassau in the Bahamas, even at that early date a hotbed of blockade-running activities. Nearly sinking twice on the trip across the Atlantic, the slow deep-draft vessel showed that it was not really the sort of ship Taylor needed to successfully run the blockade, a fact confirmed by "old hands" in Nassau. After some adventures with the *Dispatch*, Taylor returned to England and was given command of another, more suitable vessel. The *Astoria* was another bark sent by Taylor's firm to help bring Southern cotton back to England. Taylor had spent some time dealing with Union authorities in New York City (most early blockade-runners had little compunction about dealing with the devil, so to speak, if a profit was to be realized).

The *Banshee* had been built to specifications determined by these early blockade-running attempts and was in fact the very first steel-hulled vessel built as such from the keel up. She was a long-slung and graceful two-funneled paddle steamer, 214 feet long with a twenty-foot beam, displacing 217 tons fully loaded, but drawing only eight feet of water, so she could easily slide over the sand bars blocking alternative routes into the ports of Wilmington, Charleston, and Galveston. However, she could only maintain the not exactly blazing speed of eleven knots on the open sea. Her rather small crew consisted of only thirty-six men, a fraction of those usually found on similar-sized vessels, but this was par for the course on blockade ships. When profits from the trips were distributed, the smaller size of the crew resulted in a larger individual prize for each member.

Taylor was blessed with more than just a fine ship. The *Banshee*'s captain, J. W. Steele, was well-recognized even by early 1863 as one of the best blockade-running captains, and their pilot, Tom Burroughs of Wilmington, both knew the irregular coastline well and had sufficient courage to suffer through the nerve-wracking runs, a rare quality as it turned out.

The *Banshee* was modified and upgraded in Nassau, according to the latest intelligence coming in from the blockade-running community. By this time, late April 1863, it had become quite obvious that the only hope any vessel had for slipping through the blockade was to do so on a completely moonless night, and to make the vessel as low-profile as possible. The *Banshee* had all her topside rigging removed, save for one small crosstree on a single foremast for a lookout's post. Additionally, the lifeboats were rigged to hang directly alongside the gunwales, which would also aid them in a quick escape should disaster strike, and the entire craft was painted a dull gray, very similar to today's U.S. Navy standard color. Hard experience had shown that light colors reflected too much starlight, and a solid black color stood out as well on the wine-dark sea.

On Thursday, April 16, 1863, Taylor and the *Banshee* set out from Nassau on their first attempt to run the Union blockade gauntlet, with a heavy cargo of gunpowder, rifles, bayonets, lead for bullets, boots, and uniforms. For two days they ran northwest through the Bahamas chain, carefully avoiding the Union Navy's heavy battle cruisers in the area (the blockade by this time extended in three great bands as far offshore as the Bahamas and Cuba). As midnight approached on Saturday, April 18, they began their dangerous run inshore to the New Inlet of the Cape Fear

River, the northern entrance to Wilmington, which was well-guarded by Confederate-manned Fort Fisher. Taylor later remarked on his sense of excitement and anticipation:

> Now the real excitement began, and nothing I have ever experienced can compare with it. Hunting, pig sticking, big-game shooting, polo—I have done a little of each—all have their thrilling moments, but none can approach "running the blockade": and perhaps my readers can sympathize with my enthusiasm when they consider the dangers we encountered, after three days of constant anxiety and little sleep, in threading our way through a swarm of blockaders and the accuracy to hit in the nick of time the mouth of a river only a half a mile wide, without lights and with a coastline so low and featureless, that as a rule the first indication we had of its nearness was the dim white line of the surf.

With every light doused and every man ordered to be as quiet as possible, the *Banshee* crept nearer and nearer to the North Carolina coast, fully expecting an armed confrontation at any moment. As they moved slowly toward the safety of the shore, two Union cruisers moved in just off their port and starboard quarter, then another sailed directly in front of the *Banshee*'s bow. None of them were more than a football field's length away, but all passed silently, without noticing the runner. Instead of passing around to the north of the picket fleet, Steele had inadvertently sailed right into the midst of it.

Turning southward, Steele kept the *Banshee* just off the breakers, until, just as dawn began lighting up the waters, Burroughs called out that he could see the river entrance. Unfortunately, Union gunboats spotted them at nearly the same time, and a quick chase ensued. As shot splashed on either side of the *Banshee*, Taylor heard the beautiful sound of outgoing rounds coming from the shore—they had finally pulled within range of Fort Fisher's guns, and their pursuers were soon driven off. Taylor wrote in his memoirs, "For my part I was mighty proud of my first attempt and my baptism of fire. Blockade running seemed the pleasantest and most exhilarating of pastimes."

Pausing only long enough in Wilmington to load an outgoing cargo of tobacco and cotton, so as not to lose the advantage of the new moon, Taylor and his crew slipped back out to sea, this time taking a seemingly insane route that brought them within hailing distance of Admiral Dahlgren's flagship, the USS *Pawnee*. This was actually a brilliant idea, inspired by intelligence obtained from their friend Col. William Lamb, commander of Fort Fisher. As with nearly all headquarters units, the *Pawnee*'s own crew was too busy with their tasks to pay much attention and keep a good watch of the waters, while subordinate units tended to keep as far away from the brass as prudent and possible (some things never change in military circles!). Steele and Taylor successfully threaded their way past the *Pawnee* and then past the two outlying belts of blockading cruisers, making it back to Nassau without further incident. Although he was careful to never reveal exactly how much he earned on any run, Taylor exclaimed in a letter home his great good fortune on his first run:

> *Besides the inward freight of £50 a ton on the war material I had earned by the tobacco ballast alone £7000 the freight for which had also paid at the rate of £70 a ton. But this was a fleabite compared to the profit on the five hundred odd bales of cotton we had on board, which was at least £50 a bale.*

The profits made by the blockade-runners make that of today's Internet and housing market speculators seem almost trivial in comparison. One successful round trip, outbound-loaded with an average cargo of 700 to 800 bales of raw cotton, could fetch the ship's owner a profit of over $400,000 in 1865 dollars, or about $4.5 million in today's dollars! This cotton, which sold in the South for about 6 cents per pound, would easily sell for 50 to 60 cents per pound in Europe, where there was a large, eager market for it. Taylor remarked later that he had made a 350 percent profit on a single haul of foodstuffs in late 1864, while his firm returned to their investors a profit of 700 percent of their investment in the *Banshee* alone.

The lure of money had exactly the same effect then as it does now, and not many months passed before speculators and business cheats of all types arrived in Nassau, bound to make their thirty pieces of silver on the backs of the Confederacy. Due entirely to their relative shortage in the South, most highly prized speculations were in medicine, salt, and nails. At one point in 1861, four speculators controlled every available nail in the Confederacy. Needless to say, prices were not consumer friendly. A keg of nails in June of 1861 sold for as much as $10 per keg, nearly a 1,000 percent markup. Prices for salt, an essential substance in those pre-refrigeration days, soared ever higher, going from the long-standard 1 cent per pound to over 50 cents per pound within six months of the war's start.

Taylor made only seven trips on the *Banshee* before taking on another blockade-runner, the *Night Hawk*; a good thing, too, as his former craft fell into the hands of the blockaders on its very next voyage. His subsequent boats were far superior and faster. The *Night Hawk* was another two-funneled, side-wheeler steamer with a greater load capacity (600 tons), but it still drew only eleven feet of water. It was 220 feet long with a twenty-one-foot beam, and it proved to be a splendid craft on the open waters, something the *Banshee* had not exactly excelled in. It was replaced by the *Banshee No. 2*, which was yet another two-funneled, side-wheeler steamer, 252 feet long with a thirty-one-foot beam, carrying 439 tons of cargo with a fifty-three-man crew, able to make a relatively fast speed of fifteen knots.

All in all Taylor made twenty-eight trips through the blockade, earning a nice profit that would have allowed him to retire with style in nearly any land he chose, but he stayed loyal to his job and his company. In early 1865 he moved his operations to Havana, running a fleet of small steamers into Galveston, but moved back to Nassau shortly before the end of the war. With the Confederate surrender eliminating his profitable work, he returned to England, for a long recovery period from the yellow fever and "ague" he had suffered from for months. The last records available show that his grateful company gave him a partnership and a position in Bombay, India.

The relative success of the blockade and the blockade-runners is a mixed bag. Confederate runners were able to penetrate the blockade an estimated 8,000 times during the war, with an average of five out of six runners achieving success, even going in and out of Galveston with near impunity throughout the war years, but this contrasts sharply with the fact that all Southern ports had operated more than 20,000 shiploads during the four years before the war. Wilmington alone was able to bring in $65 million to the Confederate governmental coffers by outgoing shipments of cotton in the last year of the war, but this was seriously offset by the fact that incoming cargo had incredibly inflated prices. Matters were further complicated by the problems in shipping these essential supplies throughout the Confederacy, with Sherman and other Union army commanders tearing up the railroad infrastructures in nearly every direction.

Roughly 1,500 ships ran the blockade at one time or another during the four years of the war. They provided the Confederacy with almost three-fourths of its rifles and ammunition, as well as nearly all the food, clothing, and medicine Lee relied on to sustain his army during the last year of the war. The captains and officers provided both a link to hope and a source for fanciful tales; Taylor in fact is believed to have been Margaret Mitchell's inspiration for the character Rhett Butler in *Gone with the Wind*. In the end, as with nearly every other aspect of the Confederate military machine, it proved to be a gallant effort overwhelmed by the superior numbers and capabilities of the Union.

9

THE EVERLASTING FIRE: AMERICAN INDIANS

Col. Daniel Newman McIntosh, 1st Creek Mounted Volunteers
(1st Creek Cavalry Regiment, CSA)

ON THE MORNING OF JUNE 23, 1865, A COLUMN OF CONFEDERATE cavalrymen slowly rode down the dirt road into Doaksville, near Fort Towson in Indian Territory. At the head of the column was Brig. Gen. Stand Watie, a full-blooded Cherokee. Behind him in the column, at the head of his own battle-reduced regiment of Creeks, was Col. Daniel N. McIntosh, a mixed Cherokee, Creek, and Scot. These were the very last Confederates to surrender as a unit; more than six weeks had passed since Lee and his Army of Northern Virginia had laid down their arms, 1,300 miles to the east. With the stroke of a pen, Watie would end the major combat actions of that war, but he could not stop another one, a war that had begun forty years before the Civil War itself.

It is often remarked that the American Civil War pitted "brother against brother," but in no regard was this truer than within the Native American nations. As William Trotter pointed out in his excellent book on guerilla warfare in North Carolina, *Bushwhackers,* for the most part, families did not split up and fight among themselves, but instead usually favored one side or the other as a clan. Families in New Hampshire did not usually send one man South and one into the Union army, for example, nor did many southern Georgia sons make the trek north to Michigan to put on the blue suit. However, this cliché was absolutely correct when it came to many Native American nations, in particular those of the "five civilized tribes" (according to the antebellum U.S. government): the Cherokee, Creek, Choctaw, Chickasaw, and Seminole. Interestingly enough, it was these five "civilized" nations that were the only ones to divide up and fight as nations during the war.

Daniel Newman McIntosh was born at Indian Springs, Georgia, just north of Macon, on September 20, 1822. He was the youngest son of Susannah and William McIntosh, who was the principal chief of the Lower Creeks. His great-grandfather was Captain John "Nor" McIntosh of Scotland, one of Oglethorpe's officers, who led a company of Scottish Highlanders at Darien (under the command, coincidentally, of one of the author's ancestors, Gen. Hugh MacKay). Daniel's grandfather, William, was a captain in the Colonial army, and had married a Creek princess, Senoia Henneha. Some of Daniel's other ancestors included chiefs and important figures of both the Creek and Cherokee nations. This was considered very unusual for the time, because these two nations were long-standing enemies.

After the Battle of Horseshoe Bend in 1815, which pitted U.S. troops supported by Cherokees and some Creeks under Gen. Andrew Jackson against the pro-British "Red Stick" band of Creeks in Alabama, the public pressure to rid the Deep South of all Indians, always a background issue in every treaty negotiation, grew to a fever pitch. William McIntosh was heavily embroiled in these land disputes and under great pressure, he signed the Treaty of Indian Springs in February 1825. This treaty essentially ceded all remaining Creek land in Georgia, belonging both to the Upper (which he did not control) and Lower bands, to the state. This was a move violently opposed by other, more militant Upper Creeks, and less than two months later, William paid for his agreement with his life.

Stand Watie himself had faced a very similar situation. He had agreed to relinquish all Cherokee lands in Georgia to the state, after a gold rush and subsequent land grab had made the point essentially moot. Militant Cherokees threatened his life as well, underscoring the civil war that had been brewing for centuries in most of the Eastern Indian nations. Watie managed to make it to Indian Territory (now Oklahoma) unscathed, but buried his wife on the infamous "Trail of Tears" in 1837. The opposition to Watie's actions followed him to the new land.

Daniel McIntosh moved west to Indian Territory with the surviving members of his family in 1828, entering the territory at Fort Gibson and eventually settling in a designated Creek Nation site between the Verdigris and Grand Rivers. The move, and the murder of Chief William McIntosh, did little to affect the fortunes and standing of the McIntosh family, who remained one of the most influential forces in the relocated Creek Nation. Like Watie, the seething hatred toward the McIntoshes followed them to Indian Territory, but as long as the opposing bands of Creeks stayed in their separate areas, there was very little violence. Daniel settled into a life of farming and tribal politics. He was a member of the Council of Warriors, the Creek Supreme Court, and other tribal councils. He married his first wife, Elsie Otterlifter, a Cherokee, around 1842. Not only was Elsie a Cherokee, the hereditary enemy of his people, she was also a direct descendent of Nancy Ward.

Nancy Ward had first gained fame as a female warrior and tribal leader when she accompanied her husband on a raid against the Northern Creeks in 1755, known as the Battle of Taliwa. When her husband was killed during the action, she grabbed his rifle and led the Cherokee warriors in an assault, scattering the Creeks. This occurred during a time when the Cherokees, an offshoot of the New England Iroquois, were pushing south and encroaching into traditional Creek lands, located in what is today North Carolina, Tennessee, and North Georgia. Even after a hundred years, the ill feelings from the protracted Cherokee-Creek wars had not subsided, making McIntosh's union all the more remarkable.

Elsie died in 1847 after bearing two children, and McIntosh soon remarried. His new wife, Jane Ward (not thought to be related to Nancy Ward), bore him four more children before the start of the war.

After the secession of most Southern states, and the fall of Fort Sumter underscoring that a fight was brewing, the displaced nations in the Indian Territory faced yet another quandary: which side would they support? Neutrality was not much of an option. The natural inclination was to side with the Confederacy, against the very Federal authorities who had moved them west to begin with. But the situation was not that simple. Agents assigned by the government were largely from the South and had begun urging the nations to side with the fledgling Confederacy for some time before the war broke out. However, there were very serious antagonisms still festering from the treaty signings that had lost the Indian nations their lands. Other issues had sprung up concerning land and property rights in the Territory, and a whole other group of issues existed relating to ancient tribal hatreds that prevented any possibility of cooperation, whether it would ultimately mean their destruction or not.

The Cherokee Nation was already split into several major factions. One was led by John Ross, who initially urged his people to show just how civilized they were by remaining loyal to their Union masters. Another was led by Stand Watie, the highest-ranking surviving member of the group led by Major Ridge that had signed the Treaty of New Echota in 1835, ceding all the Cherokee lands in the East for land in the Indian Territory. Unfortunately, like William McIntosh, Ridge neither had the permission nor support of a large number of Cherokee to give away their land, no matter how good a deal it was for all of them. Ridge paid for his act with his life. Interestingly, and to underscore just how complicated politics were in these nations, Ridge himself had been part of a party that murdered Cherokee Chief Doublehead for signing a similar treaty in 1807 and personally murdered another Cherokee who had denounced this act.

A third major Cherokee faction had hidden away in the North Carolina mountains during the Removal. They organized quickly under the leadership of their close friend and the only white man ever made chief of an Indian nation, William Holland Thomas. Thomas raised an all-Cherokee "regiment" of about 200 warriors, dubbing it the "Junaluska Zouaves," but there is no record of it ever actually doing anything other than showing up for muster once or twice. He later raised a mixed-Cherokee-and-white unit, which would prove to be something entirely different.

While a number of Native Americans served individually as part of both Union and Confederate regiments, relatively few served together as specially designated units outside the Territory. This was primarily due to agreements that had been made within both armies that it would be better not to bring the Indians back east again. The only eastern Union all-Indian unit was Company K of the 1st Michigan Sharpshooters Regiment, which consisted of 145 men from the Ottawa, Delaware, Huron, Oneida, Potawami, and Ojibwa nations. The 1st Michigan was prominent in fighting around Petersburg, and was one of the regiments decimated at the Crater (one of the battles at Petersburg).

One source claims that Powhatans served as scouts for McClellan during the Peninsular Campaign, while several sources claim that Lumbees in North Carolina gave similar assistance to Sherman during his war-ending campaign there. Their Confederate opponents are reported to have had a number of Catawbas in two or three South Carolina infantry regiments, but the records to support this are sketchy. In any case the Catawbas couldn't have played a very large part in any unit, as a census revealed only 110 men, women, and children in 1826.

Interestingly, in the emancipated, abolitionist, enlightened and liberal North, where only a relative handful of Union Army generals still owned their slaves, these Native Americans had a very tough time even joining up to serve as cannon fodder in the ranks. Newspapers of the day illustrated the problems of racial heritage, including this November 30, 1861 article from the Detroit Tribune:

> Shall the Indians be armed? The question of arming the Indians is under discussion and its determination will probably be dependant upon the ascertained course of the rebels. The topic may be averted to in a report of the Superintendent of Indian Affairs, that will contain the facts showing that the great majority of full-blooded Indians are loyal, while the rebels have worked with more success upon half-breeds.

This was representative of a widespread and popular attitude, even in some parts of the South. The Union Army high command had a very similar view as well, confining presumably "full-blooded" Native American volunteers to "colored" regiments. A rare exception to this policy was Company D, 132nd New York Infantry, the "Tuscarora Company." Featuring twenty-four Iroquois from the Allegany, Cattaraugus, and Tuscarora clans, this integrated unit was led by one of the Tuscarora chiefs, USA Lt. Cornelius Cusick. The 132nd fought primarily in coastal actions in North Carolina. In addition, although not identified as such in the official records, the 31st United States Colored Troops had many Pequot in the ranks.

Soon after Fort Sumter, the former Federal agent for Indian Affairs to the Choctaw, Douglas H. Cooper, resigned from U.S. service. Within a few days he accepted a colonelcy in the Confederate Army, commissioned in charge of the Confederate Department of Indian Affairs, and was given the task of organizing as many Indians as possible for the cause. In the fall of 1861, he approached both Creek factions with great care, seeking to build support for a reunion, to fight together against the Union forces that would undoubtedly come their way. Daniel McIntosh enthusiastically agreed and immediately set about organizing a regiment of cavalry for service to the Confederacy, the 1st Creek Mounted Volunteers. His half-brother, Chilly McIntosh, shortly afterward raised another such regiment. Both units were soon renamed as the 1st and 2nd Creek Cavalry Regiments, respectively. These regiments drew their men from the Lower Creek and Seminole nations. Although the Upper Creeks, led by a chief named Hopoeithleyohola (sometimes Opothleyahola) had pledged to

Cooper that they preferred to remain neutral, this call to arms among their tribal foes caused not a small amount of consternation among the opposing, much larger faction of mostly Upper Creeks, led by a chief named Hopoeithleyohola, who incited them to set about raising a similar-sized cavalry force for service to the Union.

In the Cherokee lands, John Ross had reluctantly concluded that the Confederacy offered the best chance for their survival as a nation, after the Union withdrew both their agents and their logistical support, and after Confederate victories at Manassas and Wilson's Creek. He authorized John Drew, an avowed secessionist, to organize a regiment of "Pin" (full-blooded) clan warriors for the cause. Stand Watie had already raised a regiment of "half-breeds," the 1st Regiment Cherokee Mounted Rifles, and had accepted a Confederate commission as a colonel to lead it. Even as Drew was organizing his own 2nd Regiment Cherokee Mounted Rifles, Watie was joining forces with CSA Brig. Gen. Ben McCulloch's Texas Cavalry, patrolling the northern border of the Territory to keep Union "irregulars" from Kansas out of the Confederate zone.

By the end of October, Cooper had over 1,400 men in the saddle under his command, including the 500-strong 9th Texas Cavalry (an all-white unit), both McIntosh Creek Regiments, and six companies of Choctaw and Chickasaw cavalrymen.

Hopoeithleyohola (also known as Opothleyahola), was encamped with his 2,000 Upper Creek and Seminole warriors and their families, at the junction of the North Fork and Deep Fork of the Canadian River, at the present-day site of Eufaula, Oklahoma. He was alarmed over the rapid buildup of Creek forces under the McIntosh brothers, and feared that they, along with the other Confederate units in the Territory, would be used to settle the old score against him. On November 5, 1861, he broke camp along with his followers, and set out for more friendly Unionist territory north in Kansas. Dropping by the old camp for a visit a week later, Cooper discovered the move and quickly ordered his mixed-bag force, reinforced now with Drew's Regiment of Cherokee Mounted Rifles, to pursue, close, and either compel Hopoeithleyohola's force to remain neutral, or destroy them.

Cooper's cavalrymen caught up with Hopoeithleyohola's band at Round Mountain, near the Red Fork of the Arkansas River (modern day town site of Yale, west of Tulsa), and while pursuing stragglers, stumbled into his main force shortly after sunset. A short but vicious fight broke out in the dark, which ended with Hopoeithleyohola's men hastily retreating. Cooper kept the pressure on, attacking the new Unionist encampment at dawn, only to find that they had already moved further north. Cooper moved out behind them cautiously, knowing that Hopoeithleyohola's force was made up of men who specialized in guerilla warfare and ambush, and that rumor had it was even then being reinforced with Kansas Jayhawks (untrue, as it turned out).

Hopoeithleyohola had established another camp at Chusto-Talasah, on the banks of Bird Creek, a place also known as Caving Banks. As Cooper slowly drew near in early December, Hopoeithleyohola sent word that he was ready to negotiate for peace. Cooper ordered Maj. Thomas Pegg, a Cherokee in Drew's Regiment, to take three companies and speak with Hopoeithleyohola. Pegg took some of his own men, all Pin Indians, and met with the aged chief on December 8. Instead of a humbled leader of a defeated band on the run, Pegg found Hopoeithleyohola to be a strong, skilled, and gifted orator, who ignored any overtures Pegg made and instead spoke almost exclusively to his men, reminding them of the supposedly strong ties and close friendships they had enjoyed back in the good old days. Most of the young cavalrymen had been born in the Territory and were not old enough to remember the savage warfare between the two nations back in North Carolina and Georgia. They bought the story completely, and deserted Pegg on the spot to join their Upper Creek "brethren." When Pegg returned to his own camp and reported what had happened, most of the Cherokee contingent fled the camp, some for parts unknown, some for Fort Gibson. Many of the force of "full-blooded" Cherokee went over to Hopoeithleyohola's encampment, throwing their lot in with him in time for the next day's battle. Drew and only twenty-eight of his officers and men remained by the next morning.

Cooper's force was somewhat reduced by the sudden desertion of most of Drew's regiment, and Hopoeithleyohola had picked an extremely good defensive ground, but Cooper still ordered an all-out assault on Hopoeithleyohola's camp. Cooper remarked what a good ground the old chief had picked in his after-action report:

> The position taken up by the enemy presented almost insurmountable obstacles. The creek made up to the prairie on the side of our approach in an abrupt, precipitous bank some 30 feet in height, in places cut into steps reaching near the top and forming a parapet, while the creek, being deep, was fordable but at certain points known only to the enemy.

The approach side, which was occupied by hostile forces, was densely covered with heavy timber, matted underbrush and thickets and fortified additionally by prostrate logs. Near the center of the enemy's lines was a dwelling, a small corn crib and a rail fence situated in a recess of the prairie at the gorge at the bend of the creek of horseshoe form, about 400 or about 500 yards in length. This bend was thickly wooded and covered in front near the house with long interwoven weeds and grass extending to a bench behind which the enemy could lie and pour upon the advancing line his deadly fire in comparative safety, while the creek banks on either side covered the house by flank and reverse.

At about 2:00 P.M. on December 9, over a thousand Confederate dismounted cavalrymen attacked the Unionist encampment head-on, the terrain making a flanking attack impossible. The battle raged for over four hours, moving back and forth over the river bottom flat as one side or the other gained momentary advantage, until Hopoeithleyohola's men broke for good just before dark and fled east across the creek. Most of the Unionist warriors went through the Osage Hills, to the northwest of the battleground, picking up their families and baggage before rejoining Hopoeithleyohola's column. Cooper's men were too exhausted to pursue, and simply made camp in the same place that night.

Cooper reported that he believed his men had killed or wounded about 500 of the Union sympathizers, but the real count was most likely confined to the twenty-seven dead found in the camp, and another 300 or so wounded, as the situation would have precluded the removal of the dead or seriously wounded. Hopoeithleyohola kept the remains of his scattered force moving northwest through the night and found a strong defensive position in a cove of the aptly named Battle Creek, near Chustenahlah, in an area also known as Hominy Falls. There they heavily entrenched and waited again for the rumored reinforcements supposed to be heading to join them from Kansas.

Cooper, promoted in the midst of the campaign to overall command of the Indian Department, requested help from Col. James McQueen McIntosh's Texas cavalrymen. James McIntosh, no relation to the two Creek brothers, quickly responded with a force of 1,380 men, of the South Kansas-Texas Regiment (also known as the 3rd Texas Cavalry), the 6th Texas Cavalry, the 11th Texas Cavalry, and the 2nd Arkansas

Mounted Riflemen. McIntosh's scratch force left Fort Gibson, now the main area headquarters, on December 22. While he had planned to follow a two-pronged attack to crush Hopoeithleyohola once and for all, Cooper informed James McIntosh on December 25 that his own force was going to be delayed in refitting and allowed the fresh Texas and Arkansas cavalrymen to initiate the attack on their own.

James McIntosh's command reached Hopoeithleyohola's position around noon on December 26. Although the Unionist encampment was well placed, with good lines of fire and well protected by the hilly terrain, McIntosh ordered an immediate frontal assault. The charging Texans soon routed Hopoeithleyohola's men from every position, while Captain Gibson's Arkansans dismounted and drove the remnants from the thick brush alongside the river. About 4:00 P.M., with Stand Watie's Confederate Cherokees pounding up to join the battle at a full gallop and the Creek regiments not far behind, the Unionist fire slackened and then stopped, leaving McIntosh and his men inside the camp, piles of dead and dying Creek, Cherokees, and Seminoles all around them. As the exhausted Texans rested, the remaining Confederate Cherokee, Creek, and Seminole warriors swept through the camp, whooping and screaming war cries, pausing only long enough to ascertain which direction Hopoeithleyohola and his supporters had fled. McIntosh wrote in his after-action report:

> The loss sustained by the enemy was very severe. Their killed amounted to upwards of 250. Our loss was 8 killed and 32 wounded. The brave and gallant Lieutenant Fitzhue was shot in the head, and fell while gallantly leading his company. Capt. J.D. Young, of Young's regiment, and Lieutenant Durham, of the South Kansas-Texas Regiment, were both wounded while in the thick of the battle. We captured 160 women and children, 20 negroes, 30 wagons, 70 yoke of oxen, about 500 Indian horses, several hundred head of cattle, 100 sheep, and a great quantity of property of much value to the enemy. The stronghold of Hopoeithleyohola was completely broken up, and his force scattered in every direction, destitute of the simplest elements of subsistence.

Hopoeithleyohola and his primary force made a beeline for Kansas, while his other followers fled in different directions. In the midst of a raging blizzard, they ran through the night and on into the next day, with Waite's Cherokees and the McIntosh brothers' Creeks following closely, blood up for the kill, gunning down every straggler and rear guard attempt they ran across. When the old Creek chief reached the relative safety of the Sac and Fox Agency headquarters outpost, just across the border in southern Kansas, Waite's column broke off their pursuit and returned to Fort Gibson. But Hopoeithleyohola's followers had achieved only a partial salvation. There was no room at the inn, so to speak, and the Union Army garrison had few supplies and little motivation to spare anything. The remaining Upper Creek, Unionist Cherokee, and loyalist Seminole warriors were left to find whatever shelter they could in the storm-ravaged landscape. Most had left behind all of their extra clothing, tents, and even food at the Chustenahlah encampment. Over the next few weeks, more than 250 warriors died of exposure.

With the Unionist Indian bands militarily smashed, remaining loyalists gradually left the Territory and made the hard trek up to Kansas. Around 10,000 of them arrived by the summer of 1862. The Indian Territory was largely free of serious Unionist influences by the end of 1863, but that situation would not last.

In late January 1862, while the majority of attention in Washington and Richmond was focused on the developments in the east, Maj. Gen. Earl Van Dorn, commander of the reorganized Confederate Trans-Mississippi District of Department Number 2 (basically everything west of the Mississippi River), consolidated his feuding Arkansas and Missouri forces into a newly created Army of the West, adding the Indian forces in the Territory to the mix as well. This made many of the Indian commanders and men uncomfortable, as their treaty with the Confederate government specified that they were not to be used outside of the Indian Territory. The problem was that USA Brig. Gen. Samuel Ryan Curtis's Federal Southwestern District had powerful forces in Kansas and Missouri. They were embarking on a campaign to drive all Confederate forces south into Arkansas and Louisiana, and Van Dorn could only muster a far weaker force.

CSA Brig. Gen. Albert Pike, another former Federal Indian agent, had assumed overall command of the Indian regiments and ordered them out in February in support of Van Dorn's operation. Drew's desertions had put a serious damper on the already tentative relationship his regiment had with the other Indian regiments, and as a precaution, Chief John Ross traveled part of the way to Arkansas with the Confederate force, proclaiming loudly and frequently along the way his personal and his regiment's corporal devotion to the Confederacy. Neither Stand Watie nor the McIntosh brothers bought the story, and their later desertion under fire made the white Confederates even less willing to trust any of them.

One Texas cavalryman wrote to his hometown newspaper,

> *I do not like to fight with the Indians very much, for you do not know what moment they will turn over to the opposite side, and if you get in a fight with them and the enemy pours in a pretty heavy fire, they will go away with them.*

It did not help in the slightest that a number of the Cherokees who had deserted over to Hopoeithleyohola had straggled back into Drew's encampment just before they moved out on the Arkansas Campaign. Instead of being shot as deserters (an almost mandated punishment in both armies at the time, under those circumstances), Ross had overruled any such actions and forgiven the men. These same despicable, but "full-blooded" turncoats now rode in the same column with the "mixed-blood" Cherokees, Creeks, Seminoles, Chickasaws, and Choctaws who they had been fighting less than two months before.

The Arkansas and Missouri contingents had their own internal problems as well, mostly having to do with the seniority of rank and power of their respective commanding officers, but both were in accord against the outrages being perpetuated against Confederate-leaning homes and families in Missouri by the "Dutch." USA Brig. Gen. Franz Sigel, an immigrant from Baden, Germany, had raised five regiments of all-German immigrants for service to the Union in Missouri, and they had taken to their task with no small enthusiasm. His countrymen had not shown much stock to that point for full-on combat, retreating in terror after a Confederate charge at Wilson's Creek (and earning a nickname they would fight the rest of the war, the "flying Dutchmen"), but they had shown much more backbone in burning the homes and property of Confederate civilians in southwest Missouri.

Early in February 1862, Curtis moved south with his 12,000-man force, driving the remaining Confederate forces completely out of Missouri over the next three weeks. He prepared to move ahead to northwestern Arkansas to continue the job. Curtis had a serous logistical problem, however, which Van Dorn soon learned and plotted to exploit. The Union force was low on supplies, far from their home base, and forced to forage for food in a mountainous area, spreading their lines of communication and support dangerously thin. Van Dorn immediately ordered his own forces to prepare three days of cooked rations and be ready to move out, in the middle of a harsh winter storm.

Van Dorn's army departed on March 4 along the Telegraph Road, collecting his scattered brigades and regiments as the column traveled north. Within a few days he had been joined by 7,000 Missourians under Maj. Gen. Sterling Price, mostly ill-equipped and loosely disciplined, but combat-hardened state militiamen. Another 8,000 troops from Arkansas, Texas, and Louisiana, under the command of Brig. Gen. Ben McCulloch, a former Texas Ranger, also joined Van Dorn's army. Pike soon came aboard with his 1,000-strong Indian Brigade at Elm Springs, where his troops' appearance astonished the other men. One soldier in the First Missouri Infantry wrote:

> They came trotting gaily into camp yelling forth a wild war whoop that startled the army out of all its propriety. Their faces were painted for they were 'on the warpath,' their long black hair qued in clubs hung down their backs, buckskin shirts, leggings, and moccasins adorned with little bells and rattles, together with bright colored turkey feathers fastened on their heads completed unique uniforms not strictly cut according to military regulations.

Although their appearance, and the fact that they were visibly armed with clubs and tomahawks, gave the impression that these were wild, hostile Plains Indians, they were, in fact, just the same five "civilized tribes" that had been adapting to the white men's ways for the better part of a century. Even though their deliberately "savage" dress was for appearances only, it undoubtedly made many in the other ranks glad they were on the same side!

Curtis soon learned of Van Dorn's moves and pulled back north to a good defensive ground outside of Leesburg, at the base of Pea Ridge Mountain. He ordered a strong line of breastworks dug across Telegraph Road, the only obvious lane of approach in this wilderness. With good lines of fire for his fifty artillery pieces, he prepared to simply hold his position, counting on the terrain and weather to work in his favor. His 10,500 men were divided into four divisions, under the commands of Brig. Gen. Alexander Asboth, Col. Eugene A. Carr, Col. Jefferson C.

Davis, and Col. Peter J. Osterhaus. Curtis personally controlled Carr's and Davis's divisions, at the Telegraph Road breastworks. His second-in-command, Sigel, took command over Asboth and Osterhaus, who were south of his headquarters in Bentonville. This split-off, isolated position was a serious mistake on Sigel's behalf, and Van Dorn quickly saw an opportunity to strike the divided force. He ordered a general attack to begin on March 6.

The cold, icy weather and bad roads worked to Sigel's advantage, however, and Van Dorn's men took far too long working their way up the narrow road to catch him. Sigel didn't take full advantage of the Confederate delay, not fully pulling out of town on the north while the Confederate vanguard was entering from the south. McIntosh's Texas Cavalry, part of McCulloch's Division, chased after the retreating Union force, but to no avail. One source waggishly claimed that this was due to the fact that Sigel "specialized in retreating". The weather and approaching darkness made it impossible for Van Dorn to consolidate his lines, and as evening fell, his army was strung out on the road between Bentonville and Sugar Creek, a tempting but un-assailed target for Curtis, who remained in his entrenchments. It snowed heavily that night, causing untold misery for the infantrymen and cavalrymen on both sides, huddled in their holes or wrapped up on the roads.

The next day, Van Dorn's scouts reported the tactical situation. Curtis was well dug-in across the main road, the obvious avenue of attack, with heavy breastworks thrown up and the smaller forest roads around his position blocked by felled trees. The scouts had discovered a way to get around to Curtis's rear, however, and Van Dorn ordered an immediate move to a new line of departure position in that northern part of the Union line at a small intersection known as Elkhorn Tavern. On the late afternoon of March 6, he ordered Price's Division to light campfires, as if they were settling down for the night, along Telegraph Road, then to slip away after midnight down the small, rough forest lane to the north. McCulloch was ordered to take his division the next morning and make a diversionary attack to Curtis's front.

The road proved more difficult to negotiate than anyone had thought possible, due mostly to the snow and cold weather, and it was almost noon before Price was in position. McCulloch also had problems deploying his forces in the hilly woods, delaying his own assault. It was after 11:30 in the morning before he was fully on line. He ordered a charge, and the sudden crash of artillery signaled to his Union foes that things were about to get hot. Price's Division climbed up on the ridge itself as soon as they were in position, and the crackle of rifle and artillery fire alerted Curtis to the fact that his line was not as secure as he had believed.

McCulloch personally led a direct assault on the dug-in Union line and was shot from his saddle and killed just a few minutes into the attack. The Indian Brigade attacked in the middle of the line, directly toward an artillery battery, led personally by Daniel McIntosh's Texans fighting mounted. Stand Watie's Cherokees charged dismounted, and Pike himself led a mixed group including the McIntosh brothers and Drew's regiments all mounted up, all of them screaming and whooping at the top of their lungs. After several charges and one last, desperate hand-to-hand engagement, in which Daniel McIntosh was killed, the Indian Brigade managed to capture the battery.

The Indian regiments turned to savagery after the battery fell into their hands; they scalped the wounded and dead, and mutilated their bodies with knives and tomahawks. When this was reported later in the Northern press, Drew tried to claim that it was the "mixed-bloods" of Watie's and the McIntosh brothers' regiments that were responsible, further deepening the divide between them and his "pure-bloods." However, it was well established, even at the time of the battle, that this had been a free-for-all gore-fest, where nearly all the Indian regiments participated. This was repulsive to both army's commanders, who later viewed the inclusion of Indians in a "white man's fight" as not entirely desirable.

The death of McCulloch and a renewed defensive action by Curtis's troops took the momentum out of the attack. Price swept the Union forces away from Elkhorn Tavern and attempted to make his own attack on Curtis's lines, but was repulsed under heavy infantry fire, which his own artillery could not dislodge. The situation remained static as night fell, with sporadic infantry and artillery fire continuing all night. The next day's battle resumed primarily as an all-artillery affair, the energy of the infantry on both sides spent to the exhaustion point. Curtis did attempt a late-afternoon attack on Price's men, succeeding in pushing them back a few hundred yards, at the cost of very heavy casualties on both sides. Van Dorn realized his men were almost out of ammunition, and having left his supply trains back in Bentonville due to the poor road conditions, was forced to break contact and pull south to a safe distance.

On March 9, with the fighting ended, Van Dorn sent a message to Curtis requesting a truce to bury the dead and exchange the wounded. Curtis readily agreed, stating his men had captured a number of

Confederate surgeons and wounded, which he was eager to hand back, but he also noted that the matter of the mutilated artillerymen had "come to his attention." This wasn't the only atrocity committed during the two-day battle, by any stretch of the imagination, and Van Dorn's adjutant, Col. D.H. Maury, replied to Curtis as such:

> General: I am instructed by Major-General Van Dorn, commanding this district, to express to you his thanks and gratification on account of the courtesy extended by yourself and the officers under your command to the burial party sent by him to your camp on the 9th inst. He is pained to learn, by your letter brought to him by the commanding officer of the party, that the remains of some of your soldiers have been reported to you to have been scalped, tomahawked and otherwise mutilated. He hopes you have been misinformed. The Indians who formed part of his forces have for many years been regarded as a civilized people. He will, however, most cordially unite with you in repressing the horrors of this unnatural war. That you may cooperate with him to this end more effectually, he desires me to inform you that many of our men who surrendered themselves prisoners of war were reported to him as having been murdered in cold blood by their captors, who were alleged to be Germans. The privileges which you extend to our medical officers will be reciprocated, and as soon as possible, means will be taken for an exchange of prisoners.

This proved to be the first and last battle that any Indian regiment from the Territory participated in outside that area, by mutual agreement of both armies.

BACK IN THE TERRITORY

After Pea Ridge, popular dissent against the media-promoted "outrages" caused civilians in the North to fear for their lives, with visions of wild Indians running through the streets of Chicago and New York. Not for the first time, the Northern papers claimed the Union's fight for all that was good and right was against the evil South, which used barely human savages who scalped their wounded, mutilated their dead, and, presumably, looked the wrong way at the white women while they were doing it. This line of reasoning continued in the papers for several months, until the Battle of Sharpsburg (Antietam) and Lincoln's subsequent Emancipation Proclamation gave the braying jackals of the press something fresher to bash the South with. The South, bereft of any popular need to build a reason for fighting or not fighting the war, did report the incident in the larger papers, to a general approval, but remarked on a bit of concern that, like Drew's men, their Indian allies might switch sides at any given time. CSA General Beauregard, briefly in command of the western department after Shiloh, later ordered that the Indian Brigade be reserved for service in the Trans-Mississippi, where their style of fighting was more to the usual method of both sides.

Stand Watie and the McIntosh brothers stayed together under Cooper's command in 1862, along with the Choctaw, Chickasaw, and some Cherokee regiments, battalions, and companies of the Indian Brigade, skirmishing heavily with Union forces and guerillas all across the Indian Territory and parts of western Missouri. John Ross kept up his old political intrigues against Watie, first trying to get Drew promoted to general in charge of all the Indian regiments, and finally allowing himself to be "captured" during a Union raid in July. Drew's regiment was broken up the same month with most opting to go north and join pro-Union Indian formations in Kansas, and a relative few drifting over to Cooper's command.

Only two more major battles were fought in the Territory: Cabin Creek on July 1–2, 1863; and Honey Springs on July 17, 1863. Both were Union victories that gave them access and control over most of the Indian tribal settlements. Watie was promoted to brigadier general and given command of the combined Indian Cavalry Brigade in May 1864, which conducted raids and skirmishes against the Union supply columns and outposts until the end of the war. John Ross went to Washington and spent the remaining war years loudly proclaiming the loyalty of his Cherokees to each and every politician who gave him an audience.

INDIANS OUTSIDE THE TERRITORY

Back in the east, William Thomas had raised an actual fighting force of mixed whites and Cherokees, dubbing it "Thomas's Legion," and mustering in at Knoxville, Tennessee, on September 25, 1862, with 1,125 infantry and cavalrymen. His men were first assigned to the protection of eastern Tennessee, where they had a small unit action that same month.

At the end of the action, some of the Union dead were scalped, which renewed the headlines up North. Thomas, aware that the Confederate government might disband his unit rather than suffer another round of bad press in the enemy's newspapers, sternly ordered that no more of this sort of mutilation be allowed on the enemy dead. Live enemies, presumably, were still allowed to be attacked as necessary.

Thomas's Legion played roles in both USA Maj. Gen. Ambrose Burnside's 1863–64 Knoxville Campaign, and the 1864 Shenandoah Valley Campaign against USA Maj. Gen. David Hunter, where they sustained crippling casualties. Thomas was allowed to take the remains of his legion, now numbering less than one hundred, back to Cherokee country in North Carolina in early 1865, where they, like their western brethren, conducted raids and skirmishes. Even at the seeming end of the war, Thomas tirelessly recruited to refill his ranks, reporting that he had 1,100 men available for duty by April 1. His last action was against the 2nd North Carolina Mounted Infantry at Waynesville on May 9, a full month after Lee had surrendered. The next day, Thomas escorted the area commander, CSA Gen. James G. Martin, to a meeting with the same Southern loyalists, all agreeing that it was futile to resist any longer.

SURRENDER IN THE TRANS-MISSISSIPPI

CSA Gen. Edmund Kirby Smith, given the command of the Trans-Mississippi in October 1862, held out for a bit longer, finally ordering a general surrender of his force on May 26. Smith himself did not participate, leaving the formality of the paperwork to a subordinate, and personally leading a force of 2,000 cavalrymen south into Mexico rather than submit to Union authority. He quietly returned to the U.S. in November, but many of the men he led south did not, settling instead in Brazil.

Nearly a full month later, on June 23, Watie led the remnants of his brigade, with Daniel McIntosh riding just in front of his brother, Chilly, into the Union outpost at Doaksville. With great reluctance he signed the surrender of the last major Confederate unit still in the field.

Watie was a divisive figure in Cherokee politics after the war, just as he had been before and during it. He moved away to a new encampment on the Canadian River, setting up a tobacco company with one of his nephews to try and rebuild his family fortunes. Instead he soon became embroiled in politics once again, this time over a Federal excise tax aimed specifically at the Indian Territory farmers. He unsuccessfully fought the government all the way to the Supreme Court. Eventually, his tobacco business failed, he fell into bankruptcy, and he died penniless and abandoned by most of his people in September 1871.

The Cherokee Nation was devastated during the war, losing nearly half its population in both the eastern and western bands. Although Watie had negotiated an agreement with Union army officials to pardon any actions they had performed for the Confederacy, the Federal government reneged, and the nation was declared as a whole disloyal. All land and property rights were stripped from the 11,000 remaining Cherokees, and all treaties with the nations were declared officially null and void.

The Indian Territory itself was broken and destitute after years of raids. Unemployed bands of heavily armed war veterans roamed the countryside, robbing and killing at will in the lawless atmosphere. The Northern press did not deem this worthy of reporting anymore.

Daniel McIntosh fared a little better. His wife Jane had borne him another child during the war, and they added a sixth child in 1867. Jane, unfortunately, died in childbirth with this last addition. Daniel soon married his third wife, Winnie Canard, who bore him a son before dying herself in 1872. He married for a fourth time, in 1874, to Emma Belle Gawler, who bore him eight children. His last child was born only two years before he died.

Daniel served as a representative from the Creek Nation during treaty talks in Washington shortly after the war, continuing the family tradition of agreeing to what little the government offered, not that there was much in the way of an alternative. He settled into a life of farming and tribal politics near the town of Fame, where he died on April 10, 1896. Daniel had held every political office in the Creek Nation, except that of Principal Chief, and was very involved in his local Masonic lodge.

The very last official act of the war in the Eastern Theater was conducted by another Native American, USA (Bvt.) Brig. Gen. Ely Samuel Parker, a Seneca Indian on the staff of Lt. Gen. Ulysses S. Grant. Parker was a lawyer who had initially been refused acceptance for military service solely because of his race. Grant asked Parker to write up the article of surrender, and he presented it to Lee at Appomattox Courthouse.

There is a legend, not confirmed by any known document, that Lee looked at Parker and remarked, "I am glad to see one real American here."

Parker is said to have answered, "We are all real Americans."

All told, somewhere around 20,000 Native Americans served on one side or the other (or both, in a few cases) during the war years, with roughly 3,600 in the Union armies and 16,400 in the Confederacy's. Unsurprisingly, at war's end, popular sentiment to remove the scourge of Indians from the land once and for all had increased, despite the loyal service of some, and the incredible decimation of the Confederate-sympathizing nations.

10

"I GOES TO FIGHT MIT SIGEL": IMMIGRANT SOLDIERS

Cpl. Anton Steffens, Co. C, 20th Massachusetts
Volunteer Infantry Regiment

I willingly give my life for South Carolina. Oh! That I could
have died for Ireland.

—LAST WORDS OF IRISH-BORN CSA CAPTAIN JOHN MITCHELL, 1ST SOUTH
CAROLINA ARTILLERY, FORT SUMTER, SOUTH CAROLINA, JULY 20, 1864

LATE IN THE AFTERNOON OF DECEMBER 11, 1862, THREE UNION INFANTRY regiments volunteered to try and force their way across the Rappahannock River into Fredericksburg, where Lee's Army of Northern Virginia had established two tight lines of defense. All morning, men of the 50th New York Engineers had tried to construct a pontoon bridge across the freezing cold river, but had suffered crippling casualties from infantrymen of CSA Brig. Gen. William Barksdale's Mississippi Brigade, who were well emplaced and barricaded in cellars and houses near the riverbank. A long bombardment from 150 heavy guns had done nothing to lessen the accuracy of the Confederate fire, as a follow-up company of engineers on the half-completed bridge discovered, to their fatal distress.

Infantrymen of the 7th Michigan were the first to row across and land on the far shore, at the foot of Hawke Street, where they suffered horrifying casualties from the point-blank fire of the Mississippians. They were followed in short order by men of the 19th Massachusetts Infantry. Survivors of both regiments quickly began kicking in doors and entering cellars of the houses on Sophia Street, clearing out nests of Confederate infantry and establishing a tenacious toehold for other regiments to exploit. The third regiment to land was the 20th Massachusetts Infantry, the "Harvard Regiment," whose ranks will filled in part with the sons of Boston's most prominent families. The 7th Michigan had cleared out a few houses to the left of the beachhead, and the 19th Massachusetts occupied a house to the right. As the three regiments fought in the streets, houses, and cellars, Union engineers returned to their work, and in short order had finished the first pontoon bridge across the river.

With the beachhead established and reinforcements swiftly coming across, orders came down to clear out the town. The 20th Massachusetts formed up in ranks and prepared to advance into the town in column formation. Standing next to Company I's commanding officer, USA Capt. George N. Macy, who was leading the assault, was the color-bearer, Cpl. Anton Steffens of Company C.

Ordering "Forward!" and turning onto Caroline Street, Macy led his men at the column march into town. As they turned, however, the entire formation was raked by a heavy and deadly accurate fire from Barksdale's Mississippians. According to one of the lieutenants, "almost every ball struck." Macy urged them on and his men obeyed, though they soon had Confederates firing down on them from three sides, and casualties were mounting at an alarming rate. Sending word back for reinforcements, the 20th stopped in the street and held their ground, deploying companies to clear the houses on each side. The 59th New York ran up to support, but just as quickly fell back under the withering fire.

As darkness fell, the volume of fire did not let up, with some of Barksdale's men re-occupying one of the adjacent houses. The street was heaped with the bodies of the slain. Macy sent some of his companies up the left side of the street, while others stayed in the middle and took the houses on the right, but the fighting had been so protracted that many men's rifles were becoming fouled and were unable to load. Finally, as the blackness of night made it impossible to tell friend from foe, Macy ordered a slight retreat back to the intersection nearest the beachhead, and the Confederate fire gradually slackened, before petering out completely.

As Barksdale's Mississippians pulled out during the night, withdrawing to the strong line of defense on Marye's Heights above the town, the Union infantry cautiously checked the piles of dead for any wounded. Ninety-three men of the 20th had been killed or mortally wounded for a gain of less than fifty yards of ground. It was the "most useless slaughter I ever witnessed," according to one eyewitness. The regiment, however, had accomplished its primary mission. Sprawled out on the street, among the heaps of other dead and dying, they found the body of Corporal Steffens, killed during the vicious brawl.

Anton Steffens was not from one of the wealthy and prominent families of Boston, nor was he from a wealthy and prominent family anywhere else for that matter. He was the first of five children of Petronella Schmitz and Peter Joseph Steffens, and was born in Koblentz, Prussia, in 1843. He immigrated to the United States with his family in 1852, and settled in Boston, where he began working as a brass finisher. Shortly after the war broke out, he volunteered for service with the 20th Massachusetts and was present at their initial mustering-in on September 9, 1861, at Readville. Steffens was assigned to Company C, one of two companies in the 20th Massachusetts that filled its ranks with German and Prussian immigrants. His war service was lamentably short in number of years, but very long in the number of battles he fought. He had taken part in hand-to-hand combat during the disastrous day at Ball's Bluff, and was present through McClellan's Peninsular Campaign, the long, bloody day at Sharpsburg (Antietam), and finally, this last savage fight at Fredericksburg.

IMMIGRANTS IN THE WAR

Primarily due to political unrest and a revolution in Germany, a potato famine in Ireland, and assorted political troubles in Italy and France, the United States had witnessed a boom in immigration shortly before the outbreak of the Civil War. The overwhelming majority of these immigrants relocated in the northeast, in New York, Boston, and Philadelphia, though a good percentage moved out west almost immediately. A smaller percentage landed in North Carolina and Georgia, as their Irish and Scottish predecessors had been doing for well over a hundred years.

With the outbreak of war in 1861, these same groups of immigrants faced some very hard choices. Should they join the Union forces, representative of the country they had immigrated into? Should they join the Confederacy, emblematic of the struggle against entrenched powers that they had fled in so many cases back in the "old country"? Or should they try to remain neutral, moving west to the frontier, where land was cheaper and more available, and where the stirrings of war drums were more distant? Even this last choice was a bitter one to make. Whereas the eastern part of the country was consumed by preparations for war, the far west was still far from being peaceably settled, with another, even more savage war being fought against the various Indian nations. Mass slaughters of civilian settlers in the Plains and parts farther west were far from rare occurrences.

Even with all these issues to consider, quite a few immigrants answered the call. Of the roughly two million Union soldiers who served, about 500,000 had immigrated to the U.S. before the war. Small percentages, mostly Germans, were even recruited into the Union Army from overseas, in the dark days of late 1863 and 1864.

STRIKE FOR THE SOUTH

The Confederacy did have a sprinkling of immigrants in its ranks, almost all of them from Ireland. This was due primarily to the fact that so many Irish had immigrated into various parts of the South, and the countryside was a known quality for the newer immigrants as a result. Both Scots and Irish had fled or been kicked out of their respective countries after losing a long series of revolts against their English occupiers; they had flooded into the new country, well before the nation had even gained its own independence from Great Britain. There were so many men in the Southern ranks whose families originally hailed from these Celtic countries that it has been presented as one of the primary reasons for their own defeat. Grady McWhiney's landmark study, *Attack and Die: Civil War Tactics and the Southern Heritage*, held that the old Celtic ways of constant offense, using cold steel and blade in frontal assaults, were "programmed in" to the largely Scottish- and Irish-heritaged Confederate high command. While this method worked very well in the days of muskets and pikes, modernized weaponry, including rifles and accurate long-range artillery, caused massive casualties in such attacks.

A separate, but related reason why so many Irish went south was due to their Democratic leanings. Most had little to no sympathy for slaves, but greatly feared the work of Northern abolitionists, who they saw as no different from the English lords who had stripped them of their rights and property back in Eire. In fact, it was Irish immigrants in the north, who were violently opposed to military service based on political beliefs, who helped start the 1863 New York Draft Riot, where 103 people lost their lives.

According to one source, about 40,000 Irishmen served in the Confederacy. The best known and most prominent by far was the Western Theater corps commander, Maj. Gen. Patrick Ronayne Cleburne, who was killed in action at Franklin, while leading his men into battle in the old Celtic manner. There was no major unit in the Confederate army that was Irish by specific designation, but a number of them did carry the colors, symbols, and names of old Ireland in their devices, and some had a full complement or nearly so of Irish in the ranks.

Due in part to certain Hollywood productions, perhaps the best known "Confederate Irish" unit was the 24th Georgia Infantry, commanded by Antrim, Ireland, native Col. Robert McMillan, and including many native-born Irishmen in the ranks. They were present at Fredericksburg that terrible day in December 1862, lined up along the Sunken Road behind a stout stone wall, at the foot of Marye's Heights, just west of town. To their left was a unit with another strong Irish connection, the 19th Georgia Infantry, with its Irish-themed colors bearing Company B, "Jackson's Guards," then-commanded by Irish born Capt. John P. Kelly.

Quite a number of other Confederate units claimed an Irish connection, justified or not, including: Company H of the 8th Alabama Infantry, known as the "Emerald Guard"; Company B of the 27th Virginia Infantry, the "Virginia Hibernians"; and Company K of the 1st South Carolina Infantry (Gregg's), the "Irish Volunteers." This last company, raised in Charleston early in the war as part of an intended "Irish Battalion," had a beautiful silk battle flag of white and green silk, with an Irish harp and cross surrounded by a wreath of oak leaves, palmetto leaves, and shamrocks. It was adorned with eleven silver stars and a silver silk fringe. Over the cross in silver script was the motto, *In Hoc Signo Vinces* (By This Sign You Conquer).

One other Confederate regiment with a strong Irish connection was the 10th Tennessee Infantry, claimed by one source to be known as the "Bloody Tenth." Most unusually, it had a large population of Irish Catholics in the ranks—most Catholics had tended to immigrate to the North. The regiment saw good service at Forts Henry and Donelson early in Grant's Western Rivers Campaign, and surrendered after the fall of Donelson. While they were being held at Camp Douglas, awaiting parole, an officer from the Union Irish Brigade tried to convince the lads to switch sides and join his brigade. A few accepted the offer, but it was overturned in any stead by higher command. Their battle flag was as spectacular as the South Carolinians, was made of light green silk outlined in Kelly green. Emblazoned with a gold Irish harp, its motto stood out in white lettering trimmed in maroon: "Sons of Erin, Where Glory Awaits You."

All for the Union

The Irish in the Union armies were a whole different story, with many full companies and regiments consisting of nothing but sons of Eire. About 170,000 volunteered for the ranks, and many of them did so for precisely the opposite reason of their Southern brothers. They saw in the Southern planter class, who ran politics down South, the same sorts of people as the lords and landowners of Ireland—who had starved and abused them nearly to the point of death. The families in old Ireland and Scotland alike had long before organized into clans, with wealthy hereditary chiefs and chieftains controlling all aspects of the lives of those living in their territories. Too often these privileged few men born into such power amused themselves by warring with surrounding clans, bringing death and misery to the impoverished people who filled the ranks, and weakening both countries through internal strife to the point that even the despised English could invade and take them over without much trouble.

The Union's best known and most easily recognizable all-Irish formation was the 2nd Brigade of the 1st Division, 2nd Army Corps, Army of the Potomac, consisting of the 63rd New York, 69th New York, 88th New York, 28th Massachusetts, and the 116th Pennsylvania Infantry Regiments, known collectively as the "Irish Brigade." They were under the command of their flamboyant Irish-born commander, Brig. Gen. Thomas Francis Meagher, and they earned their battlefield reputation the hardest way possible, during bloody assaults on two well protected Confederate positions. The first was at Sharpsburg (Antietam), where they suffered over 500 casualties. The second was against the stone wall on Telegraph Road at Fredericksburg.

At Fredericksburg, 1,200 men of Meagher's Irish Brigade marched past the site where Steffens had fallen two days earlier, on through the shattered, battle-scarred town, then across a small canal and upward on a slope toward Lee's positions, atop a low hill called Marye's Heights about a mile west of the town. Most of the brigade's beautiful emerald green battle flags had been torn and ripped to shreds in the previous campaigns, and on that fateful day, only the Twenty-eighth Massachusetts still carried their flag. In the center of the line of battle, it waved gently in the breeze above their heads. After a short pause, Meagher gave the order, "Men of the Irish Brigade! Forward at the double-quick, guide center, March!"

The Irish Brigade never really had a chance. It constituted the third assault of the day up that deadly space, and the Confederate artillerymen by then had the range dialed in to near perfection. Solid shot and shell were falling in their ranks even before they got into the line of departure, and as they came at a slow trot up the slope, great holes were ripped in their ranks by exploding case shot. Because the Confederate infantry were below the artillery position, on the military crest of the hill, the Southern artillerymen didn't even have to pause their deadly work when it came time for the infantry to begin theirs.

Just to the front, across the wide, upward sloping ground, were the Irishmen of the 24th Georgia. Despite Hollywood's pretensions and oft-told tales to the contrary, Colonel McMillan had no qualms about firing on "brother" Irishmen, and he did so with gusto that day. He was recorded as noticing the green flag of the 28th Massachusetts through the flash and smoke of falling artillery, and remarking aloud, "That's Meagher's Brigade!" He may have indeed paused and entertained brief thoughts about fratricide of his Irish brethren. But as soon as the Irish bluecoats came into rifle range, he gave the command to fire, shouting over the incredible din, "Give it to them now, boys! Now's the time! Give it to them!" The Confederates were four ranks deep behind that stone wall, nearly impervious to incoming fire as they worked like an assembly line to load and pass up rifle-muskets to men on the line, who picked off the onrushing Union Irish like tin ducks in a county fair target-shoot.

The Union Irish Brigade moved forward on the upward slope of the shell-blasted hillside, naked to Confederate fire, without so much as a shrub to hide behind, while a hurricane of lead balls, iron shot, and exploding shells tore through the ranks. The heavy fire decapitated company officers, thudded through soldiers who were desperately trying to reload, dropped others by the dozen, until only half their number remained in line. The survivors dropped to the ground, clawing for cover, as the Confederates still raked their lines, stopping only to fire on the fol-lowing brigades as they in turn tried to gain the heights. All the rest of the afternoon until well after dark, the Irishmen stayed under that hell-ish fire, until they were able to crawl back down the slope to the relative safety of Fredericksburg, in some cases dragging bodies of the dead behind them as a sort of macabre sandbag, to absorb the rounds still being fired by Confederate sharpshooters. At a cost of over 540 of their own, the best they could later claim was that they had made it the farthest up the hill toward the Confederate position.

The Irish Brigade didn't survive to the end of the war as a unit, either. Meagher, wounded severely at Sharpsburg, rebuilt his shattered ranks as well as he could, then led them into more hellish battles in the Wheat Field at Gettysburg, and finally the swirling mess at Chancellorsville. Meagher asked permission in May 1863 to pull his brigade out of the field and rebuild it through recruitment efforts in New York. When this was refused, he resigned his commission, losing command of the brigade for good. The whole brigade by then was reduced to approximately the strength of a normal regiment—about 1,000 men and officers—and was finally broken up in June 1864.

Over the course of two years of service, and in the midst of some of the heaviest fighting in the Eastern Theater, the Irish Brigade had a total muster of over 7,000, and suffered over 4,000 casualties, more than had ever served in the ranks at any given time. The 69th New York, almost always on the right of the line, suffered the most, losing sixteen of nineteen officers, and suffering 75 percent casualties over those two deadly years.

Meagher, like so many combat veterans, fought a losing battle trying to adjust to civilian life back in New York. He tried for a time to raise support for a group called the Irish Republican Brotherhood, which intended to invade and seize Canada to try and force the English to let Ireland be free again. Meagher's fiery personality and take-no-prisoners approach probably did more to harm this movement than to help it. After a few years wandering around New York, he moved to Montana Territory, where, on the basis of his war reputation, he gained an appointment as territorial secretary. When the territorial governor resigned over a political scandal, Meagher was tapped to take his place. About a year later, on July 5, 1887, while traveling on the riverboat *Thompson* down the Missouri River, he fell overboard and drowned. His body was never recovered.

OTHER IMMIGRANT SOLDIERS

About 20,000 French immigrants, and another 40,000 French-Canadians served in the Union Army, despite the tensions caused by the *Trent* Affair and the subsequent threat by Great Britain to invade the U.S. from Canada. These tensions were exasperated by the ill-considered rumblings of William Seward, who remarked on several occasions his desire to use the Union Army to invade and annex Canada. One entirely French regiment was formed in the Union ranks, the 55th New York Infantry, the "Lafayette Guards," who were commanded by Colonel Philippe Regis de Trobriand. One company of the supposedly all-Italian "Garibaldi Guard" was composed mostly of Frenchmen, as well.

At least five Australian and three New Zealand natives enlisted in the Union navy. One, a twenty-eight-year-old black man named John Jackson, died on March 24, 1862, aboard the USS *Ohio*.

Many Scandinavians, particularly Norwegians and Swedes, had immigrated to the frontier parts of the upper Midwest, Minnesota, and Wisconsin, in the 1850s, and many readily answered the call to arms. Several all-Swedish and all-Norwegian company-sized units formed up in the western armies, but the only regimental size force of Scandinavians in either army was the 15th Wisconsin Volunteer Infantry, the "Scandinavian Regiment."

The 15th Wisconsin entered service in February 1862 with 801 officers and men. Almost all of them were Norwegian by birth, but there was a scattering of Swedes and Danes in the ranks as well. They received only 105 replacements over the next three years, all Scandinavians. The unit served with the Army of the Cumberland at Stones River and Chickamauga, where its beloved commanding officer, Col. Hans C. Heg, was killed in action. They also participated in all the major actions of Sherman's 1864 Atlanta Campaign, where the regiment was decimated crossing the field at Pickett's Mill. After staying in reserve for the rest of the campaign, the 15th was reassigned to the garrison at Chattanooga and mustered out in December 1864. This unit performed well under harrowing conditions, losing 267 killed in action and dead from disease, 204 severely wounded in action, and twenty-two made prisoner. Most of these men later died at Andersonville. Just 320 were still standing by the colors when they were discharged.

One of the POWs who survived was Ole Steensland, who was born in Hjelmeland, Norway, in 1842. He was captured at Chickamauga, held at Belle Island, and later transferred to the new prison camp at Andersonville. He survived nineteen months in various Confederate POW camps, and later described the physical appearance of him and his friends upon their release:

> We were a hard looking bunch. Some of us almost naked, unshaved, with our louse eaten hair hanging down to our shoulders. My ankles were so stiff and my feet so swollen that I could hardly hobble around.

Steensland finally made it home in May 1865, and died of "a stroke of apoplexy" in 1903. He had survived over eleven months in the stockade at Andersonville, one of only a handful of prisoners to last through such a long stretch.

The largest immigrant group by far in the Union army came from Germany and Prussia. About 216,000 served in the ranks, in a number of German-speaking companies and regiments. One of these was actually a Polish unit, the 58th New York Infantry, known as the "Pulaski Guard," which was composed of German-speaking Poles from the Prussian and Austrian ruled sections of Poland.

There was even one entire "Dutch" (a popular nickname for German-speaking immigrants, a corruption of the proper name for German: "Deutsche") division: Blenker's German Division, commanded by USA Brig. Gen. Ludwig (Louis) Blenker of Worms, Hesse-Darmstadt, Germany. This unit was under the command of yet another famed German soldier, Maj. Gen. Franz Sigel of Baden, who commanded a corps in Pope's Army of Virginia at the time. This division was composed of eight New York infantry regiments (the 8th, 29th, 39th, 41st, 45th, 54th, 58th and 68th), four Pennsylvania infantry regiments (the 27th, 73rd, 74th and 75th), the 4th New York Cavalry, and three artillery batteries (Schirmer's, Wiedrich's, and Sturmfels'), all of whom gave their orders and commands strictly in German. However, shortly after the disaster at Sharpsburg (Antietam), the division was reorganized and reassigned and lost its all-German status.

One regiment in Blenker's Division is worthy of note for another reason. The 39th New York Infantry, the "Garibaldi Guards," started off as an all-Italian unit, and showed up for its first muster wearing green plumes atop their headgear—the distinctive badge, worn even today, of Italian light infantry, known as "Bersaglieri." They quickly became a sort of hodge-podge, multi-ethnic unit, containing Germans, Italians, Swiss, Austrians, Spaniards, Slavs, Turks, Russian Cossacks, Indian sepoys, ex-French Foreign Legionnaires with apparently no discernable nationalities, and even a few French-Algerian Zouaves. They all, however, spoke German like the rest of the division, by the time they were included. The regiment's first commanding officer, Colonel Frederick George D'Utassy, was a Hungarian who had formerly worked as a trick horse rider in a circus.

The most famous German soldier in the Union ranks by far was Maj. Gen. Franz Sigel. He was born in Baden in 1824, and was a well-regarded German army officer who had graduated from the Karlsruhe Military Academy. He earned his reputation as both a combat officer and liberal politician by resigning his commission in 1847, and helping lead the revolution against Prussia the following year. He was forced to flee the country after the revolution failed. In 1851, he arrived in the United States, where he soon settled into the life of a schoolteacher in St. Louis. There, he became a forceful abolitionist political influence among the many German immigrants settling in the area, and shortly after the war began, he accepted a brigadier general's commission personally from Abraham Lincoln.

Sigel served in the West for the first year of the war, successfully raising many German-speaking regiments, but not showing much in the way of battlefield prowess at first. His command broke and ran at Wilson's Creek, on August 10, 1861, leading to the derogatory nickname for German troops that stuck to the end of the war: "Flying Dutchmen." His command showed much more tenacity at the follow-up confrontation at Pea Ridge, where their stubborn stand helped defeat Gen. Earl Van Dorn's effort to drive Union forces out of Arkansas. Sigel was promoted to major general and transferred to the Eastern Theater in March 1862, rising quickly to command of the I and XI Corps. His forces were defeated in the Shenandoah Valley, during a campaign against CSA Lt. Gen. "Stonewall" Jackson (to be perfectly fair, no one did very well against "ol' Blue Light"!) and were soundly thrashed at 2nd Manassas. His reputation suffered another blow, this time a fatal one, in his loss at the Battle of New Market, on May 15, 1864, which featured a Confederate charge led by college cadets from the nearby Virginia Military Academy. (Stonewall's former place of employment—no doubt they were inspired by his earlier success against Sigel!). Sigel was stripped of his command, and he tendered his resignation shortly after the battle. After the war, Sigel dabbled in publishing and politics. He died in New York City in 1902.

He was no doubt one of the worst of an already bad bunch of Union general officers, but his men absolutely adored him, and his personal charisma and reputation in the German community was priceless in helping to fill the ranks in the tough, early days of the war. A popular song of the day was written around a sort of unofficial motto of the German-speaking troops of the Union. Most could speak very little English, but proudly boasted of what they did alongside their well-regarded countryman, in "I Goes to Fight Mit Sigel." It is hard to say today if this was intended to be an ethnic joke at the German's expense or a true tribute to the man:

I GOES TO FIGHT MIT SIGEL
(To the tune of "The Girl I Left Behind Me")

I've come shust now to tells you how,
I goes mit regimentals,
To schlauch dem voes of Liberty,
Like dem old Continentals,
Vot fights mit England long ago,
To save der Yankee Eagle;
Und now I gets my soldier clothes;
I'm going to fight mit Sigel.

CHORUS:
Ya! Das ist drue, I shpeaks mit you,
I'm going to fight mit Sigel.

When I comes from der Deutsche Countree,
I vorks sometimes at baking;
Den I keeps a lager beer saloon,
Und den I goes shoemaking;
But now I was a sojer been
To save der Yankee Eagle;
To schlauch dem tam secesion volks,
I'm going to fight mit Sigel.

I gets ein tam big rifle guns,
Und puts him to mine shoulder,
Den march so bold, like a big jack-horse,
Und may been someding bolder;
I goes off mit de volunteers,
To save de Yankee Eagle;
To give dem Rebel vellers fits,
I'm going to fight mit Sigel.

Dem Deutshen mens mit Sigel's band,
At fighting have no rival;
Un ven Cheff Davis' mens we meet,
Ve Schlauch em like de tuyvil;
Dere's only one ting vot I fear,
Ven pattling for de Eagle;
I vont get not no lager bier,
Ven I goes to fight mit Sigel.

For rations dey gives salty pork,
I dinks dat was a great sell;
I petter likes de Sour Kraut,
De Switzer Kaize un Pretzel.
If Fighting Joe (or Liddle Mac.)
Will give us dem,
Ve'll save de Yankee Eagle;
Und I'll put mine Frau in breechaloons,
I'm go un fight mit Sigel.

11

WE ARE MEN, AREN'T WE?: BLACK SOLDIERS

Pvt. Scott Green, 1st United States Colored Troops (USCT)

"Now," the flag-sergeant cried,
"Though death and hell betide,
Let the whole nation see
If we are fit to be
Free in this land; or bound
Down, like the whining hound,
Bound with red stripes of pain
In our old chains again!"
O, what a shout there went
From the black regiment!

—FROM *THE BLACK REGIMENT*, BY GEORGE H. BOKER

EARLY JANUARY IN THE ATLANTIC OCEAN OFF THE NORTH CAROLINA coast is rarely anything but stormy and cold, and January of 1865 was no exception. Aboard a troopship, pitching in the rough waters, was Pvt. Scott Green, 1st United States Colored Troops (USCT). Two weeks earlier, another force had tried to storm the Confederate outpost of Fort Fisher, which he could now see in the distance. The fort guarded the entrance to the Cape Fear River, and 10 miles up that river was the last remaining major port open to the entire Confederacy, Wilmington. That earlier assault had failed miserably. The Union general in charge, Benjamin "Spoons" Butler, had returned to his early-war roots and fled the battlefield in panic when the Confederate garrison had proven to be manned with stout men. Now, it was up to Green's 1st USCT (part of a full division of black soldiers), and three more divisions of white soldiers to take that last remaining coastal fort.

Green had mustered in to the newly formed 1st USCT in Washington, D.C., in June 1863. Within a few months the unit was assigned to the unfortunate General Butler's command, and Green was in mopping-up operations along the northern North Carolina coast. The critical situation around Petersburg, however, demanded their reassignment. Green entered his first real combat on May 24 at Wilson's Wharf, where his 1st USCT and another black regiment successfully defended the supply depot there against a raid by CSA Maj. Gen. Fitzhugh Lee's Cavalry Division. At the same time, Grant was moving his great armies against Lee near Petersburg. This city is where Lee ultimately stopped Grant's advance, nearly for good, as both sides settled in for what would turn out to be the longest siege in American military history.

Green and his compatriots were assigned to a series of duties during the first part of the nine-month siege, mostly picket and rear-area guard duties, but they were on the line near the Cemetery Hill section of the 20-mile-long line of battle on July 30. For two months engineers had been building a tunnel that extended to underneath the Confederate trench lines, intending to pack it full of explosives and quite literally blow a hole in the line that they could then exploit with infantry. When the mine was blown just before 5:00 A.M. on July 30, a huge crater was blasted out of the Confederate redoubt, nearly 200 feet long, sixty feet wide, and thirty feet deep, with nearly vertical sides. Almost 300 Confederates were killed instantly, and the main artillery battery at the site was destroyed, but the follow-up attack was not mounted for nearly an hour, allowing the Confederates a chance to regroup and prepare.

Green and the rest of the 1st watched then as three all-white infantry divisions tried to break through, but were easily repulsed. Then, at 8:00 A.M., USA Brig. Gen. Edward Ferrero's 4th (Colored) Division launched its attack, with 4,200 black troops and white officers, organized into two brigades and nine regiments (the 19th, 23rd, 27th, 28th, 29th, 30th, 31st, 39th and 43rd U.S. Colored Troops). At first they did quite well, moving forward into the breached wall through murderous, point-blank rifle and artillery fire. They captured the last line of Confederate trench lines in front of the remains of the hilltop redoubt, but finally were repulsed. A second attempt to regroup and assault up the left side of the crater ended the same way, this time met by two full Confederate brigades, (Weisiger's Virginia and Wright's Georgia, of CSA Brig. Gen. William Mahone's Division) who slammed into them with a great fury. The situation in the crater quickly deteriorated into an outright melee, with the Confederates in no mood to give any quarter (which may have been inspired by the black troop's own battle cry, "No quarter!"), and there was no good way for any of the Union soldiers to withdraw under the murderous fire. Four more Confederate assaults, the last starting after 1:00 P.M., finally ended the Union attack.

The vicious brawl at the Crater has long been regarded as a one-sided slaughter, even a massacre, of the black Union infantrymen, and some accounts do support that charge. Several white Union officers later reported witnessing the bayoneting of wounded black troops, and the shooting of others who attempted to surrender. One Confederate soldier, Pvt. Henry Van Lewvenigh of the 12th Virginia Infantry, wrote home:

> *Saturday's fight was a bitter struggle. No furlough wounds given there and no quarter either . . . The negro's charging cry of "No quarter" was met with the stern cry of "amen" and without firing a single shot we closed with them. They fought like bulldogs and died like soldiers. Southern bayonets dripped with blood and after a brief but bloody struggle the works were ours. The only sounds which now broke the stillness was some poor wounded wretch begging for water and quieted by a bayonet thrust which said unmistakably "Bois ton sang. Tu n'aurais plus de soif." (Drink your blood. You will have no more thirst.)*

In all fairness, though this was a vicious, close-quarters brawl where any remaining niceties of war were forsaken, it was not the massacre of black troops it has gained the reputation for being. The Confederate forces reported a loss of 1,032 men, while over 5,000 casualties were reported out of the four Union divisions that attacked. Of the 4,400 men in Ferrero's 4th Division, 219 were killed in action, 957 were wounded, and 410 were made prisoner, with 2,895 making it back safely to the Union trenches.

Still, this is the world Scott Green entered when he enlisted in 1863, where his very presence on the battlefield inspired discomfort and shunning by other, white Union units. He received lower pay than those same white infantrymen and encountered violent reactions from Confederate troops. Were he to surrender, he had no guarantee (at first, at least) of being treated as any other soldier would have been treated. Finally, he had to endure the postwar enmity of millions of veterans and civilians, who considered him part and parcel the cause of so many deaths and so much destruction.

NORTH CAROLINA

After the disaster at the Crater, Grant reorganized his army, firing the incredibly incompetent Butler, who had commanded the Army of the James at Petersburg. Mostly to prevent him from hanging around Washington and causing more mischief, Grant ordered Butler to a new command attempting to take on the last Confederate holdout on the Atlantic coast, in North Carolina. As part of this massive reorganization, Green and the 1st USCT were reassigned as well, going with Butler to the North Carolina coast, where they were assigned to Brig. Gen. Charles J. Paine's all-black 3rd Division (part of Major General G. Wietzel's all-black 25th Army Corps, the last corps organized during the war). They were charged with assaulting and taking control of the last stretch of usable coastline from the Confederacy, as well as taking its last open seaport, Wilmington. This would in turn shut down the blockade-runners who had made the Union navy's life so miserable for the past three years. It would also end the last tenacious thread of logistics for the two great Confederate armies still in the field.

Onboard a bucking and swaying troopship, up on deck in the freezing cold January wind, recalling what he had witnessed at the Crater, and looking across the rough surf at low-slung Fort Fisher, bristling with heavy guns, it is not hard to imagine the thoughts that must have been going through Green's mind.

WILMINGTON, 1864–65

After USA Maj. Gen. Ambrose Burnside's successful 1861–62 campaign in the eastern portion of the state had cut off supply and transport routes into Virginia, Wilmington inherited a vital role as the most important safe port for blockade-runners. The supplies they managed to sneak past the Union fleet were transferred to trains on the Wilmington &Weldon Railroad and sent north to Lee's army. Lee remarked on several occasions that he would not have been able to fight for so long without this steady flow of supplies. Two other railroads carried some supplies to the western portion of the state, then on to Tennessee and Georgia, and down to Charleston and Columbia in South Carolina.

Wilmington had a very favorable and easily defended location, 26 miles inland on the wide and deep Cape Fear River, whose twin entrances from the Atlantic Ocean were well fortified. To the Union Navy's grief, it was very nearly impossible to sail into the river inlet without the use of local, firmly Confederate-sympathizing guides to show the way through the treacherous Frying Pan Shoals.

To guard against even the remote possibility of a Union attempt to assault the city by water, there were no less than six forts. The two channels into the Cape Fear River were separated by Smith's Island, which contained Fort Holmes. On the west bank of the river above the island were Forts Johnston and Anderson. The lesser-used Old Inlet was guarded by Fort Caswell and Battery Campbell. To guard the much heavier used New Inlet, a massive sand-work fortification called Fort Fisher was constructed on Federal Point starting in the summer of 1861. Fisher was not a true fort, in the classic sense, as it did not have encompassing walls. Instead, it was L-shaped, with the longest side facing the expected avenue of attack, the Atlantic Ocean. Fort Fisher mounted forty-four heavy guns guarding the river entrance, with 150 more of various calibers protecting every avenue of approach. Several earthwork redoubts and batteries surrounded each fort, adding to an already impressive amount of available firepower.

The Union blockade fleet had at first considered Wilmington an insignificant port and ignored it. They later placed only a single ship, the USS *Daylight*, off the coast in July of 1861. But by late 1864, its importance had become clear even to Union planners in Washington, and by that time, more than fifty blockade ships lay just offshore. Even with this tight noose around the supply lanes, blockade-runners managed to slip through up until the time of the battle here itself.

THE BATTLES FOR WILMINGTON

While Grant was tied up in the months-long battle around Petersburg, he realized that in order to bring the stalemated fight to a successful conclusion, he was going to have to cut Lee's supply lines. Until the only remaining port supplying the Army of Northern Virginia, Wilmington, could be cut off or taken over, this was not going to be possible. Grant ordered Butler and Rear Adm. David Dixon Porter to take their forces south and capture the city. Butler had two divisions of infantry, Brig. Gen. Adelbert Ames's 2nd of the XXIV Corps and Paine's 3rd of the XXV Corps, along with two batteries of artillery, for a grand total of nearly 8,000 men. Porter commanded the largest force of ships ever assembled at that time in the U.S. under one command—nearly 60 ships mounting a total of 627 guns.

As attack on the port city was likely at some point, Confederate President Davis sent Gen. Braxton Bragg to take over command of the defenses. The previous area commander, Maj. Gen. William Henry Chase Whiting, was a competent officer and was well liked by both his troops and the local citizens. Davis's choice of the notoriously inept Bragg to replace him (he was actually placed over Whiting, who stayed on to directly command the garrison) was loudly protested. The size of the command then around Wilmington is highly debatable, but it can be safely assumed that Bragg initially commanded somewhere around 3,000 men.

Lee was fully aware of the critical and vulnerable nature of the port city, and warned Davis that if the city fell, he would be forced to pull back and abandon Richmond itself. When the Virginia general learned of Butler and Porter's advance down the coast, he sent Maj. Gen. Robert Frederick Hoke's Division to help defend the vital port, adding another 6,000 men to the line.

THE FIRST BATTLE FOR FORT FISHER

Butler, considered by many on both sides to be Bragg's equal in ineptness, was determined to open the Cape Fear River by reducing its strongest defense, Fort Fisher. On December 20, 1864, the Union fleet began arriving off the Wilmington coast in the midst of a severe storm, taking nearly three days to get organized. Finally, on the night of December 23, with nearly all his command present and ready to assault, Butler sprang his "secret weapon" on the unsuspecting Confederates.

Butler had decided that a ship loaded to the gills with gunpowder, floated to the outer defenses of Fort Fisher, and then exploded, would reduce at least one wall of the sand-work post to dust, and allow his troops to pour in through the opening. Amazingly, he had managed to sell Porter on the idea and got Grant's grudging approval to go ahead. Butler and Grant were mortal enemies, and the supreme Union commander had simply wanted to fire Butler rather than allow him another chance to screw up, but could not due to Butler's political connections. At 1:45 A.M. on December 24, an unnamed "powder ship" loaded with 215 tons of gunpowder was sailed to within 200 yards of the fort, and then exploded. The resulting massive blast failed to even superficially damage the well-constructed fort, and the sleepy defenders peered out, wondering if one of the Union ships had suffered a boiler explosion, or something of a similarly innocuous nature. Despite the failure of his "secret weapon," Butler ordered the planned attack to proceed.

As dawn crept over the horizon, Porter's gunboats began a heavy bombardment of the fort, while Butler ordered his troops ashore on the peninsula just north of the Confederate stronghold. Capturing two small batteries and pushing back Confederate skirmishers, the Union troops had made it to within 75 yards of the fort by Christmas morning. Butler learned that Hoke was then only 5 miles away and moving in fast. Panicking, Butler ordered his troops to break off and return to the troop transports, which he in turn ordered to hoist anchor and sail away so fast that over 600 infantrymen were left stranded on the beach. Porter, who had no idea what Butler was up to, was forced to send his own ships and sailors to the beachhead, under fire from the defenders of Fort Fisher, in order to rescue the stranded troops. Butler reported a loss of fifteen wounded and one killed in action (by drowning), while the Confederates suffered about 300 killed, wounded, and captured, as well as the loss of four precious artillery pieces.

A furious Grant immediately fired Butler, damning the political consequences (which were, by then, moot, with Lincoln's re-election a fact), hurriedly assembled another, stronger assault force under Maj. Gen. Alfred Howe Terry, and sent Porter a message, "Hold on, if you please, a few days longer, and I'll send you more troops, with a different general." Porter pulled about 25 miles offshore, to the general line of the Union blockade fleet, to await Terry's arrival.

THE SECOND BATTLE FOR FORT FISHER

Porter did not have long to wait. Terry left Bermuda Landing, Virginia, on January 4, 1865, with a total of 8,000 soldiers. Joining Porter's squadron just off Beaufort, the force sailed once again for the Cape Fear River, through yet another strong storm, arriving late on the afternoon of January 12.

Whiting had received word that the Union force was en route to try again, and fearing that this attempt would be much stronger, he personally led 600 North Carolina troops to reinforce Col. William Lamb's garrison of 1,200. Hoke's newly arrived command deployed on the peninsula north of the fort, in case the second assault followed Butler's attempted route.

A few hours after the Union fleet arrived, Porter ordered all guns to open fire on the Confederate fort while Paine's 3rd Division, with Green and the 1st USCT in the ranks, landed unopposed north of Hoke's line. They quickly set to work building a strong line of breastworks and trenches across the peninsula, cutting off the forts to the west from another Confederate relief column then en route from Wilmington. Terry spent the next two days carefully bringing the rest of his two forces ashore and deploying them in a semi-circle around the fort. One brigade, under Col. Newton Martin Curtis was sent to the western end of the peninsula, where they captured a small redoubt and dug in close to the fort.

At dawn on January 15, Porter's ships once again opened up a massive fire, lasting over five hours, until Terry signaled his men to advance. Riflemen from the 13th Indiana Infantry Regiment led the assault, dashing forward under fire to dig in less than 200 yards from the fort, and then raking the parapets with a deadly, accurate fire.

While this rifle fire kept the Confederate defenders' heads down, Terry ordered forward Curtis's brigade, now reinforced with Colonel Galusha Pennypacker's Brigade, against the western face of the fort. As the Union troops cut through the wooden palisades and dashed up the sand walls, Lamb's men rose out of their shelters and met the Union soldiers with fixed bayonets and drawn swords.

As the western wall defenses broke down into a massive hand-to-hand melee, 2,200 sailors and marines from Porter's command sprang forward to assault the northeastern corner of the fort. There, the Confederate defenders were able to return a disciplined fire, killing or wounding over 300 of the naval command, and forcing them to quickly retreat.

Terry left the rest of his command, which consisted mostly of Paine's 3rd Division (Colored), before Hoke's line, and Hoke never sent any of his men to help relieve the fort's defenders, at Bragg's direct order. About 10:00 P.M., after hours of unrelenting and vicious hand-to-hand combat and the commitment of the last Union reserves, the seriously wounded Lamb finally surrendered his post. The exact numbers of dead and wounded Confederates are difficult to assess, as records of this fight are spotty and highly debatable on accuracy, but somewhere between 500 and 700 were killed or wounded, and another approximately 2,000 were captured. Whiting himself was mortally wounded during the assault, and died less than two months later. Terry reported losses of 184 killed, 749 captured, and twenty-two missing—including the seriously wounded Curtis, who had been shot three times while leading the way over the ramparts. Porter reported the loss of 386, in addition to the casualties in his marine assault force.

As a sort of morbid postscript to the hard-fought battle, on the morning of January 16, two drunken sailors (sometimes identified as U.S. Marines) were walking around, looking for something worth stealing, when they came to a heavy bunker door. Opening it, they lit a torch and stuck it in the dark opening. The resulting explosion of about 13,000 pounds of gunpowder killed twenty-five more Union soldiers, wounded another sixty-six, and killed an unknown number of wounded Confederate prisoners in the next bunker.

Although Green and the rest of the all-black division saw no direct combat in the fight for Fort Fisher, the fact that they were there, in uniform, armed and ready to do harm perhaps had as much affect as if they had. Henry M. Turner, Chaplain of the 1st USCT, described later what it was like out on that line of battle:

> The land forces on our [right] . . . in no instance broke nor exhibited any cowardice . . . . At one time I thought they could never stand it, neither do I believe they would have stood, but for the fact that they knew the black troops were in the rear, and if [the white troops] failed, the colored troops would take the fort and claim the honor. Indeed, the white troops told the rebels that if they did not surrender they would let the negroes loose on them . . .

THE FALL OF WILMINGTON

With the main defense post now in Union hands, Bragg wasted little time mounting any sort of renewed defense. The next day Fort Caswell's garrison was withdrawn and the walls blown up, followed in quick order by most of the remaining forts, batteries, and redoubts. Fort Anderson was left manned to cover Bragg's withdrawal. This post stayed until February 20, when USA Maj. Gen. Jacob Dolson Cox's XXIII Corps moved up river and forced them out without much of a fight. The next day Hoke's troops were finally withdrawn and escaped north with the last remnants of Bragg's force to Goldsboro. On February 22, Wilmington Mayor John Dawson rode out to surrender his city to the Union invaders.

African American Soldiers

When the war broke out, ostensibly over the issue of slavery (though that reason was muted or even denied by Northern politicians and newspapers, at least until after Sharpsburg), Northern politicians and military leaders made a tacit agreement that it was to be a "white man's war." Despite claims to the contrary by a hundred years of bad textbooks, there was at least as much, or probably more, in the way of racism in the North than in the South, and this quickly cooled any of the sporadic attempts to form black regiments early in the war.

The South, slave holding as it was, and presumably the last place on earth any sane white man would put a rifle into the hands of a black man, was in fact the very place it happened first. The *Charleston Mercury*, a fiery pro-secession newspaper of the day, reported in an issue two weeks after the fall of Fort Sumter, in April 1861, the interesting sight of the passage through Augusta, Georgia, of a column of troops heading for Virginia, including "one Negro company" from Tennessee. Another secessionist newspaper, the *Memphis Avalanche*, gave notice in several May 1861 editions of the appointment of a committee to "to organize a volunteer company composed of our patriotic freemen of color of the city of Memphis, for the service of our common defense." Finally, the February 9, 1862, *New Orleans Picayune* wrote in an article concerning a grand review of local troops for the war, that "We must also pay a deserved compliment to the companies of free colored men, all very well drilled and comfortably equipped." An adjacent article mentioned that these companies numbered some "1,400 colored men," a good regiment-and-a-half strength.

These stunning notices confirming the presence of black Confederates under arms are made even more startling by their source; USA Sgt. Maj. Christian A. Fleetwood, a black soldier in the 4th United States Colored Troops, who won the Medal of Honor for his heroics as a color-bearer at the Battle of New Market Heights (Chaffin's Farm), Virginia. In one of his postwar writings, *The Negro as a Soldier,* he pointed out how the Confederacy had been the first to raise and deploy black soldiers, lamenting that it took over two years before the Union, presumably fighting for their cause, bothered to do so themselves. Fleetwood wrote the thin booklet for the Negro Congress at the Cotton States and International Exposition, held in Atlanta, Georgia, in November of 1895.

Back up North, several prominent men repeatedly called for Lincoln to allow the raising of black regiments, none louder or more frequently than the abolitionist Frederick Douglass, an escaped slave himself. He frequently pointed out that there had been many blacks in the ranks of the Continental Army, during the American Revolutionary War, commenting that, "Colored men were good enough to fight under Washington, but they are not good enough to fight under McClellan." He later bitterly added, "Liberty won only by white men would lose half of its luster."

One other problem that arose in the supposedly enlightened "we are marching to make men free" North was the fact that prewar fugitive slave laws had never been overturned, and were at least in theory still in effect. When freed slaves entered the Union army lines, some local commanders kicked them back out and tried to return them to their Southern masters, or even allowed slave catchers or, in a few cases, the masters themselves to come into camp to pick them up. One of these unhappy Union army commanders was none other than "Spoons" Butler himself. When his command in Fort Monroe, Virginia, accepted a large number of ex-slaves into their lines, he declared them to be "contraband," and set them to work building up his own fortifications. The name, "contraband," and this precedent of treatment, stuck for the rest of the war.

USA Brig. Gen. David Hunter, then-commander of the Union Department of the South, issued his own "emancipation proclamation" in May 1862, freeing all slaves in the Carolinas, Georgia, and Florida, and shortly afterward, he recruited and equipped the first Union black infantry regiment, the 1st South Carolina Volunteers (African Descent). Lincoln ordered both the proclamation revoked and the unit disbanded, but eventually allowed Hunter to keep a single company of it under arms. Three months later, another officer tried it again. USA Brig. Gen. James Henry Lane organized the all-black 1st Kansas Colored Volunteer Infantry Regiment from ex-slaves in the Western Department. This time, under strong political objections from Washington, the unit was allowed to serve, fighting in Missouri and Arkansas, and eventually being redesignated as the 79th USCT.

Seeing both the writing on the wall and the thinning Union ranks, Butler finally reversed his own position, and with Washington's blessing, he raised three black regiments in late 1862 from the New Orleans area his forces had just conquered—the 1st, 2nd, and 3rd Louisiana Native Guard.

After issuing his Emancipation Proclamation on January 1, 1863, Lincoln ordered the army to reverse his former policy and raise as many black regiments "as practicable." The fact that his call the summer before for 300,000 volunteers had only gone half met was likely one of the reasons for his sudden change of heart. Whatever the reason, Douglass and other prominent black political leaders were delighted, and quickly set about touring all through the northeastern states on a grand recruiting drive. One of the first full regiments thus raised was the famed 54th Massachusetts Infantry, who won their initial fame at Battery Wagner, South Carolina (the setting for the movie *Glory*), but whose outstanding battlefield actions later at Olustee and Honey Hill showed just how effective the highly motivated men in those ranks could be, when given a real chance. Two other all-black regiments were quickly raised in the Boston area—another infantry and a cavalry regiment—and both were sent into action just as quickly.

The situation finally and permanently reversed in May 1863, when the War Department set up the Bureau of Colored Troops, to both oversee the recruitment of men for the newly established regiments, and to coordinate the conversion of state formations to Union ones. All the new and converted regiments would be designated as numbered United States Colored Troops (USCT) regiments. One overriding consideration remained, and would for many years after the war: these black units would always be commanded by white officers.

By the end of the war, 165 all-black infantry, cavalry, and artillery regiments and batteries were established, with a total of slightly over 178,000 men in the ranks. Another 100,000 or so served as civilians in the camps—as cooks, nurses, corpsmen, and teamsters. Approximately 94,000 were ex-slaves from Confederate states; another 44,000 were from the border states, both freed men and escaped slaves, from a total of thirty-five states and territories and several foreign nations. Most had worked in a variety of skilled and unskilled manual labor, only a relative few were literate, and only the barest handful had any formal schooling at all. "Black" or "colored" soldiers are terms now considered to be archaic, at best, or even somewhat obscene, but the modern-day politically-correct term of "African American" would not apply very well for these men, as very few of them were citizens of the United States, even the ones who had been born and lived all their lives in the states. The Fourteenth Amendment, ratified three years after the war ended, would take care of that once and for all.

These men fought in 449 of the roughly 10,000 engagements at some level, including 39 major battles. Thirteen of these men were awarded the Medal of Honor, then, as now, the nation's highest award for valor on the battlefield. One of these men, the aforementioned Sergeant Major Fleetwood, was awarded his medal for what he did on a terrible day in Virginia, snatching up his regiment's colors and carrying them forward in a storm of flying shot and steel, rallying the men to keep going forward in the face of overwhelming fire from the Confederate line, after eleven previous color-bearers had been shot down. More than 1,700 of these men were killed in action.

The 1st Regiment USCT survived both the fight for Fort Fisher and the short campaign for Wilmington itself, then moved into North Carolina in support of Sherman's war-ending campaign. They were standing in the ranks outside the Bennett House at Durham Station on April 26, 1865, when Gen. Joseph Eggleston Johnston surrendered his once-invincible Army of Tennessee. They were mustered out of service on September 29, 1865. During their period of service, the 1st USCT lost seventy-one officers and men killed in action, and another 114 felled by disease.

Almost nothing personal is known about Private Green, other than the fact that he was present in the ranks of the 1st USCT all through their service and was still standing at the end. We have no written record as to what he looked like, where he came from, and where he went after the war. Other than the possibility of a faded picture in some forgotten bureau, or a few half-remembered stories from aged grandchildren, if he in fact ever had any, everything about him, including all his stories of battle and camp are now lost. All we know about him, like so many other men we have discussed in this book, was what he did when it counted: he stood up, took the oath, and did his service with honor and without accolade.

He was a brave man in a desperate time.

References and Bibliography

Primary Sources

Ambrose, Stephen E., ed. *A Wisconsin Boy in Dixie: Civil War Letters of James K. Newton*. Madison: University of Wisconsin Press, 1961.

Baird, W.D., ed. *A Creek Warrior for the Confederacy: the Autobiography of Chief G.W. Grayson*. Norman: University of Oklahoma Press, 1991.

Billings, John D. *Hardtack and Coffee: Or, The Unwritten Story of Army Life*. Boston: George M. Smith, 1887.

Cate, Wirt Armistead, ed. *Two Soldiers: The Campaign Diaries of Thomas J. Key, C.S.A. and Robert J. Campbell, U.S.A.* Chapel Hill: University of North Carolina Press, 1938.

Confederate Veteran Magazine, 40 vols. Nashville: Confederate Veteran Press, 1893–1932.

Hautmann, Laurence M., ed. *A Seneca Indian in the Union Army. The Civil War Letters of Sgt. Isaac Newton Parker, 1861–65*. Shippensburg, PA: Burd Street Press, 1995.

Johnson, Robert U. and Clarence C. Buel, eds. *Battles and Leaders of the Civil War*, 4 vols. New York: The Century Company, 1887–88.

McPherson, James M. and Patricia R. McPherson, eds. *Lamson of the Gettysburg: The Civil War Letters of Lieutenant Roswell H. Lamson, U.S. Navy*. New York: Oxford, 1997.

Military Order of the Loyal Legion of the United States War Papers, 70 vols. Philadelphia: MOLLUS, 1887–1915.

Ransom, John L. *John Ransom's Diary*. New York: Paul Erikson, 1963.

Selfridge, Thomas O., Jr. *What Finer Tradition: The Memoirs of T.O. Selfridge, Jr., Rear Admiral, USN*. Columbia: University of South Carolina Press, 1987.

Skinner, Arthur N. and James L. Skinner, eds. *The Death of a Confederate: Selections from the Letters of the Archibald Smith Family of Roswell, Georgia, 1864–1956*. Athens: University of Georgia Press, 1996.

The Southern Historical Society Papers, 49 vols. Richmond: The Southern Historical Society, 1876–1943.

War of Rebellion: Official Records of the Union and Confederate Armies 1861-1865, 128 parts in 70 vols. Washington, DC: U.S. War Department, 1880–1901.

Watkins, Sam R. *Company Aytch: Maury Grays, First Tennessee Regiment, or A Side Show of the Big Show*. Nashville: Cumberland Presbyterian Publishing House, 1882.

Secondary Sources

Barrow, Charles Kelly, et al. *Forgotten Confederates: An Anthology About Black Southerners*. Atlanta: Southern Heritage Press, 1995.

Barrow, Hugh W. *Private James R. Barrow and Company B, Cobb's Legion Infantry*. Privately published, 2003.

Baumann, Ken. *Arming the Suckers, 1861–1865*. Dayton, OH: Morningside, 1989.

Bragg, William Harris. *Joe Brown's Army: The Georgia State Line, 1862–1865*. Macon, GA: Mercer University Press, 1987.

———. *Griswoldville*. Macon, GA: Mercer University Press, 2000.

Cain, Andrew W. *History of Lumpkin County for the First Hundred Years, 1832–1932*. Atlanta: Stein, 1932.

Castel, Albert: *Decision in the West: The Atlanta Campaign of 1864*. Lawrence: University Press of Kansas, 1992.

Cochran, Hamilton. *Blockade Runners of the Confederacy*. Indianapolis: Bobbs-Merrill, 1958.

Coombe, Jack D. *Gunfire Around the Gulf: The Last Major Naval Actions of the Civil War*. New York: Bantam Books, 1999.

———. *Thunder Along the Mississippi: The River Battles That Split the Confederacy*. New York: Bantam Books, 1996.

Crow, Vernon H. *Storm in the Mountains: Thomas' Confederate Legion of Cherokee Indians and Mountaineers*. Cherokee, NC: Press of the Museum of the Cherokee Indian, 1982.

Crute, Joseph H., Jr. *Units of the Confederate States Army*. Privately published, 1987.

Cunningham, H. H. *Doctors in Gray: the Confederate Medical Service*. Gloucester: Peter Smith, 1970.

Daniel, Larry J. *Cannoneers in Gray: The Field Artillery of the Army of Tennessee 1861–1865*. Tuscaloosa: University of Alabama Press, 1984.

Davis, Stephen. *Atlanta Will Fall: Sherman, Joe Johnston and the Yankee Heavy Battalions*. Wilmington: Scholarly Resources, 2001.

Dyer, Frederick H. *A Compendium of the War of the Rebellion*, 3 vols. Des Moines, IA: Dyer Pub. Co., 1908.

Evans, Clement A., ed. *Confederate Military History*, 12 vols. New York: Thomas Yoseloff, 1962.

Gaines, W. Craig. *The Confederate Cherokees: John Drew's Regiment of Mounted Rifles*. Baton Rouge: Louisiana State University Press, 1989.

Hicks, Brian and Schuyler Kropf. *Raising the Hunley: The Remarkable History and Recovery of the Lost Confederate Submarine*. New York: Ballantine Books, 2002.

Jones, James Pickett. *Yankee Blitzkrieg: Wilson's Raid Through Alabama and Georgia*. Athens: University of Georgia Press, 1976.

Jordan, Ervin L., Jr. *Black Confederates and Afro-Yankees in Civil War Virginia*. Charlottesville: University Press of Virginia, 1995.

Kimball, Charles B. *History of Battery "A," First Illinois Light Artillery Volunteers*. Chicago: Cushing, 1899.

Lane, Julian C. *Key and Allied Families*. Macon, GA: J.W. Burke, 1931.

McWhiney, Grady and Perry D. Jamieson. *Attack and Die: Civil War Military Tactics and the Southern Heritage*. Tuscaloosa: University of Alabama Press, 1982.

O'Brien, Sean Michael. *Mountain Partisans: Guerilla Warfare in the Southern Appalachians, 1861–1865*. Westport, CT: Praeger, 1999.

O'Kelley, Harold. E. *Dahlonega's Blue Ridge Rangers in the Civil War, 1863–1865*. Privately published, 1992.

Priest, John Michael. *Before Antietam: the Battle for South Mountain*. New York: Oxford University Press, 1992.

Robertson, James I. *The Civil War's Common Soldier*. Washington: Eastern National, 1998.

Rogers, Robert L. *Report of Robert L. Rogers, Historian to the Atlanta Camp, Number 159, United Confederate Veterans On the Capture of the DeGress Battery and Battery A, 1st Illinois Light Artillery in the Battle of Atlanta, July 22, 1864*. Atlanta: United Confederate Veterans Camp #159, 1898.

Scaife, William R. *The Campaign for Atlanta*. Privately published, 1987.

————. *Civil War Atlas and Order of Battle*. Privately published, 1997.

Scaife, William R. and William Harris Bragg. *Joe Brown's Pets: the Georgia Militia in the Civil War*. Privately published, 1999.

Scharf, J. Thomas. *History of the Confederate States Navy: From its Organization to the Surrender of its Last Vessel*. New York: Rogers & Sherwood. 1887.

Soderberg, Susan Cook. *A Guide to Civil War Sites in Maryland: Blue and Gray in a Border State*. Shippensburg, PA: White Mane Books, 1998.

Speer, Lonnie R. *Portals to Hell: Military Prisons of the Civil War*. Mechanicsburg, PA: Stackpole Books, 1997.

Still, William N., Jr., et al. *Raiders and Blockaders: The American Civil War Afloat*. Dulles, VA: Brassy's, 1998.

Taylor, Thomas E. *Running the Blockade: A Personal Narrative of Adventures, Risks, and Escapes during the American Civil War*. London: John Murray, 1896. Reprint Annapolis, MD: Naval Institute Press, 1995.

Trotter, William R. *Bushwhackers: The Civil War in North Carolina: The Mountains*. Winston-Salem, NC: John F. Blair, 1988.

————. *Ironclads and Columbiads: The Civil War in North Carolina: The Coast*. Winston-Salem, NC: John F. Blair, 1989.

Tsouras, Peter G. *Military Quotations from the Civil War: In the Words of the Commanders*. New York: Sterling Publishing, 1998.

Tucker, Spencer. *Arming the Fleet: U.S. Navy Ordnance in the Muzzle-Loading Era*. Annapolis: U.S. Naval Institute Press, 1989.

Wideman, John C. *The Sinking of the USS Cairo*. Jackson: University of Mississippi Press, 1993.

Wiley, Bell Irvin. *The Life of Billy Yank: The Common Soldier of the Union*. Baton Rouge: Louisiana State University Press, 1952.

———. *The Life of Johnny Reb: The Common Soldier of the Confederacy*. Baton Rouge: Louisiana State University Press, 1943.

Wise, Stephen R. *Lifeline of the Confederacy: Blockade Running During the Civil War*. Columbia: University of South Carolina, 1991.

Journals

Joslyn, Mauriel. "Who Caused Andersonville?" *Journal of Confederate History* 8, (1995): 181–91.

Oxley, Robert M. "The Civil War Blockade: The Unpublished Journal of a U.S. Navy Warrant Officer Aboard the USS Vincennes, 1861–1864" *International Journal of Naval History* 1, no. 1 (April 2002).

Peery, Charles. "Clandestine Commerce: Yankee Blockade Running." *Journal of Confederate History* 4, (1991): 89–111.

Rollins, Richard, ed., "Black Southerners in Gray: Essays on Afro Americans in Confederate Armies" *Journal of Confederate History* (1994): Special issue, whole issue.

Tucker, Spencer "Confederate Naval Ordnance" *Journal of Confederate History* 4, (1991): 133–52.

Wise, Stephen R "Greyhounds and Cavaliers of the Sea: Confederate Blockade Running During the Civil War" *Journal of Confederate History* 4, (1991): 61–76.

Worthington, W. Curtis, MD. "Confederate Surgeon: The Letters of Thomas Smith Waring, A South Carolina Planter-Physician at War" *Journal of Confederate History* 2, (1989): 55–92.

INDEX

John McKay spent fifteen years as a firefighter and paramedic before turning his interests into teaching and writing history. His main inspirations were his great-grandfathers on both sides of his family, Confederate veterans almost killed or badly wounded during the war. McKay has been a freelance writer and photographer for commercial magazines, newspapers, and academic and literary publications.